T0155646

Azure Arc Systems Management

Governance and Administration of Multi-cloud and Hybrid IT Estates

Ramona Maxwell

Apress®

Azure Arc Systems Management: Governance and Administration of Multi-cloud and Hybrid IT Estates

Ramona Maxwell
Redwood City, CA, USA

ISBN-13 (pbk): 978-1-4842-9479-6
https://doi.org/10.1007/978-1-4842-9480-2

ISBN-13 (electronic): 978-1-4842-9480-2

Managing Director, Apress Media LLC: Welmoed Spahr
Acquisitions Editor: Ryan Byrnes
Development Editor: Laura Berendson
Editorial Assistant: Gryffin Winkler

Cover image designed by Arnon Thaneepoon at Dreamstime.com

Distributed to the book trade worldwide by Springer Science+Business Media New York, 1 New York Plaza, 1 FDR Dr, New York, NY 10004. Phone 1-800-SPRINGER, fax (201) 348-4505, e-mail orders-ny@springer-sbm.com, or visit www.springeronline.com. Apress Media, LLC is a California LLC and the sole member (owner) is Springer Science + Business Media Finance Inc (SSBM Finance Inc). SSBM Finance Inc is a **Delaware** corporation.

For information on translations, please e-mail booktranslations@springernature.com; for reprint, paperback, or audio rights, please e-mail bookpermissions@springernature.com.

Apress titles may be purchased in bulk for academic, corporate, or promotional use. eBook versions and licenses are also available for most titles. For more information, reference our Print and eBook Bulk Sales web page at http://www.apress.com/bulk-sales.

Any source code or other supplementary material referenced by the author in this book is available to readers on GitHub (https://www.apress.com/gp/services/source-code).

Paper in this product is recyclable

In honor of my bold and spirited adventurer
Charity "Cha Cha" Cassady (1974–2016)

put your finger right in the middle of the cake
refuse to give up
refuse to let anyone you care about give up
pursue your dreams relentlessly

Table of Contents

About the Author

Ramona Maxwell is an experienced Enterprise Solution Architect who has worked with clients across a broad spectrum of the Fortune 100 such as utilities, finance, and healthcare organizations. She is certified by Microsoft as an Azure Solutions Architect Expert and is an AWS Certified Solutions Architect, Microsoft Certified Trainer (MCT), Associate as well as a 2020 graduate of VMware's Platform Acceleration Lab training for application architects. She has expertise in container technologies such as Kubernetes and Docker and extensive experience extending line-of-business systems across multiple technology stacks. Ramona is an occasional presenter at industry events on enterprise computing strategies and techniques. The author's full profile can be viewed at `https://ramonamaxwell.com`.

About the Technical Reviewer

Mike DeLuca is a recognized expert in public, private, and hybrid cloud. With seven patents, numerous cloud-related innovations, and a long career at Avanade and Microsoft, he has deep expertise helping the world's premier enterprises and online properties understand the journey to cloud. Mike currently serves as the leader for Avanade's suite of cloud-related tooling globally. He lives in the San Francisco Bay Area with his wife and four kids. He is also a contributor to the blog www.cryingcloud.com.

Introduction

The necessity of the methods and products covered in this book stands as a testament to the celerity with which enterprise IT estates have sprawled across multiple public clouds while never entirely leaving corporate-owned data centers. Exponential growth of data requires efficient access and processing methods, along with protection against corruption or exfiltration. Accomplishing these tasks manually is no longer possible; thus, tools and methodologies which are equal to these challenges are considered in this book. While Microsoft's Azure Arc is the primary focus, the principles of enterprise IT management discussed should serve to inform even those readers who are not currently in the market for an enterprise control plane. The book may be read topically if a particular area is of interest to you, with the caveat that earlier chapters are foundational to understanding more complex subjects that follow. Both business and IT leaders should find answers to their particular concerns around governing and securing technology assets in a fashion that promotes the objectives of the business.

CHAPTER 1

The Challenges of Enterprise-Scale Hybrid and Multi-cloud Architectures

The innovation of technology solutions available to enterprise-scale organizations continues to grow exponentially and at an astonishing pace. While adopting new technology is a vital strategy for profitability and growth, it also creates significant hurdles with transitions between product stacks, integration with existing solutions, and the critical need to observe and control the entire information technology [IT] estate of an organization. This book aims to investigate what the author believes to be the most comprehensive control plane for IT systems governance available on the market today, Azure Arc. It will cover the product's capabilities across management of database systems, Kubernetes, governance and policy, security, and its contributions to industry best practices such as DevOps. While focusing on Arc, some comparisons will be made to other products that have similar objectives. Finally, it will offer some historical context as to how the platforms impacted by Arc developed and what fostered the need for a product like Arc.

© Ramona Maxwell 2024
R. Maxwell, *Azure Arc Systems Management*,
https://doi.org/10.1007/978-1-4842-9480-2_1

CHAPTER 1   THE CHALLENGES OF ENTERPRISE-SCALE HYBRID AND MULTI-CLOUD
ARCHITECTURES

In the world of enterprise architecture and the IT systems it creates, a use case or problem statement often generates a premise for the design. In the case of hybrid and multi-cloud system DevOps, governance, security, modernization, upgrades, monitoring, and management are all key areas of concern which we can examine before proposing any solution.

Over the last decade, the rush to the cloud has moved many enterprises to undertake large modernization projects. Motivating these behemoth efforts have been factors such as speed to market, adopting agile project methodologies in hopes of simplifying upgrades and expansion of technology stacks, shedding the large capital expense of running a data center, and more.

Commercial considerations may also influence which cloud an organization utilizes. The famous resistance of Walmart to use cloud services from Amazon, a chief competitor in the retail space, has led them to develop a hybrid solution combining their own infrastructure with services from Google Cloud Platform [GCP] and Microsoft Azure – but not Amazon Web Services [AWS].[1] Companies making acquisitions may find their new subsidiaries are already fully built out on a specific cloud platform, offering little justification to immediately rebuild on the parent company's provider platform. One of Azure Arc's key features, which will be covered extensively in this book, is its ability to manage IT assets on multiple clouds as well as in private data centers from one dashboard, thus enabling centralized governance and cost control.

Unfortunately, attempts to modernize and migrate IT workloads have a significant risk of failure. The UK consulting firm Advanced publishes an annual report surveying mainframe modernization initiatives in companies with more than 1B in revenue. In 2020, 74% of companies reported failed

---

[1] www.bloomberg.com/news/newsletters/2022-07-12/walmart-cloud-weans-itself-off-of-microsoft-azure-google-cloud

modernization projects,[2] and in 2021 that number had increased to 78%.[3] At the time of this writing their most recent update to the report was commissioned from Coleman Parkes early in 2022.[4] The summary noted progress as its subjects had gone beyond "embracing cloud hyperscalers as infrastructure providers" and begun "inviting them into the critical operations of their businesses" with multi-cloud identified as a strategy that would "predictably emerge as an organization's cloud maturity rises." Thirty-three percent of respondents to *Unisys'* detailed Cloud Success Barometer[5] report unsatisfactory outcomes in terms of organizational effectiveness following cloud migrations. As a result, vendors like Dell are seizing the opportunity to "repatriate" customers back to their own data centers,[6] an offering likely to entice the 54% of respondents to Advanced's latest survey that identified private cloud as part of their mainframe migration strategy.

Microsoft's answer to these throes of transition has not been not to abandon their cloud-first strategy and revert to selling server-based solutions. Instead, they looked at how the Azure cloud itself runs on Azure Resource Manager and began to extend this configuration-based approach to create a control plane capable of managing resources no matter where the customer hosted them including competitor's clouds, on-premise data centers, and edge locations. Over a period of experimenting with various control technologies (which will be detailed in the chapter covering Arc's history), Microsoft constructed and continues to expand upon Azure Arc.

---

[2] https://www.businesswire.com/news/home/20200528005186/en/74-Organizations-Fail-Complete-Legacy-System-Modernization

[3] https://modernsystems.oneadvanced.com/globalassets/modern-systems-assets/resources/reports/advanced_mainframe_report_2021.pdf

[4] https://modernsystems.oneadvanced.com/globalassets/modern-systems-assets/resources/reports/2022-mainframe-modernization-business-barometer-report.pdf

[5] https://www.unisys.com/siteassets/microsites/cloudbarometer/report_unisyscloudsuccessbarometer.pdf

[6] https://www.crn.com/news/data-center/michael-dell-it-s-prime-time-for-public-cloud-repatriation

The three primary cloud vendors (Google, Azure, and AWS) have each responded with offerings that allow customers to retain some critical workloads in-house while still benefiting from their platform's proprietary tools including deployment pipelines and administration consoles. Google Anthos offers an extension of Google Kubernetes Engine (GKE) to instances running on a competitor's clouds, edge locations, and bare metal running on the customer's hardware, while AWS Outposts use only AWS hardware that is shipped to the customer. While each of Google Anthos, AWS Outposts, and Azure Arc share Kubernetes management as a large part of their DNA, only Arc encapsulates the data center in its administration capabilities – a key differentiator which we will also devote a chapter to.

Microsoft does not even make a pretense of humility regarding Arc's capabilities and importance, with the page header in Arc's section of the Azure portal declaring, *"Govern and manage all your infrastructure, anywhere."* Thus, while ordering an Outpost will ship your own AWS world with a subset of their services, and Google will let you run its industry-leading Kubernetes offering no matter where you park your servers, Microsoft's claim is that Arc can manage Kubernetes, SQL Servers, virtual machines, and more on any cloud or in your data center from a single control plane while additionally opening the doors to a plethora of Azure services to workloads not actually running on Azure.

The Challenges of Hybrid and Multi-cloud Architectures in a Modern Application Stack

What are some of the specific challenges posed in terms of implementing governance, DevOps, and security where systems are disparate and spread across large IT landscapes? How can existing workloads that are core to

business operations be modernized in order to be secure and competitive
in their market? In the next few paragraphs, we will examine some of
the barriers to success, while subsequent chapters will delve into how
control plane technologies and specifically Azure Arc can offer steps to
remediate them.

DevOps

Core principles of DevOps practice such as continuous integration, testing,
deployment, and monitoring are made challenging by the very nature of
distributed infrastructure. Reducing complexity and keeping work visible
are extremely difficult as the number of systems and locations in large
enterprise architectures continuously proliferate. A lack of compatible
interfaces between disparate environments, product-specific management
tools, and the need to have teams specializing in particular products or
technology stacks raise up barriers against DevOps best practices such
as minimizing handoffs and swarming in response to failures in order to
prevent their impacting downstream systems (where the cause of failure
may be difficult or impossible to diagnose).

The introduction of DevOps in the IT industry is generally attributed
to examples of success in the automobile manufacturing industry where
utter failures to consistently produce vehicles meeting safety and design
specifications at a speed that was profitable led companies like Toyota to
completely redesign their manufacturing process. Likewise, the software
pipeline has been improved to prevent defective modules from entering
the final product and speed time to market so that business can profit from
software initiatives. Being able to see the product as a whole, eliminating
barriers between teams, and shortening handoffs are only possible when
infrastructure can be fully managed. In this way, the "Ops" side of the
pipeline becomes a predictable target for "Dev" to deploy to.

Governance

Properly implemented enterprise IT governance does not start in the
part of the organization being governed. Rather, it is a business initiative
that protects assets such as personnel and financial information, trade
secrets, client and distribution data, and many more adjuvant resources
that information technology processes. Consequently, an organization
generally has a steering committee and written policies within a
governance plan that specify how all of the digital capital of a company will
be managed.

When a mature IT organization implements a governance plan, they
will choose technology and processes that allow them to implement
its guidelines successfully. Monitoring of multiple facets of these IT
systems such as security, performance, usability, and more must also be
implemented and utilized to provide feedback to the steering committee
on how the governing standards are being applied. This implies a
mapping between a governing standard and all systems affected by the
rule. For instance, a rule requiring all personally identifying (PI) data be
encrypted would require monitoring of finance databases, front-end web
applications, messaging systems, caching mechanisms, and more.

When an organization has assets distributed across multiple and
diverse systems, capturing and analyzing the level of compliance may
become so burdensome that if it cannot be "baked in" in the form of
automated processes, its cost can weigh heavily against the revenue of the
systems being governed.

Further, large IT landscapes may have legacy systems that cannot
be successfully migrated or shadow IT initiatives that have sprung up
to manage pain points or weak integrations. Accurate reporting around
compliance and eDiscovery becomes excessively difficult not only due
to disparate systems but also has origins in poor Enterprise Content
Management [ECM].

Security

In terms of security, the difficulty of managing hybrid or multi-cloud infrastructures as a single unit cannot be overstated. One of the most valuable tools in terms of both governance and security is the ability to automatically apply consistent policies throughout an organization's IT assets, with the goal of 100% coverage.

For example, in August 2021, Microsoft took urgent action on reports of a critical flaw which allowed attackers to gain access to the primary account key for Azure Cosmos DB customers via vulnerable Jupyter notebooks with access to the database.[7] A classic conundrum of enterprise security is that some products, such as Jupyter notebooks, exist for the very purpose of open sharing and collaboration, while the enterprise data stores which they access are not intended to be open. It was estimated that 30% of Microsoft's customers utilizing Cosmos DB and Jupyter were forced into an emergency reset of account keys in order to reestablish database security, as well as forensic research to determine whether private data had been compromised. The ability to consistently monitor access patterns, enforce network security by requiring database instances live behind firewalls or within protected virtual networks, and regularly update account keys are just a few of the ramparts that must be continually built to ward off the onslaught of attacks targeting companies threatened by this and similar vulnerabilities.

The risk to a company of a data breach[8] can range from a loss of customer confidence and market share to failure and fines.[9] RiskIQ, a cybersecurity firm recently acquired by Microsoft, estimates in its 2021 Evil Internet Minute[10] report that cybercrime is currently costing organizations

---

[7] https://chaosdb.wiz.io

[8] https://www.upguard.com/blog/biggest-data-breaches

[9] https://www.linkedin.com/pulse/
most-expensive-fines-companies-faced-due-security-failures-andre/

[10] https://www.riskiq.com/wp-content/uploads/2021/07/Evil-Internet-
Minute-RiskIQ-Infographic-2021.pdf

roughly $1.8M per minute, while McAfee's faned 2020 whitepaper on
the hidden cost of cybercrime estimated more than trillion dollars lost
each year,[11] a figure some disputed as far too low.[12] Further, small and
medium businesses may be forced to shutter entirely in the face of a single
cybercrime attack.[13]

The onslaught of cybersecurity risk is contributing to a more severe
regulatory environment. In July of 2023, the US Securities and Exchange
Commission [SEC] imposed new reporting requirements on public
companies,[14] as well as some private and foreign entities, requiring them to
disclose certain cybersecurity incidents within just four days of identifying
them as material to avoid being subject to fines and potential legal action
by the SEC. While not requiring companies to engage board members with
cybersecurity expertise, as was postulated by many while the rules were
being formulated, the ruling calls out the necessity of competent security
leadership and mandates that companies identify both their process for
responding to incidents and list the potential impact of a security breach
on the company. Are companies prepared? Forbes noted in February of
2023 that only 51% of Fortune 100 companies benefit from a qualified
cybersecurity professional serving as a director on their boards, and the
situation becomes increasingly grim as companies decrease in size and
resources.[15] The SEC regulations are only one thread in a large net of
compliance obligations being cast by governmental authorities as Forbes[16]

---

[11] https://www.businesswire.com/news/home/20201206005011/en/New-McAfee-
Report-Estimates-Global-Cybercrime-Losses-to-Exceed-1-Trillion

[12] https://cybersecurityventures.com/mcafee-vastly-underestimates-
the-cost-of-cybercrime/

[13] https://cybersecurityventures.com/60-percent-of-small-companies-
close-within-6-months-of-being-hacked/

[14] www.sec.gov/news/press-release/2023-139

[15] www.forbes.com/sites/forbestechcouncil/2023/02/06/90-of-boards-are-
not-ready-for-sec-cyber-regulations/?sh=665fcff588e7

[16] https://fortune.com/2023/12/20/quiet-cybersecurity-revolution-
economy-us-allies-new-threats-regulation-politics-tech-eric-noonan/

also notes, "the federal government is quietly directing a seismic shift in the economy by mandating stringent cybersecurity compliance across all 16 critical infrastructure sectors,"[17] meaning that very few businesses will be exempt from these new requirements.

Modernization

As we head into the foreseeable future, enterprise modernization efforts that feature multi-cloud and hybrid systems have nearly a decade of experiential learning to draw on. Monumental failures in these attempts have been well documented, for instance, those in several of the State of California's governmental systems[18] and the national embarrassment suffered in the rollout of Healthcare.gov which was initially unable to enroll users or even remain accessible for them to attempt that process. Per the Brookings Institution,[19] "... the Centers for Medicare and Medicaid Services (CMS) eschewed four management practices recommended by the Software Engineering Institute and the GAO: scheduling, estimating the effort needed for project tasks, data management monitoring practices, and milestone project reviews." Despite that blunt assessment of CMS, the blame for the site's woes extended far beyond that agency. A comprehensive retrospective featured in the Harvard Business Review's Cold Call podcast[20] pointed out that support from key participants was subject to political whims and that base requirements for how the site should function were undefined. Robinson Meyer in *The Atlantic*[21] notes

---

[17] www.cisa.gov/topics/critical-infrastructure-security-and-resilience/critical-infrastructure-sectors

[18] https://www.linkedin.com/pulse/risk-mitigation-through-successful-consulting-ramona-maxwell/

[19] www.brookings.edu/blog/techtank/2015/04/09/a-look-back-at-technical-issues-with-healthcare-gov/

[20] https://bit.ly/4ON5UIx

[21] www.theatlantic.com/technology/archive/2015/07/the-secret-startup-saved-healthcare-gov-the-worst-website-in-america/397784/

that the project was ultimately rescued by "a team of young people" who applied agile software development principles in order to fix issues ranging from logins and security to the user interface in order to eventually deliver a working website.

The lack of publicity around enterprise project failures is not because they don't occur in a similarly dramatic fashion. It is largely because there has historically been less regulatory compulsion for them to disclose mistakes unless there has been a data breach or other injury to outside parties, but a review of industry survey statistics published in Computerworld[22] indicates that keeping pace the massive evolution of the computing industry is a struggle for businesses of all sorts.

Enterprise applications may be constructed as large monoliths, hundreds or thousands of individual applications, be using a service- oriented architecture, or even have graduated to a microservice model – but they all have one thing in common: *data*. Risks of data migration are risks to the heart of a running business, and those risks are multiple. Data quality, security, and the compatibility of data types between old and new systems are some of the first items that must be examined in the assessment phase of a data migration. The risk of corruption, undocumented dependencies, application downtime, and the impact of all of these issues on the flow of business illustrate why Ernst & Young Analytics partner Chris Michell states that data migration is not a technology project, but a "business-critical risk mitigation program."[23]

Finally, you cannot modernize what you cannot catalog. Some enterprise systems age gracefully due to consistent governance throughout their lifespan, while others degrade into byzantine morass of complexity. In these cases, documenting what the output of the system

---

[22] https://www.cio.com/article/221827/14-reasons-why-software-projects-fail.html

[23] https://www.ey.com/en_lu/consulting/why-data-migration-is-about-risk-mitigation-not-technology

is, replacing that functionality, and starting fresh may be the only way
to provide a secure and performant platform which meets the business
need. Whichever approach of reformation or replacement is chosen,
the problem remains that many business-critical systems must remain
operational while the transformation is accomplished.

Upgrades

Anyone with a history in enterprise IT has a war story or two about
sacrificing a weekend for a marathon upgrade session that required
downtime for production systems. The cadence of upgrades has increased
with the need to meet ever-growing security threats and assure technical
stacks for crucial applications remain inside support windows for specific
product versions.

Because of that, a longtime industry goal has been zero-downtime
upgrades, also known as Evergreen IT. IaaS, PaaS, and serverless
computing models have come reasonably close to achieving that (with
varying degrees of completeness). In the case of hybrid and multi-cloud
systems though, some of the old paradigms of calling an outage still apply.

Regardless of where an upgrade is performed, certain protective steps
must be taken to reach that moment of relief when all systems are back
online, and high among these is monitoring. Similar to data migrations,
application compatibility is a risk, and testing must be done before and
after an upgrade is completed. This is particularly true in scenarios where
an upgrade cannot be rolled back once it is performed. If incompatibility
is discovered after a nonreversible action is taken, then remediation will
likely be required that may not have been anticipated in terms of the
operational costs of performing the upgrade.

Whether software is upgradeable can often depend on how well an
application has been maintained and documented during its lifetime. I
personally witnessed a core application at a major bank that became so
prone to failure that updates were only made through stored procedures

in its database and deployed through feature flags in production. The
risk of an application drifting into such a dysfunctional state cannot be
overstated, and effective monitoring coupled with timely remediation is
a proven strategy for preventing upgrade debacles – which is exactly the
approach taken by Azure Arc.

Monitoring

As mentioned, monitoring is a cornerstone of successful modernization
and upgrade efforts, but its value extends to the entire enterprise
ecosystem from governance and implementation to application
consumption. Without effective monitoring, it is impossible to create the
continuous feedback loop between intent and outcome to gauge success.
No matter the topic – be it performance of a web application, protection
from DDOS, or whether traffic between internal applications is properly
secured – what is not being monitored can be assumed to be at risk, if not
in a state of failure.

Obstacles to effective monitoring are numerous. Middleware products
are inclined to customize their output to fit their tool's design, and this
output may not be consumable by a particular monitoring tool without
extra transformative steps. Problems also occur with too much or too
little information being outputted; there is a reason some log emitters are
referred to as fire hoses! Logs have to be segregated and filtered for noise
or sometimes composed into something that is meaningful for whomever
is responsible for auditing their output. Transactional data, for instance,
might go through extensive analytical processing after being shipped
to a data warehouse. If these challenges are not met correctly, then
organizations can be left "flying blind" in key areas of governance, security,
and profitability of business objectives.

Management

A final and not insignificant pain point in having IT infrastructure spread across multi-cloud and hybrid systems is the inability to manage sprawling assets from a single point of view. While individual teams can and should manage systems nearest to them, a high-level view is still critical because of interdependencies throughout disparate systems. Even though an operationally mature organization will have strategies for maintaining high availability of critical systems, downstream systems should also be prepared to manage failure if their operation would be interrupted or perhaps fail also in the event of an outage.

System administrators with deep experience in topics such as networking, virtualization, or databases will still face entirely new paradigms when moving to cloud. Despite the fact that mega-cloud infrastructure is composed of roughly the same components, the parlance and the perspective from which they manage will be much different. Further complicating matters are attempted modernizations or upgrades that are stuck for long periods in an incomplete state, requiring management of "accidental hybrid" systems. When a multi-cloud approach is taken, the processes and tools will vary between vendors, adding yet another facet of management complexity.

Finally, management requires visibility and thus depends on accurate monitoring. Whether the metrics are financial, operational, or project based, there must be visibility into the entire corpus of an organization's IT assets if management is to successfully steer toward the business' objectives.

Throughout this book, we'll explore what Azure Arc is, its capabilities, and how it can lessen the hardships associated with development, governance, security, modernization, upgrades, monitoring, and management in multi-cloud and hybrid environments.

CHAPTER 2

What Is Azure Arc?

Arc – A Single Control Plane Across Multi-cloud and Hybrid Architectures

The unification of IT infrastructure management under a "single pane of glass" has been an end of the rainbow objective since the beginning of enterprise computing. The Jenga tower of interdependent resources that is created as organizations grow can be read like tree rings to examine what led to the current health of IT systems – the thin year when we didn't have sufficient staff and nothing was documented, the fat year when many new products were purchased but without sufficient time for integration testing, or the steady years when there was a consolidated stack working relatively well followed by the evidence of fire when a major security breach occurred.

In every case, both business and IT are seeking visibility not only for failure analysis but also to gather the data around what will support an optimal growth pattern. Classic IT Service Management [ITSM] processes and frameworks, notably Information Technology Infrastructure Library [ITIL], were initially seen as contrary to a modern DevOps approach as their elongated process flows and reduced agility hampered the speed of iteration despite the governance they provided being undeniably necessary. The principles for managing change processes across not only

© Ramona Maxwell 2024
R. Maxwell, *Azure Arc Systems Management*,
https://doi.org/10.1007/978-1-4842-9480-2_2

services but also infrastructure had to be blended with agile practice so that the ability to move faster would not jeopardize the outcome, and tools to accomplish this were not always readily available or mature.

Azure Arc is revolutionary in its ability to realize the goal of gathering assets into a single theater for observation and management. Its comprehensive approach to asset management uses the tools, processes, and approaches pioneered by Microsoft in the Azure cloud and allows you to leverage these same processes, tools, and approaches on any workload anywhere, even other cloud providers. For instance, along with Azure Stack Portfolio, Azure Stack IoT, and SQL Server, things like Kubernetes clusters or servers running in your own data centers or on competitor clouds are all viable targets.

What are some of the benefits? I recently gave a talk on container support for AWS Lambda (a compute service offering a runtime on which to execute functions to process data.[1] The function outputs can be consumed by various types of workloads), in which I noted I used a total of four command line interfaces (Docker, AWS, ECS, and SAM) to deploy my containerized function. Using Azure Arc as the management plane, you are able to use its CLI and APIs consistently across the entire catalog of managed assets (e.g., not switching to AWS CLI to manage a server located there). Not only that, but the view of asset inventory outside of the Azure portal is not segregated – instead, you can view all assets of a particular type together (see Figure 2-1) and manage them as a group. Further, you can apply policies and then monitor compliance since tools like Azure Policy and Azure Monitor are included.

---

[1] https://docs.aws.amazon.com/lambda/latest/dg/welcome.html

Figure 2-1. *Monitoring AWS policy compliance, including AWS CIS in Azure Security Center by means of Azure Arc analytics agent[2]*

Internal Architecture

The genesis of Arc is an interesting history that will be touched upon throughout this book. Here, though, I'd like to dive into the functional pieces of Arc and how the capabilities under discussion are achieved. To understand Arc, it's helpful to understand the core pieces of Azure itself. Long before operational visibility came along as icing, the Azure cake was baked into its current form with a couple of its key ingredients being Azure's Fabric Controller and Resource Manager.

The Fabric Controller reminds me most of the Diego Brain utilized by Cloud Foundry to spin up container instances on virtual machines based on requests from Cloud Foundry's Cloud Controller such as "give

---

[2] https://docs.microsoft.com/en-us/azure/security-center/quickstart-onboard-aws

me a Windows instance for this .Net Core app horizontally scalable by x factor" or an Alpine Linux instance for a Ruby app and many more combinations. Diego auctions off the app's request for a home to the server farm where the machine with the correct supporting OS and capacity can be selected. Next, Diego creates the container instance and runs the app, begins emitting its routing data to service requests, and sends its logs to an aggregator. If health checks are configured for an application, Diego also monitors whether the application is healthy and reports failures back to the Cloud Controller, so a new container instance to run the application can be created.

Initially, Azure also focused on cloud hosting of applications, and so its Fabric Controller, like Diego, serves as an intermediary mapping container requests to the hardware layer and continually monitors their health status in case any need to be replaced. Today, though, its purview is much broader than hosting applications since Azure provides not only PaaS but also IaaS services. Thus, the fabric controller also regulates other types of hardware, including networking and storage controllers.

The Fabric Controller itself sits on dedicated hardware in each cluster of approximately a thousand servers within an Azure Data Center.[3] The Fabric Controller servers are configured to be highly available, as are the clusters themselves organized according to what Microsoft refers to as "fault domains," which are at every crucial intersect where a hardware failure may occur (typically server racks which share a NIC and power supply, but since their definition is hierarchical, subsidiary components like disks may also belong to a fault domain). The Fabric Controller uses agent-based communication to manage guests, and this communication is always initiated by the host with responses from the guest assumed to be untrusted. This inability for a guest OS to initiate communications

---

[3] https://learn.microsoft.com/en-us/azure/security/fundamentals/
infrastructure-components#azure-management-by-fabric-controllers

with the host is just one of the security boundaries that protects Azure infrastructure from the vulnerabilities that virtual machines running on nodes (physical servers) in the cluster may be exposed to. The Fabric Controller itself runs on VMs, allowing it to take advantage of security isolation provided by the virtual machine hypervisor including protection of the node's physical hardware and memory space.[4] Additionally, the hypervisor provides critical isolation of VMs, not only for the hardware layer but also limiting network communications to VMs within the same VNet so that "side channel" incursions where a malicious VM is used to attack other VMs in the same cluster are prevented.

The Fabric Controller manages three different operating systems, including Host OS (which is a minified and hardened version of Windows Server) on the node's root VM, Native OS which is the operating system for the Fabric Controller itself (as well as some Azure services that do not run under a hypervisor such as storage), and thirdly a guest OS which provides the runtime for the VM workload. The guest OS may be chosen from a variety of Linux distributions as well as recent versions of both Windows Server and consumer editions of Windows. The Fabric Controller also provides health monitoring and actively searches for a new host and restores a guest VM that goes down for any reason.

If you are one of those people who exercises the liberty to make fun of Hyper-V, you might reconsider when you understand how a modified version of the same hypervisor is foundational to Azure cloud infrastructure. The role of a hypervisor is of course to distribute the resources of a powerful server among as many virtualized server instances as the machine can comfortably host. The Azure hypervisor goes beyond this core task to provide security isolation so that no virtual machine can communicate with others on the same host, and additionally it is minimized to what is required to operate Azure so that its attack surface is shrunken.

---

[4] https://learn.microsoft.com/en-us/azure/azure-government/azure-secure-isolation-guidance#strongly-defined-security-boundaries

While the hardware platform itself is not under the control of the hypervisor, it is still constructed in such a way as to minimize risk. A dedicated microcontroller, Cerberus,[5] monitors boot processes and blocks malicious attacks against BIOS firmware and communication with hardware peripherals. Some organizations might assume they are safe from attacks on a cloud provider's underlying platform; however, Microsoft itself is well aware of the need to protect Azure from the ceaseless menace and threats pounding on its virtual doors. This book will cover the concept of a zero trust security model as it applies to various topics discussed, and it's worth noting that the construction of Azure itself provides one of the largest examples of its implementation on the planet today.

Azure Resource Manager [ARM] supplies the instructions the Fabric Controller needs to execute operations on the hardware layer. When a request is sent to ARM using the Azure CLI, PowerShell, Azure SDKs, or the Azure Portal interface, ARM authenticates the request and also provides authorization to subscription assets according to the role assumed by the requestor. ARM then sends this request through an API to the Fabric Controller to execute. Many adjunct tasks are performed such as configuring guest agents that will be required for post-deployment software installations and other jobs. The artifacts defined in a request then reach Fabric Controller's own front end for translation into commands understood by the Fabric Controller's root operating system.

ARM templates are the templating engine native to Azure which allow large environment builds to be configured as code so that while you could execute a line or two in the console to deploy a server or application, you would typically avoid that in favor of creating configuration files in JSON or Microsoft's new YAML templating engine Bicep. This allows for consistent repeatable builds that can be designed according to proper security and

---

[5]www.dailyhostnews.com/microsoft-open-sources-project-cerberus-protect-firmware-cyberthreats

performance standards before the infrastructure is stood up. ARM is powerfully equipped as a central control plane for Azure, with components on the platform each having their own resource definition within ARM's ecosystem of resource providers.[6]

So where does Arc fit in this landscape? Simply put, Arc extends the ARM control plane beyond the confines of Azure and allows incorporation of IT estates on cloud providers such as Google and AWS or on-premise data centers to be brought under management by Azure. The extensible design of ARM is the bedrock of Arc capabilities, and it's built upon with the ability of the Fabric Controller to manage the artifacts that ARM defines. This allows Arc to manage the Fabric-Based Infrastructure[7] [FBI] of not only Azure but to extend the reach of the Fabric Controller to perform operations on the FBI of other clouds, such as creating, updating, and deleting resources.

Live in a Managed World – On-Premise

Now imagine you can not only manage public cloud infrastructure from Azure, but also you can begin to manage your on-prem data center as though it were on Azure. You can become a PaaS provider offering database as a service from servers running on your own infrastructure or provide IaaS so that your on-premise workloads can be deployed using ARM templates just as they would if running on Azure's hardware.

Data is the heart of the application. Thus, storing, organizing, optimizing, and protecting databases from their physical machinery to software updates and security are the nuclear football that is the

---

[6] https://docs.microsoft.com/en-us/azure/azure-resource-manager/management/azure-services-resource-providers#match-resource-provider-to-service

[7] www.gartner.com/en/information-technology/glossary/fabric-based-infrastructure-fbi

responsibility of the data center to maintain and protect. Some of the obstacles routinely faced in this endeavor include the physical aspects of running a data center such as water, power, and cooling as well as expert staff to manage equipment failures and provisioning. Further, the maintenance of the servers containing the databases and the databases themselves will require upgrades and patches along with both physical and logical security. Finally, the data itself requires maintenance in order to assure consistency and avoid duplication which could call into question whether data is a truthful source.

Managed data services take away much of the complexity and pain of the aforementioned points, allowing the data to become the core focus. This ideal state contributes to rapid development cycles and the health of workloads running on PaaS. In some scenarios, it can also be a more cost-effective option when a workload has occasional spikes in volume as it avoids the trap of overprovisioning hardware to account for exceptional loads.

However, if your organization is motivated to continue to run its own infrastructure, Azure Arc provides substantial benefits in that it extends your ability to maintain, monitor, and secure assets living outside Microsoft's hardware ecosystem to competitor's clouds or in customer-owned data centers. These benefits include fully automated patching and upgrades, as well as the ability to scale server instances as one might with a managed service (within the limits of the target data center's infrastructure).

Another key benefit to Azure Arc managed data centers is the ability to safely migrate large workloads without taking down the database. This topic will be covered in detail in Chapter 4 examining the protected migration of SQL Servers.

Advanced Usage Scenarios

Depending upon many factors including the size of an organization and the complexity of IT assets being governed, Arc may be used as an overarching tool or applied in a targeted way to specific assets or processes. A high overview of potential use cases might include DevOps, machine learning, edge computing, and more. Microsoft offers a plethora of case studies, one being the mega accounting firm EY.[8] EY's business is multi-tenant at its core and requires strict security to prevent any type of leakage between clients. As a worldwide firm, they are also subject to regulatory and compliance requirements that differ based on the geographic region of the client. As the reference in the footnote explains, not only was EY able to attain a consolidated management view of their sprawling infrastructure, they were also able to leverage edge computing to create private cloud Kubernetes installations in regions where deploying to a commercial cloud provider is not an option. Let's take a tour of Arc's usage scenarios, starting with DevOps.

DevOps

Cloud-native development support is an adjunct benefit of Arc. Compare the ease of pushing your application to Azure App Service where all of the deployment mechanisms are abstracted away to a local build process requiring containerizing your application and adding it to the container management system manually. The manual approach would likely require developers to create a Dockerfile, YAML deployment scripts, secure keys, connection strings, and an operations team to stand up the infrastructure on which your workloads will run – be that Kubernetes clusters, Docker

---

[8] https://customers.microsoft.com/en-us/story/1343635293322291084-ey-professional-services-azure-arc

Swarm, or something else. The App Service by contrast allows developers to simply write application logic and push it to the appropriate repository. The remaining steps will be triggered by that push – no Dockerfile or YAML required unless you want to deploy your app in a container. Just to add gravy here, as mentioned earlier with managed SQL, you can also offer Azure App Services on other public clouds or in your data center using Azure Arc.[9]

Managing infrastructure with Azure Arc enables GitOps and policy-based creation and management of new assets, blessing the Ops side of DevOps with the same continuous integration and improvement capabilities enjoyed by the Dev side of the house. Imagine an edge computing scenario where hardware must be adjacent to equipment, such as factory or field operations. You have registered edge compute locations with Azure Arc such as a maintenance hub in the Midwest, a production line in the Southwest and a transportation hub near shipping ports on the West coast. Now you push an automated deployment of Kubernetes infrastructure to each one that incorporates uniform builds, security, and policies across your enterprise. Since the desired state of your installation is fully defined in the code from which it is deployed, changing the environment to better suit its workload becomes almost trivial, and further, the systems you deploy are continuously monitored for configuration drift and largely self-healing. In the Arc dashboard, you now see the edge infrastructure you've deployed as if it were hosted on the Azure cloud. Additionally, your workloads can take advantage of additional PaaS services running either on the Azure cloud or locally via Azure Arc, meaning you can choose which portions of your data center you will manage locally and which are advantageous to host in Azure data centers.

---

[9] https://learn.microsoft.com/en-us/azure/app-service/overview-arc-integration

So how is this model of free administration of assets in data centers it doesn't own advantageous to Microsoft? While ensuring that you find the Azure stack indispensable, it also makes it easy for Microsoft customers to purchase cloud resources that will be intertwined with their on-premise computing assets as described in the preceding example. Further, with cloud computing growing at a breakneck pace that challenges even big players in this space, it offers stretched capacity by relying on a hybrid compute model that makes hardware purchasing, provisioning, and maintenance of the edge location the responsibility of the customer. This is a key differentiator between the approach taken by AWS Outposts, which includes provisioned hardware, and Azure which extends its Arc management layer across the customer's hardware. This option has particular appeal for companies that've already made capital investments in their own data center and have not yet recouped depreciation of those assets by forestalling a move out of the data center until they've reached end of life. Whether emulating Jeff Hollan's flamboyant demonstration of Arc managing a Kubernetes cluster running on a laptop under the podium at Build 2021,[10] running stretched clusters on validated hardware that you own with Azure HCI, or even just deploying vanilla virtual machines on an existing ESXi cluster, it's clear that what you manage with Arc does not have to be owned by Microsoft.

Azure Stack HCI, Edge, and Hub

The operational methodologies of Azure Arc are not new; rather, they are a mature outflow of Azure Stack. Azure Stack extends the Azure cloud in three principal ways:

---

[10] https://learn.microsoft.com/en-us/events/build-may-2021/azure/featured-sessions/ts03/?ocid=AID3032299

- HCI or Hyperconverged Infrastructure refers to a cluster of Hyper-V hosts running on validated hardware that you purchase directly from a vendor. Each cluster consists of between 1 and 16 servers. Initially, these clusters had to be collocated, but they can now be stretched geographically to provide resiliency in the case of natural disasters or other disruptive events. You can run Kubernetes clusters hosting either Linux or Windows workloads on HCI,[11] and this use case is typical for applications that must be replicated at hundreds or thousands of branch offices, scaling storage or running high-performance instances of SQL Server. It is also possible to create a seamless hybrid data center with some assets running on the Azure cloud and some on Azure Stack HCI. As the flagship for the Azure Stack family, HCI tends to lead the way in showing what's possible, and the newest preview version as of this writing makes Azure the single source of truth for HCI infrastructure with near full automation. According to the release announcement for 23H2,[12] new edge deployments are as simple as "plug them in" and allow them to be remotely provisioned in your network with proper security, policy, and desired features already in place and on par with your existing installations.

---

[11] https://learn.microsoft.com/en-us/azure/aks/hybrid/overview#why-use-aks-on-azure-stack-hci-and-windows-server-for-containerized-applications

[12] https://techcommunity.microsoft.com/t5/azure-stack-blog/accelerate-edge-deployments-with-cloud-managed-infrastructure/ba-p/3982951

- Azure Stack Edge is a network data transfer device provided by Microsoft, but it does much more than transfer data – it brings the power of the Azure cloud to you including Kubernetes for Azure Stack Edge as well as offering Edge versions of many popular Azure Services including Functions, Event Grid, and more. Once you are running Kubernetes on your Edge device, you can manage it with Azure Arc just as you would any other on-premise Arc-enabled Kubernetes cluster.[13] The Edge device also serves as a storage gateway and provides a local cache of data for quick response times as well as intelligent data transfer to the cloud. The fun doesn't stop there, as the Edge device is also available in a GPU equipped model so that you can run machine learning and analytics processing jobs near the real-time data that you're processing.

Figure 2-2. *Azure Stack Edge 2 device comes in various configurations including GPU equipped models for AI Inferencing, Microsoft Docs[14]*

Per Alexander Ortha, a Global Black Belt Senior Specialist for Hybrid Solutions at Microsoft, Azure Stack Hub was originally released as just "Azure Stack" in 2017. It is the evolution of the private cloud model

---

[13] https://learn.microsoft.com/en-us/azure/databox-online/
azure-stack-edge-gpu-deploy-arc-kubernetes-cluster
[14] https://learn.microsoft.com/en-us/azure/databox-online/azure-stack-
edge-pro-2-overview#components

Microsoft has offered for at least 15 years beginning with provisioned data centers, then on to System Center private cloud products circa 2012, and now today is a complete hardware and software solution delivered to the customer's premises that can be used either connected to or disconnected from the Azure cloud. The option to run disconnected makes it highly suitable for scenarios where data sovereignty is mandatory or in locations where connectivity is sparse, such as ocean liners or disaster zones. Ortha notes: "With Azure Stack Hub, the customer becomes their own instance of the Azure Cloud" with a fully configured environment that includes Azure Resource Manager, an instance of the Azure Portal CLI management, and access to Azure Services. In addition to the highly regulated scenarios mentioned earlier, Ortha also points out that Hub can be useful in multi-tenant scenarios where a customer may want a discrete instance of Azure.

A key difference between offerings in the Azure Stack product suite and Azure Arc is that a hardware purchase is recommended for Stack products in order to facilitate Azure capabilities at the edge, while Arc can enable your existing infrastructure running in the DC or public cloud of your choice to function as part of an Azure ecosystem. In fact, though, you can create a reasonable facsimile of Azure Stack HCI on your own hardware using Arc-enabled technologies (as was hinted at in an Ignite 2023 announcement stating that in Azure Stack HCI 23H2, "every workload is automatically Azure Arc enabled"[15]); however, Microsoft emphasizes that using "Microsoft-validated hardware from an OEM partner [will] ensure optimal performance and reliability."[16]

---

[15] https://techcommunity.microsoft.com/t5/azure-stack-blog/accelerate-edge-deployments-with-cloud-managed-infrastructure/ba-p/3982951
[16] https://learn.microsoft.com/en-us/azure-stack/operator/compare-azure-azure-stack?view=azs-2306#azure-stack-hci

IoT and Edge Security

As noted earlier, edge computing scenarios are one of the three pillars of Azure Stack. At an internal Tech Summit a couple years ago, I spoke on SASE, or Secure Access Service Edge, using AWS Greengrass IoT as one of the best examples of a thorough implementation existing at that time. Not only was the traffic from field sensors encrypted, but if a channel to a particular sensor was opened by an analyst who then left their station to get coffee without closing it, the connection would be closed automatically, requiring it to be reopened when the analyst resumed their task. This is the type of governance that can be baked into edge computing environments when they are properly monitored and managed remotely.

Sometimes, there is an assumption that data which is not relating to PII or financials need not be protected in the thorough way that practices like SASE are designed to do, yet when it comes to proprietary business data, this is not the case. If an agriculture firm is collecting seemingly innocuous data on fertilization, rainfall, soil mineralization, and more on their industrial farming operations, any one of those data types may seem unworthy of the effort and expense of securing them in transit. Yet if a regional competitor would benefit from the same data, why should they invest in the infrastructure to monitor their crops when they can simply scrape data off of someone else's unprotected system?

Azure IoT security provides equivalent protections to harden field devices, secure traffic, and monitor an IoT installation with continuous threat detection and the ability to lock down potentially compromised devices. When you consider that a single IoT hub can support literally billions of field devices, you can see the impossibility of managing them without full automation.

How does Arc improve upon the suite of IoT management tools already offered by Microsoft? Take a look at the diagram in Figure 2-3 from Microsoft[17] illustrating its benefits.

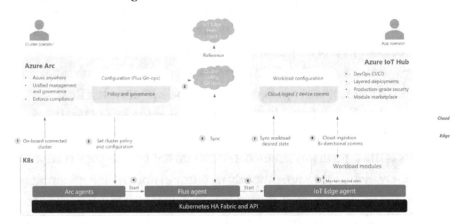

Figure 2-3. *Benefits to Azure IoT Operations*

Via Arc, you are able to apply policies to assure this cluster is compliant with your enterprise governance. Deployment can also be managed by Arc using its flex agent. Then once the cluster is created, it can be connected to Arc so that it is accessible from the consolidated view Arc provides of your enterprise landscape.

Azure Arc Enabled for Machine Learning

Arc uses an extension to enable Arc-managed Kubernetes clusters for machine learning. The managed cluster can be on-premise, on cloud, or at the edge just as any other cluster managed by Arc. The machine learning

---

[17] https://docs.microsoft.com/en-us/azure/azure-arc/kubernetes/media/ edge-arc.png

extension depends upon Arc's Kubernetes extension to deploy its agent on the target cluster. Once installed, that cluster can be a part of an Azure Machine Learning workspace.[18]

A key risk in large machine learning workloads is that the body of data being analyzed may contain personally identifying or other regulated data. Aside from configuring an Arc cluster to enable Kubernetes and machine learning, there are larger network and security concerns that must be addressed in the initial architecture for your machine learning instance, such as ensuring that data is not accessible via a public vNet, that PII data is not exposed in the model, that service accounts for processing data are set up correctly, and that meaningful monitoring is assuring that your cluster machines remain compliant with policy. Arc provides agents to accomplish those tasks, and the ability to run Azure Monitor on your cluster will also ensure the health of the machines, enable you to observe traffic, collect logs for analysis, and more. These types of automation and their relationship to effective security will be discussed in Chapter 8. Chapter 9 will examine the explosion of functional AI and the practices that will allow your organization to create and utilize machine learning models not only for their value to core lines of business (which has now far surpassed classic analytics) but also for threat detection and response.

Arc-Enabled Kubernetes

A killer feature of Azure Arc (and indeed the motivator for competitive control planes) is its ability to manage large Kubernetes farms wherever you choose to host them. As we will discuss in a chapter devoted to Arc-enabled Kubernetes, the ability to deploy, govern, and update the premier container host platform is an operational challenge that can be greatly reduced when it is possible to manage those tasks from a single vantage

---

[18] https://docs.microsoft.com/en-us/azure/machine-learning/how-to-attach-arc-kubernetes

point on the Azure platform. Particular advantages include the ability to deploy with uniformity, apply policies which ensure security of both the platform and the workloads it carries, and to continuously monitor and defend these installations whether they are hosted on AWS, Azure, Google Cloud Platform, or in an on-premise data center or edge compute location. More details, including the difference between the Azure Kubernetes Service and Arc-enabled Kubernetes, will be discussed in Chapter 6 which is devoted entirely to Kubernetes.

That concludes this chapter's exploration of some of the Arc control plane's capabilities managing on-premise and foreign cloud VMs, Kubernetes clusters, SQL and other database servers, and even hyper-converged infrastructure installations in edge locations. Beyond that, it also allows you to host many Azure PaaS services in all of these locations, a remarkable extension of cloud-native capabilities to where they are needed. In Chapter 3, we will examine some of Arc's benefits in more detail.

Overview of Benefits of Arc in the Enterprise

"Man is a tool-using animal. Without tools he is nothing, with tools he is all" was the opinion of Thomas Carlyle, a British author and philosopher who died 140 years ago. You might have thought he was a bit prescient about the evolution of technology when you consider another quote, "Go as far as you can see; when you get there you'll be able to see farther." In the enterprise, Arc is a tool to help you see farther.

What is "enterprise" computing? Gartner defines an enterprise as a business with more than a thousand employees or more than 50M in revenue.[1] Such organizations require specialized tools to scale, govern, and monitor large IT landscapes. Today, businesses of all sizes can take advantage of an enterprise computing paradigm simply by consuming

---

[1] www.gartner.com/en/information-technology/glossary/smbs-small-and-midsize-businesses

SaaS [Software as a Service] or PaaS [Platform as a Service][2] offerings from major cloud vendors. However, solutions that might be required for a large enterprise could be burdensome to a smaller business to purchase and maintain. If you don't have acres of database servers, IT assets that may have a wide geographic distribution, edge computing installations, hybrid installations, or vast farms of VMs or containers, then your organization may realize enough benefit from using Azure's many monitoring tools without the Arc umbrella.

Let's take a closer look at specific use cases for Arc in some of the problem spaces that were highlighted in Chapter 1.

DevOps

Application Lifecycle Management (ALM) is management of an application during its span of usage in an organization from its design, implementation, and day-to-day usage to its eventual retirement. It is an area that has been codified into a discipline partially in response to what happens when there is no ALM. A premier example of what can go wrong is the case where a multi-tenant application begins to be deployed in a snowflake fashion, tenant by tenant, until it is no longer a single application but hundreds of applications with varying requirements and implementations. Maintenance and upgrades become progressively more difficult and expensive the longer this situation is allowed to continue. Conversely, a defined set of requirements for what the application does and proper source code management along with continuous integration and deployment can achieve the first of the 12 factor principles[3] of "One codebase tracked in revision control, many deploys" throughout the application's lifetime.

---

[2] www.ibm.com/topics/iaas-paas-saas
[3] https://12factor.net/

Arc is a particularly apt solution to the "many deploys" aspect of maintaining large distributed applications or services that may be hosted on-premise, in a customer's data center, at the edge, or upon a public cloud since it can manage Kubernetes installations in all of those places and assure that the desired consistency is achieved.

The impact on testing and quality assurance for an application is also profound, since automated deployments allow for environments to be strictly governed for consistency. Human-readable definitions allow disparities between environments to be quickly identified and remediated. Additionally, the disposable nature of containers means that unlike virtual machines, they are not intended to be customized individually in order to support a unicorn version of an application. Containers are often described as "cattle not pets" for this reason. When a test is run on development code, there is a reasonable assurance that if it passes in dev, it will also be runnable in QA and subsequently pre-prod or production.

Eliminating friction caused by manual deployment strategies and inconsistent environments greatly contributes to the ability to establish agile release cycles, meaning that code can be released frequently as needed without risk to the platform as opposed to large cumulative releases that are difficult to troubleshoot. This level of standardization and governance is truly new and doesn't rely on human intervention to achieve once configured. While still short of full Robotic Process Automation, the use of machine learning to mine logs and metrics[4] already allows for closing the loop on some types of issues with an automated response, thus moving steadily in that direction.

A Kubernetes control plane (such as Istio[5] service mesh) provides service discovery, configuration ingestion and validation, certificate management, runtime proxies, easy blue/green or canary releases, and

---

[4] https://docs.microsoft.com/en-us/azure/machine-learning/monitor-azure-machine-learning#analyzing-logs

[5] https://istio.io/

ease of operation compared to managing Kubernetes directly. What lifts Arc above using a service mesh alone is the ability to apply the same deployment configuration and security policies to clusters running in hybrid, edge, and multi-cloud environments and manage them all from a single perspective – a truly one-world approach to Kubernetes deployments.

An application's lifecycle may be short, such as those developed for seasonal campaigns, sign-ups, or other temporary service needs within an organization. Conversely, an application may live for decades with an indefinite endpoint. The Internal Revenue Service, many state governments, and industries like insurance and banking still rely on applications that were developed in COBOL for mainframes more than 40 years ago. In the case of financial institutions, what some might view as an antiquated language still has the benefit of being designed to handle fixed-point arithmetic calculations well. In this case, the central ALM stages of maintenance and feature enhancements will be managed not by a single group, but by a series of specialists passing the baton of responsibility for that application. Can Arc manage your more than 40-year-old mainframe running its 60-year-old programming language? That's unlikely; however, if you end up migrating off the mainframe and into the Azure cloud,[6] then those legacy applications can come under a very modern control plane with Arc.

During the maintenance phase, ALM core challenges include things like dealing with application failures, maintaining integration points, feature additions and enhancements, meeting evolving security threats, and more. How does Arc address some of these ALM challenges?

Arguably, the most critical issue faced in managing an application is an outright failure. Even if the length of the outage is brief, there may be substantial cost attached in terms of lost revenue and customer goodwill, the time or overtime of incident responders, and corporate trust in the

---

[6] https://docs.microsoft.com/en-us/azure/architecture/example-scenario/
mainframe/ibm-system-i-azure-infinite-i

faulting systems. Downstream effects could include data corruption or loss, a scenario which carries its own costs (particularly if there is a breach of private information that results in legal action against the company). If the application is regulated, there may be consequences in terms of additional monitoring requirements or fines and reputational injury. If postmortem failure analysis shows security was breached, that requires a crisis response. If any of the preceding issues are encountered by a core business system that cannot be offline, then the impact is compounded.

There is confusion around the term "application" in that the singular term might make it seem there is one artifact that can be manipulated when new features or fixes are desired. In reality, what appears as a single application to a user is an orchestration of workloads that could be running on multiple systems of disparate types. The codebase itself may consist of separate repositories of application code, application variables, and environment configuration as well as deployment configurations. If the application is built using microservices, then each service will have all of these as a small stand-alone unit, and an application may have hundreds of such services. Then there is the data an application may create, consume, manipulate, or store. This could mean there are messaging systems, databases, data caches for quick retrieval, and flat file storage components. Connections between all these elements and users of the application must be made; thus, there are networking and sometimes Telco (in the case of dedicated pipes that do not traverse the public Internet) elements to also consider. Finally, all of this must have security as an integral component which can extend far beyond who or what can access a particular area and include validation of component identity with certificates, cryptographic stores for secret values like access keys, and more. Further, multiple applications might depend upon shared components or platform features compounding the risk of their failure.

This is why the objective of a product like Arc to have a very high-level view of all the elements of an application is so necessary for the maintenance phase of ALM and particularly proactively managing potential points of failure. If, for example, a messaging queue fails, but the queue is monitored and has a failover strategy in place, then those sorts of micro failures can occur without the application as a whole suffering an outage. A modern application, especially one that is intended to run on a distributed computing platform, must have resiliency built into every application component to avoid being prone to failure.

The definition of an application as an amalgamation of a tremendous number of resources is also a good indicator of why Arc is an enterprise product, and it is at that level of complexity that its value will be realized against the effort of implementation.

In both existing and new enterprise applications, project failure is a constant risk to the extent that an entire industry has sprung up around the forensic analysis of failed enterprise applications. As a consultant, I encounter projects where we may be the second or third firm called in to restructure and deliver projects that prior consulting partners had failed to complete or that are installed but experiencing an unacceptable rate of failure. This experience has been so common that it led me to write a brief article on how to mitigate risk in consulting relationships.[7]

Over the past five years, estimates of software project failures have remained at the astonishing level of about three quarters of those initiated according to multiple sources, including Forbes contributor Steve Andriole who, in a scathing send-up of this being an accepted norm, cites management commitment to IT projects but also oversight and scope as critical issues.[8]

It's the oversight piece that could most benefit from tools like Arc. Like the 1980s PSA, "Do you know where your children are?" – a project with even a slim chance of success must think about incorporating

---

[7] www.linkedin.com/pulse/risk-mitigation-through-successful-consulting-ramona-maxwell/

[8] www.forbes.com/sites/steveandriole/2021/03/25/3-main-reasons-why-big-technology-projects-fail---why-many-companies-should-just-never-do-them

visibility and accountability long before the first server is provisioned. In order for projects to come under the umbrella of corporate governance, there first has to be a working governance model to adhere to, and then it must be applied from the moment an idea enters the design phase. Which governance policies apply to a particular piece of software as well as how they will be implemented and monitored should be a prebuilt decision based on the application requirements. Thus, a tool like Arc that automates the application and monitoring of policy across all registered resources shows its value from the very beginning of the ALM process when the first development environment is set up. The management of the application can be part of its development cycle so that if in some way it's not easily aligned with existing policies, adjustments can be made before it even reaches its first round of quality assurance testing.

For a software project to have a shot at success, planning must include more than a vision of what the application will do, how it will be built, and how much it may cost. It should also assess all of the potential points of failure, their impact on both the component and the project as a whole, as well as whether or how to remediate them. A mantra of modern DevOps is to "fail fast" and thereby not have problems disappear into the deeper layers of the codebase where their origin will be much harder to diagnose. Seema Thapar explains how her team performs a "premortem"[9] in the PayPal blog in order to uncover potential points of failure, while "the team still has control to fix the problems" by inviting the execution team to create potential failure scenarios before even beginning the development of the first application components.

The God's eye view that a control plane like Arc provides is desirable in the management phase of ALM because often failures do not occur in a linear set of dependencies where a single weak link in a chain could be blamed for everything past that point. Enterprise systems far exceed the

---

[9] https://hbr.org/2007/09/performing-a-project-premortem

complexity of a vehicle, yet that might serve as a simple analogy. If you have a weak spark plug and the others still fire, you may be okay. If the weak plug is combined with a failing alternator, then you might soon be stranded. This is why there is some pushback to the idea of Root Cause Analysis being effective in a large enterprise environment. Failures are generally complex with multiple contributors and require a holistic approach to resolve. Enterprise infrastructure and software are both able to be designed with resistance to failure in mind. When individual elements are adequately monitored, and backups stand ready to take their place, it is unlikely that the system as a whole will fail.

According to the 2020 State of the Industry Report *Software Quality Analysis*[10] (SQA), a small report published by the Consortium for Information and Software Quality (CISQ), only 17% of organizations surveyed are requiring SQA tools in their development pipeline. One of the functions of such tools is to check for code compliance with known standards such as OWASP (security), HIPAA (healthcare privacy), and others. This dovetails well with Arc's policy features which will then monitor deployed applications if, for instance, you choose to extend Azure's App Service to your Kubernetes deployment running on non-Microsoft infrastructure (covered specifically in Chapter 6 of this book). Since the Health Insurance Portability and Accountability Act (HIPAA) is a standard governing how healthcare information should be managed, Azure complies with commonly recognized methods of applying those standards to IT infrastructure and provides predefined policy sets to enable adherence to this standard and many others.[11] Examples include specifying how specific application interactions must be constructed to avoid the likely compromise of private health information. Arc thus

---

[10] www.it-cisq.org/pdf/soti-report.pdf

[11] https://learn.microsoft.com/en-us/azure/governance/policy/samples/hipaa-hitrust-9-2

prevents another issue noted in CISQ's SQA report that software quality violations are often ignored by developers – a scenario that is unlikely to occur when it is known that substandard code will not be deployable.

This leads directly to another core DevOps objective, that of continuous integration of new features or modifications into the existing codebase. It is the methodology to achieve the 12-factor manifesto objective of a single codebase using frequent (sometimes multiple times per day) pushes of developer code into the main codebase for the application. In this way, new code is constantly verified to work within the context of the existing application code. When integration is not continuous, there is a significant risk that the feature branch may drift from the architectural patterns used in the application and also perhaps grow large enough that when it is finally integrated there are multiple incompatibilities to resolve. As the application continues to stray, the technical debt accrued in terms of the effort to fix or maintain it burgeons, a problem common enough that technical debt is one of the three main focuses of CISQ's 2022[12] report, where it was estimated to consume an astonishing 33% of an "average developer" workweek. Automating builds with GitOps is a primary way this tight feedback loop of continuous integration is accomplished.

GitOps

Once an organization moves toward automated deployments and configuration as code, then it becomes obvious that the configuration files are data, and the repository is roughly analogous to a database for that data and thus a candidate for applying well-known principles of data consistency. The configuration store (Git repository) becomes the single

---

[12] www.it-cisq.org/wp-content/uploads/sites/6/2022/11/CPSQ-Report-Nov-22-2.pdf

source of truth for environments and the applications deployed within them. The store also exposes the configuration to auditing and monitoring processes to assure configuration remains consistent.

Arc makes use of a CNCF project called Flux[13] to achieve what is known as desired state configuration in Kubernetes clusters.[14] Flux monitors the Git repository (polling for changes every five minutes by default) containing an application's configuration for changes in order to assure that the state you have defined for your application via a Kubernetes manifest is a match to what is running in your cluster. Flux's state management is not only additive that is pushing new configuration, but unlike many current deployment pipeline tools, it can also remove values that are no longer part of the manifest. It can be used to automatically update your configuration to the latest version of a container, thus assuring its deployment configuration will automatically remain current.

The creator and CNCF contributor of Flux, Weaveworks (who are also reputed to have coined the term GitOps), proudly noted at their 2022 GitOps conference[15] that Flux is integrated into the GitOps pipeline of major platforms, including AWS, VMware, Azure, Red Hat, and more. As we will discover in the upcoming chapter on Arc-enabled Kubernetes, Microsoft has been using Flux since version 1.0 and with the integration of version 2.0 notes that GitOps using Flux is now a "first-class citizen"[16] with Flux available as a managed service so that both Azure Kubernetes Service and Arc-enabled Kubernetes can be deployed using GitOps pipelines. In addition to facilitating swift deployments, Arc-enabled Kubernetes clusters also benefit from continuous monitoring and self-healing of deployed

---

[13] www.cncf.io/projects/flux/

[14] https://learn.microsoft.com/en-us/azure/azure-arc/kubernetes/conceptual-gitops-flux2

[15] www.weave.works/blog/gitops-days-2022-recap-major-clouds-vendors-offering-gitops-with-flux

[16] www.youtube.com/watch?v=6OjhYD2wLkY

resources, thereby creating a resilient platform for enterprise workloads. GitOps integration means all the typical deployment tools from the CLI and PowerShell to portal commands are available, and you can monitor the status of your deployment as it runs from within the Azure portal. This expeditious approach allows deployments across Azure, on-premise, and competitor's clouds to run uniformly and at scale while reaping significant cost savings by eliminating tedious and error-prone manual deployments.

Automating deployments using GitOps greatly accelerates the pace of deployments and provides operators with fast feedback. Integrations become simpler when both the infrastructure and code are predictable and visible to development and operations teams. Test and QA cycles for developers also benefit since deployment may go from hours and days to minutes and seconds.

Overall, GitOps contributes greatly to implementing continuous integration and deployment as part of an agile software development approach to ALM. Key concerns around the safety of deployments are minimized or eliminated, and the entire process comes under an organization's governance umbrella, no longer subject to the vagaries of individual approaches and preferences that are not testable, repeatable, or safe.

Governance and Policy

Enterprise-level governance is a process with known standards and accepted methodologies. Typically, it may involve an executive steering committee reporting to the highest levels of the organization, senior IT leaders such as CTO or CIO, serving as a consultative guide to the committee as well as representation from legal and compliance departments. A comprehensive governance plan will specify standards across broad categories that can have a direct impact on regulatory compliance, security, performance, profitability, and more. Almost always implementation of these standards will have some impact on IT, or in larger organizations there will be subsidiary governance manifests around technology standards.

IT implementation of these standards requires considerable planning and systems architecture since the application of a governance mandate may be extremely complex. Ideally, both the governance document and its implementation specification will be living documents versioned in lockstep with any update to policy triggering a review of the implementation plan to assure it remains compliant. Conversely, when CTOs become aware of offerings in the constantly evolving technology landscape that will more comprehensively fulfill governance objectives, the implementation specification may update without any change to the governance plan. In real-world scenarios, synchronicity between governance and operations is extremely difficult to accomplish, let alone maintain. That is why yoking them together through Arc's ability to extend the reach of Azure's policy engine to the far netherlands of large IT estates is a powerful leverage in the effort to apply governance.

Scenarios that tend to precipitate changes to governance include business growth and acquisition, evolution of threats both commercial and operational, profit opportunities requiring compliance upgrades, and the rapid changes to technology itself.

Arc lives up to its definition as an enterprise-wide control plane by facilitating monitoring and collection of data that can then be fed back into threat assessment tools. It's important to remember that Arc is not the tool performing the monitoring; rather, as a control plane, it facilitates access via an agent where that is required. That agent is performing on your behalf the activities you want applied to an asset, from monitoring to updates and application of policies.

A March 2021 Cloud Native Computing Foundation outlines an expectation that DevOps best practice will move beyond the implementation of policy defined in document repositories to Policy as Code, which the author defines as "the process of managing and provisioning policy enforcement tooling through machine-readable definition files."[17] This is not so far-fetched since in coding a template for a Kubernetes deployment things like ingress and egress rules or applying security standards are in effect implementing policy.

This obvious need to automate infrastructure controls has led to projects like Crossplane,[18] which, similarly to Arc, are attempting to extend infrastructure management, but in this case using a Kubernetes control plane in a cloud-agnostic fashion suitable for multi-cloud deployments.

Determining whether Arc or an alternate approach would be better for automated policy implementation and monitoring depends on several factors. Is the enterprise historically a consumer of Microsoft products and therefore its operations team is well equipped to manage non-Microsoft assets using familiar Azure paradigms? Organizations already invested in the Azure Stack would also find Arc to be an obvious choice. Since Crossplane is basically a Kubernetes operator, if an organization isn't running Kubernetes clusters it's an unlikely choice. Crossplane also lacks Arc's tight integration with Microsoft SQL Server, so that is likely to be a key decision factor in organizations where that database is widely used.

For companies with a long history of Linux Servers and open source software though, the CNCF Crossplane project would likely integrate much more smoothly with existing workflows. Interestingly, Crossplane claims both Red Hat, a publisher of a popular Linux distro, and Microsoft as among its supporters. While the two tools aren't mutually exclusive, for instance, you could use Arc's monitoring capabilities in conjunction with Crossplane's infrastructure; deployment chaos can sometimes result in environments overloaded with too many tools and not enough integration. Since the infrastructure landscape serves as the foundation

---

[17] www.cncf.io/blog/2021/03/29/what-is-kubernetes-policy-as-code/
[18] https://crossplane.io/

of critical line-of-business applications, its architecture must be holistic, avoiding redundant or shadow IT solutions that create more problems than they solve.

Modernization

Digital transformation, shift left, modernization, and cloud migration are just a few of the phrases reflecting global efforts to transform enterprise IT to a distributed computing model. First, there were microservices, then a stampede to the cloud, and now a more realistic hybrid approach. What causes an organization to embark upon this digital journey?

Insecure, nonperformant, and nonscalable applications often incite modernization efforts, as highlighted in Table 3-1, discussing the notorious Equifax breach of consumer credit data.

Table 3-1. *Data Breach Factors*

Risk Management ***Java Example***	The famous Equifax breach was attributed to an unpatched Struts vulnerability. Security Boulevard logged 20 years of Struts vulnerabilities and the packages they affect	Lacks built-in protection against many common security risks. Amid legacy libraries are known vulnerabilities. Weak or ineffective "security" strategies such as obscuring URLs
Scalability	Not cloud-ready OOTB. Model/ View/Controller with tightly coupled layers. Relies on a plug-in system	Accomplished by clustering and load-balancing technologies
Operability	Security options require construction of filters, expert knowledge of vulnerabilities, and remediation	Security can be misconfigured, heavily manual. Scaling approaches require ongoing configuration and administration

Many organizations have thousands of such legacy applications that are difficult to maintain and protect. Some of these may not be identified or considered in an overall risk profile due to the challenges of cataloging large infrastructures and their dependencies. Remediating security vulnerabilities is sometimes not possible on legacy platforms, and performance improvements may also face obstacles. Thus, it becomes apparent that *modernization has value independent of cloud adoption.*

Modernization has value independent of cloud adoption![19]

A principal benefit of Arc to enterprise modernization efforts is the capability it provides to catalog large infrastructures and monitor hosted application stacks running on them. Modernization projects start with an inventory of current applications and their business value. Beginning left with the value to the business is key to not recycling old tech for its own sake, but instead serving the reasons for which a particular business or nonprofit organization exists. Sometimes, initial assessments may reveal that much of the functionality of an old application is being served elsewhere, and the app itself is still living simply because it performs one calculation or is familiar to certain individuals who prefer it to adoption of newer methods and different applications. Some of the effort that was initially expected for the transformation may fall away quickly when business value is the first criteria for retention of an application.

It is extremely challenging to enumerate large corpus of applications and their supporting infrastructure, so much so that many organizations never complete a thorough audit of their IT landscape. It is key to a successful effort to consider the time required to accomplish the initial assessment. If large efforts are not undertaken concurrently with sufficient

---

[19] 2020 Magenic Masters Course on Practical Application Modernization Strategies, authored and delivered by Ramona Maxwell

team support and a good dose of automation, the risk becomes that the intended modernization strategies themselves may become outdated before they are implemented, creating a vicious cycle of always remaining in an outmoded state. The adoption of Arc can provide a dose of prevention if all new assets are required to be exposed to its control plane, but application modernization projects are often a juncture at which technical debt must be paid if success is to be achieved. Some systems aren't worth the debt acquired, so the question becomes how to replace them with whatever product is the modern standard for the company's industry in order to assure it remains competitive with its peers. Often, that product will be a SaaS solution.

As existing candidates for modernization are identified, a common approach is to perform a capability assessment[20] of inventoried items against a matrix of industry norms. This can help segregate applications by their importance, known deficits, and other key attributes before deciding how to treat each similar set. A popular industry paradigm of the "Five Rs"[21] can help to differentiate between core strategies for rationalizing a large application portfolio. These five are

- Rehost

    - A modern application will be platform agnostic

- Refactor

    - Look for opportunities to reorganize the application so that part or all of it can be migrated to microservices or even PaaS offerings

- Revise

---

[20] https://cio-wiki.org/wiki/IT_Capability

[21] https://docs.microsoft.com/en-us/azure/cloud-adoption-framework/digital-estate/5-rs-of-rationalization

- Revise the current application only to the degree
  that allows it to be hosted on a cloud platform

- Rebuild/Retain or Retire

  - Rebuild on-prem, retain existing, or retire

- Replace

  - The beauty of greenfield development with the
    constraint of assuring uninterrupted service

The Five Rs are shown in Figure 3-1.

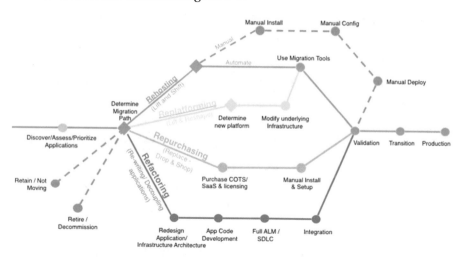

Figure 3-1. *The Five Rs – Credit: Stephen Orban, AWS*

Performing adequate capability assessments will assist in determining
which approach to take with a particular application or group of similar
applications. For instance, applications that are already platform agnostic or
containerized may simply be *rehosted*. An important goal in rehosting is to
remove manual configurations so that even if the applications themselves
are not optimized to be cloud native, their management is much less
burdensome. Sometimes, this path is taken as part of a longer-term strategy
where individual apps will be assessed for further modernization after a

cloud migration is complete, and sometimes it is the end goal. This may be the case when the reduction in operational costs significantly reduces the total cost of ownership for those applications, while modernization may have much lower returns (particularly for applications that may be near the end of their lifecycle). The operational benefits of moving select application types to a cloud provider's platform in a "lift and shift" were present before Arc, which only sweetens the deal with dramatically improved administrator overview and control plane capabilities.

Refactoring the application is often preferred for large monolithic applications that are reaching their capacity limits as to cost-effective scaling, have become entangled with internal and external dependencies that were not well managed, or may be difficult to integrate with modern software applications and effectively secure. This process is rarely quick and is sometimes fraught with unexpected pitfalls in terms of dependencies. Often, a Strangler Fig[22] pattern (originally conceived by Martin Fowler[23]) is used to peel off portions of functionality into individual microservices that will over time form the building blocks of the now modernized application. This extended timeline previously also applied to the benefit of managing the new microservices in the cloud as they gradually replaced old functionality from the original application. However, Arc's ability to manage on-premise assets as natively belonging to Azure accelerates governance, server management, and security benefits of the cloud from the moment the Arc agent is installed and management controls applied. Microsoft's implementation of the Strangler Fig pattern particularly recommends a façade over the application as a whole, both the legacy monolith and the modern services, in order to avoid dependent users or applications having to make adjustments as

---

[22] https://docs.microsoft.com/en-us/azure/architecture/patterns/strangler-fig
[23] https://martinfowler.com/bliki/StranglerFigApplication.html

to the location of app components (when that applies). In a sense, Arc accomplishes the same abstraction for the configuration and management tasks involved in administering the application.

Revision is a less common approach that touches the application only to the minimal degree needed to move it to a different host. It might apply to singular use cases where a prerequisite functionality needs to move quickly before the components that depend upon it or for a group of applications that need only one small adjustment to move.

Choosing to *rebuild* or *retain or retire* an existing application is often prudent choices. As part of the original assessment process, there are often good candidates for retirement due duplication of functionality, low usage, and other criteria. Removing these, along with any associated cost allocation, contributes to the speed and lowers the cost of the modernization project as a whole. As will be discussed in the chapter on data migration, it may be helpful to bring host servers under management as early as possible in the project so that usage patterns may be tracked. Rebuilding an application that gains little from transitioning to microservices but will still benefit from cleaning up outdated technical stacks and other typical problems can be worthwhile. The rebuild effort can include a modern deployment pipeline to reduce risk and reliance on the old-school practice of using feature flags (switching the release on if it appears to work or off if it creates issues) to add new capabilities to live systems. When the rebuilt application is brought under Arc's control plane, then its management and security as part of the enterprise application portfolio will also be assured. Even applications that are selected for retention only (e.g., do nothing) should be evaluated as candidates for consolidated management under Arc since the payback from an Arc deployment is partially tied to gathering up all stragglers. Not only the application but its operational ecosystem stand to benefit from the centralized management that Arc provides, for example, Microsoft

Defender for Cloud[24] can protect servers outside of Azure when they are Arc enabled, potentially replacing several on-premise or competitor cloud antivirus [AV] solutions, thereby reducing both complexity and cost.

The *replace* option is guaranteed to generate enthusiasm in business stakeholders, architects, and developers alike due to the opportunity to use cutting-edge technology and innovate solutions that if executed correctly may propel a business into new profit opportunities. It is also, as previously discussed, fraught with the danger of project failure or cost escalation. Even if costs are contained, it is generally an expensive option that may require extensive validation to gain approval. If designed correctly, it will be resilient (self-healing), rapidly scalable, secure, and potentially have many other enhancements, such as artificial intelligence, machine learning, and more. It provides a golden opportunity to apply governance and management strategies from the very beginning of a new application's lifecycle.

Upgrades

Since many of the options discussed earlier refer to classic hosting of applications in data centers (whether on-premise or on a cloud provider's infrastructure), the issue of how to update running systems remains critical.

Common types of updates include patches to fix security vulnerabilities or bugs in a current version of software, updates which are improvements to software that are not a new installation but usually increment the version, and lastly upgrades which usually completely uninstall an older version of software in order to reinstall a completely new version but retain the user data and preferences. The necessity of applying any of these may occur all the way through the technical stack

---

[24] https://learn.microsoft.com/en-us/azure/defender-for-cloud/quickstart-onboard-machines?pivots=azure-arc

from a server's firmware and operating system to end-user software and everything else in between, including things like network protocols, firewalls, etc. Microsoft has its tradition of "Patch Tuesday"[25] releases, and other companies also have distinct routines with an out-of-band release signaling a significant security vulnerability that must be dealt with immediately. The incredibly complex job of managing a living IT landscape has led to Herculean efforts by administrators with entire teams devoting 48 hours of their weekend to installing and validating an endless stream of items which are continuously being stapled onto software packages. Colloquial wisdom held that responsible administrators would stay six months behind Microsoft's release date before installing update packages, since the updates themselves sometimes created issues and were often impossible to roll back. An early incentive toward cloud-hosted PaaS[26] (when reluctance to abandon private data centers was rampant) was the Nirvana of living in a world relieved of the need to manage patching, and this is still a primary driver toward rehosting applications on PaaS since not only OS components are updated but also SDKs for application code as well as database and security updates.

Arc's approach to updating servers is world's away from all-night sessions of humans watching for maintenance side effects. It was designed to enable uniform patching and upgrades across hybrid and multi-cloud environments in service of a single control plane mandate for enterprise infrastructure administration.

Imagine you have Ubuntu Server running on an EC2 in AWS as part of your enterprise fleet. About as un-Microsoft as you can get, right? By installing the Arc agent on this server, it "projects" its runtime information into your Azure Arc dashboard. As with servers you may have running in Azure, it can then live up to its control plane moniker by applying updates

---

[25] www.microsoft.com/en-us/msrc/faqs-security-update-guide
[26] https://searchcloudcomputing.techtarget.com/definition/Platform-as-a-Service-PaaS

and policies, running analytics, and more. Arc can then apply policy to assure the Azure Monitor agent (required as of mid-2024, formerly the Log Analytics agent was used[27]) is installed on your Ubuntu Server. Once configured, this opens up the plethora of monitoring options that will be discussed in Chapter 8. This is one of many examples of how Arc allows administrators to benefit from their existing Azure skills to manage a diverse IT landscape.

Arc utilizes the information provided by the agent to determine whether the patch level of your Ubuntu Server matches the desired state you have configured for servers of that type. If it does not, then updates can automatically be applied to make the server compliant as shown in the diagram in Figure 3-2 from Microsoft's documentation.

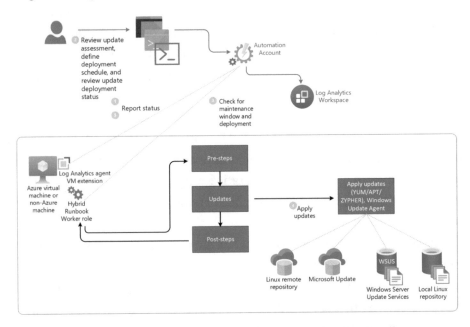

Figure 3-2. *Credit: Microsoft Azure Update Automation Documentation*

---

[27] https://learn.microsoft.com/en-us/azure/azure-monitor/agents/azure-monitor-agent-migration

This does not mean abandoning appropriate cautions including patch testing environments, proper change management practices to document each update, and subsequent thorough smoke testing to assure applications running on the newly patched server still work properly. What it does accomplish is automation to assure critical patches aren't delayed, monitoring that will raise alerts before failures can cascade into adjacent systems, flagging of troubled installations as not suitable for production, as well as discovery of what the challenges will be in applying a particular update to production systems (for instance, if a reboot is required, then a planned outage may also be necessary). An organization's security profile will be raised proportionate to the assets under active management, as today's threats aim to probe for any outlier that can provide a foothold for further intrusion. Today, systems management without automation is nearly equivalent to no management at all.

Systems management via policy is also advantageous in that effective patch and update management depends on prioritization of both the systems being updated and the changes being applied to them. Servers hosting core line-of-business applications require more vigorous oversight, detailed analytics, and prompt attention to risk than those with less critical workloads. Likewise, updates themselves have varying levels of criticality and value that must be considered in the constant rebalancing of resources and requirements that is the Wallenda walk of enterprise systems management.

In each of the aforementioned topics of this chapter, there is another layer that will ultimately determine the success or failure of the application, and that is end-to-end security. In Chapter 4, we'll examine the practical application of a zero trust security model in the enterprise and how Arc may contribute to its implementation.

CHAPTER 4

Securing the Enterprise with Arc

Security As Job One

The impact of enterprise security failures is increasing as tolerance for missteps decreases. Countless breaches of consumer data have often been met with token fines and pats on the head to injured users in the form of a year or two of credit monitoring, a tepid remedy that in no way resolves the situation for those whose identity was actually misused. As failures begin to impact national security and the internal workings of large corporations though, the reaction is becoming more proportionate. The now famous SolarWinds failure to protect corporate and government consumers of its security tools is resulting in lawsuits. A November 2021 suit filed against SolarWinds board[1] by two pension funds accuses SolarWinds of failures that are patently ridiculous for a company purporting to provide IT security, such as using "solarwinds123" as a network password.

The takeaway from this and other miscreant behaviors among companies turning a blind eye to security gaps is that negligence or hoping for luck to escape the sort of risks facing corporate IT today is undeniably

---

[1] https://news.bloomberglaw.com/employee-benefits/solarwinds-board-sued-by-pension-funds-over-massive-cyberattack

© Ramona Maxwell 2024
R. Maxwell, *Azure Arc Systems Management*,
https://doi.org/10.1007/978-1-4842-9480-2_4

a foolish strategy. Companies must employ tooling not only to protect their IT landscape and data, but must also monitor their supply chain and assure that, as happened with SolarWinds, the failure of a provider cannot become a threat to the company. Can an acceptable level of threat protection be accomplished, and if so, how is Arc an aid in the process of doing so?

Security leaders are under a lot of pressure to show quick wins while knowing full well that everything they do will be heavily scrutinized and challenged, and ultimately, they will pay the price for things that are not under their control. —Yaron Levi[2]

A commonly held view that internal threats can be managed by culture or comradery has persisted despite heaps of evidence to the contrary. Late 2021, a Senior Cloud Lead at Ubiquiti was charged with wire fraud and extortion for a convoluted scheme that began with abusing his access under cover of a virtual private network [VPN] to steal his employer's private GitHub repository contents and other confidential information. An administrative account was misused not only to leak data but to adjust log retention policies and obscure suspicious activities from monitoring. He then attempted to anonymously bribe the employer to the tune of nearly $2M in Bitcoin, and when that failed, he pretended to be a whistleblower exposing Ubiquiti's lack of transparency over the breach. He was eventually tripped up by junior crook mistakes and happenstance. An Internet outage temporarily removed the VPN's cloak of his home IP address, a rather inexpensive VPN service he had paid for with his very own PayPal account. Given that Ubiquiti deals in confidential trade data, the risks posed by a breach were extreme. They admirably refused to pay

---

[2] www.linkedin.com/in/yaronrl/

a ransom and immediately engaged the FBI. The ultimate costs to the company are in the "billions" according to the indictment[3] and include remediation, plummeting stock value and customer goodwill.

If media accounts of the illegal actions taken are correct, the losses suffered could have been prevented. The use of a service account with shared user credentials is the first red flag. Instead, the user of the service account should first have to authenticate their identity and provide a proper credential to be able to execute actions as the service account. Treating a service account as if it were a credentialed individual is an invitation to abuse. No one should be given the keys to the kingdom without showing their ID demonstrating they are members of a role with permission to execute actions as the service account. The application of this security principle is a focus for security upgrades among major cloud providers. AWS, for instance, allows a user to assume a role[4] (such as a network administrator), but on doing so, they lose all the privileges associated with roles in their own user profile. They must officially cast off the cloak of network administrator and return to their own role to again have access to its scope of access. Azure offers managed identities and service principals that work in a similar fashion and warns in its documentation against adding a service account itself to a highly privileged group such as administrators. Managed accounts on Azure thoroughly solved the problem of direct login access since "credentials are fully managed, rotated, and protected by Azure" and "No one (including any Global admin) has access to the credentials, so they cannot be accidentally leaked by, for example, being included in code."[5] This

---

[3] www.justice.gov/usao-sdny/press-release/file/1452706/download
[4] https://docs.aws.amazon.com/IAM/latest/UserGuide/id_roles.html
[5] https://docs.microsoft.com/en-us/azure/active-directory/fundamentals/service-accounts-managed-identities

platform strength directly benefits Azure Arc operations in several ways,[6] such as the ability to use RBAC to control access to any Arc-enabled server, secure credential storage in Azure, and the option to customize security roles to assure least privilege access.

The scope of a service or management account should be limited so that if unauthorized entry were gained through a service account credential, it would not be possible to use that credential everywhere, as appeared to have happened at Ubiquiti. Imagine your favorite spy show with the super-secret underground control center. Every elevator, hallway, and room have a monstrous steel door with an impenetrable lock. However, what good is that if they all share the same key as the front door? Break into one and the rest are meaningless. A managed identity is a way to put discrete locks on each door. Like those fluorescent stamps on your hand at a music venue, you only have access backstage if you possess both an entry ticket and the extra special one that indicates you're VIP. An Azure managed account, having access to all of your application's venues, including perhaps messaging, storage, or key management, is capable of issuing a token for access to one, multiple, or all areas of a given service depending upon the role of the requestor.

Finally, monitoring of access should be continuous, and policies must be centralized in an area that has its own management credentials (not shared with the assets being governed). This is the sort of governance Arc intends to simplify, and similar tools are available on AWS.

The case of Terry Childs, who as the Senior Network Administrator locked the City of San Francisco and its collaborators out of their own network in 2008,[7] is another infamous example of the dangers of ignoring

---

[6] https://learn.microsoft.com/en-us/azure/cloud-adoption-framework/scenarios/hybrid/arc-enabled-servers/eslz-identity-and-access-management

[7] www.wired.com/2008/07/sf-city-charged/

internal risk. An interesting article by Paul Venezia,[8] Senior Editor at InfoWorld, implies his behavior might have been a case of someone going digitally postal rather than greed as in the Ubiquiti hack. Nevertheless, it heavily damaged the City's reputation for information governance and created a major scandal that made headlines nationwide. As in the prior case, known principles of IT security could have been applied to make sure that one person was not the sole repository of critical infrastructure access. Across the IT admin community, there tends to be a high level of professionalism, integrity, and pride in what is viewed by most as a sacred trust in their ability to protect the interests of the enterprise IT landscape they are entrusted with. Nonetheless, humans are a big variable in the overall security posture of an organization – which leads us to another common misconception – or misnomer, the *human firewall.*

The late Kevin Mitnick[9] was a security expert who was imprisoned twice in the late 1980s and early 1990s for his adeptness at breaking into corporate IT systems partnered with Stu Sjouwerman in building KnowBe4, a consulting firm devoted to showing the emperors of IT security exactly where they can find their clothes. His classic social engineering techniques were demonstrated by KnowBe4's Roger Grimes in a presentation on the weaknesses of multifactor authentication [MFA], a strategy widely regarded as an effective way to block account impersonation. Armed with only a user's name, phone number, and email, he was able to successfully convince callers to provide enough credential information to intrude into organizations that thought they had provided sufficient training to protect against such attacks. In fact, the National Institute of Standards and Technology's Digital Identity Guidelines[10] have degraded SMS push notices to "out-of-band second authentication

---

[8] www.infoworld.com/article/2653004/why-san-francisco-s-network-admin-went-rogue.html

[9] https://gizmodo.com/kevin-mitnick-famous-hacker-dies-at-59-1850659160

[10] https://pages.nist.gov/800-63-3/

factor"[11] for the reason that it's difficult to validate that the SMS is actually going to a cellular phone in the user's possession vs. a VOIP number that may have multiple access points across any PC which the user has logged in to.

Since the human firewall has as many vulnerabilities as there are types of humans on which to practice social engineering techniques, this brings us back to automated monitoring and threat response to shutter intrusion attempts before major damage can be accomplished. Historically, there has been resistance to efforts to lock the inner doors. A decade ago, many administrators did not want to deal with implementing HTTPS to encrypt internal traffic, nor were CFOs willing to finance it – now it is a baseline standard that comes baked into the majority of infrastructure and application traffic. The Secure Access Service Edge [SASE[12]] model is now facing the same introductory pressure, but is fast becoming a standard among cloud providers and large enterprises. In practical terms, it can be thought of as integrating security into every single artifact of an IT ecosystem from a global perimeter to a tiny IoT device on the factory floor. It is the technological manifestation of the Home Alone hero Kevin's elaborate defense strategies.[13] When that pernicious nation-state burglar gleefully assumes that they're inside your infrastructure, there will be a paint can smack to the head waiting around the next corner.

As of early 2024, a retrospective of significant cyberattacks in 2023 doesn't show a reversal in the level of risk; in fact, annual reports issued by IBM,[14] Fortinet,[15] and Akamai[16] each demonstrate that attack vectors

---

[11] www.nist.gov/blogs/cybersecurity-insights/questionsand-buzz-surrounding-draft-nist-special-publication-800-63-3

[12] www.zscaler.com/resources/security-terms-glossary/what-is-sase

[13] www.imdb.com/title/tt0099785/

[14] www.ibm.com/downloads/cas/DB4GL8YM *and* www.ibm.com/downloads/cas/E3G5JMBP

[15] www.fortinet.com/resources-campaign/cloud/2023-cloud-security-report

[16] www.akamai.com/resources/state-of-the-internet/2023-year-review

and methodologies continue to expand apace with the growth of technology and that AI has become significantly more important to both cybercriminals and organizations seeking to defend against them. Both IBM and Akamai highlight IoT devices as an inherently insecure area to which special attention must be given, and Akamai cites CSO[17] in calling out insufficiently managed Internet of Medical Things [IoMT] as "some of the most vulnerable assets across all industries." IBM focused notably on the costs of a data breach reporting that it had escalated more than 50% from 2020 to its Q1 2023 assessment and that companies who neglected to involve law enforcement or discover the breach themselves were likely to incur substantially larger recovery costs. Fortinet, providers of a multi-cloud security platform, noted that more than two-thirds of their survey respondents operate on more than one public cloud and that even when facing "macroeconomic headwinds" a majority of customers are increasing their security spend. Later chapters of this book focusing on monitoring, policy, and automation capabilities enabled by Azure Arc will discuss how its control plane offers visibility into IoT workloads and integrates with security offerings capable of diminishing many of these threats.

Monitoring – Light in the Corners of the IT Universe

If one consistent message echoes through the daily barrage of security incident and breach reports, it is that danger is constantly lurking. It is also true that the volume of data most organizations must monitor is beyond human capabilities to sift through. Traditional monitoring solutions which offer reports after the fact are of low value if the horse is already out of the barn, or worse yet the wolf is inside selecting its next target. To be effective,

---

[17] www.csoonline.com/article/651075/new-research-reveals-most-attacked-vulnerable-assets.html

monitoring needs to be as near real time as is physically possible and paired with an effective threat response. Thus, in many cases, monitoring a log of what *has* occurred will be ineffective, and what is needed is to respond to events in real time. Then the response to the event can be altered to protect the system being monitored. The log, meanwhile, will contain forensic data that can be used to harden that same system against future attacks.

Arc's approach to monitoring benefits greatly from the product having its genesis in Azure. For security monitoring, Arc-enabled servers can be connected to Microsoft Sentinel,[18] a premier SIEM/SOAR[19] tool that was ranked at the top of Security Operations tools by Gartner in 2022's Magic Quadrant for that category.[20] Meanwhile, container workloads benefit from Container Insights which captures actionable performance data. We will examine usage scenarios for both of these products as part of a discussion of process automation in Chapter 8.

If you look at the InfoSec Institute's eight domains risk[21] monitoring may technically belong to Security Operations, but in practical terms, it's a nonfunctional requirement of all of them. Arc lands squarely in the Security Operations domain with its emphasis on server management for purposes of patching, application of policy, and continuous monitoring.

Integration with Lighthouse

Lighthouse is an interesting offering from Microsoft because it doesn't have any true competition from the other two major cloud vendors. It's an integrated solution to allow companies that run environments for

---

[18] https://learn.microsoft.com/en-us/azure/sentinel/overview

[19] https://www.paloaltonetworks.com/cyberpedia/what-is-soar-vs-siem

[20] https://techcommunity.microsoft.com/t5/microsoft-sentinel-blog/microsoft-is-named-a-leader-in-the-2022-gartner-magic-quadrant/ba-p/3666566

[21] https://resources.infosecinstitute.com/certification/the-cissp-cbk-domains-info-and-updates/

thousands of customers to centrally manage them. For example, huge consulting companies like EY whose suite of tax applications serve legions of tax clients, each discretely separated into their own application space,[22] could benefit from Lighthouse. Lighthouse harkens back to Microsoft's SharePoint roots and expertise in secure multi-tenancy and puts that on steroids with cloud solutions running on Azure. As the documentation for Lighthouse explains, "Authorized users, groups, and service principals can work directly in the context of a customer subscription without having an account in that customer's Azure Active Directory (formerly Azure AD, now Entra) tenant or being a co-owner of the customer's tenant."

Whether the scope being managed in the customer's tenant is the entire subscription or just a resource group, the customer's subscription ID is still required to complete registration for the assets that will be administered. Registration also requires the managing organization be assigned to roles that have RBAC to `/register/action` in the client's tenant, whether that be as a contributor or owner in the client's tenant or automated by use of a Logic App that has the appropriate permission.[23] The managing organization does not work directly in the client's tenant; rather, Lighthouse creates a shadow copy of the assets under management. When an administrator in the managing organization makes a change to their copy of the tenant, Lighthouse checks the registration and permissions before writing the change to the actual tenant in the client's organization. All activities and the identity they were performed under are also logged in the client's tenant, and the *client tenant can remove access*.[24] This is an important point to bear in mind when designing a service

---

[22] www.ey.com/en_us/tax/global-tax-platform (one example, see video for clarity)

[23] https://learn.microsoft.com/en-us/azure/lighthouse/how-to/onboard-management-group#register-the-resource-provider-across-subscriptions

[24] https://docs.microsoft.com/en-us/azure/lighthouse/concepts/architecture

portal. Are you delivering a product where the administering organization also owns all of the portals being administered? Or simply delivering an administrative service?

How does this dovetail with Arc, and in what way does Lighthouse combined with Arc enhance the ability to monitor and secure the IT landscape? We've been discussing Arc as though it lives at the pinnacle of the administration pyramid, but when managing tenants with Lighthouse, it is actually the latter in the top perch. In addition to the aforementioned scenario of an organization with many clients consuming a SaaS application, this overview also has great value in enterprises with a large number of subscriptions. While Lighthouse does not operate at the Management Group [MG] scope, a policy for the MG can specify that all of its subscriptions be registered with Lighthouse, thus gathering a vast IT landscape into a single high-level view. With Lighthouse, you can peer into Arc instances in all the managed tenants you operate for clients as well as the vast expanse of resources you utilize internally and thus extend Arc's ability to consistently manage the server's and Kubernetes clusters across your continually expanding IT galaxies.[25] Yes, go ahead and pick up your scepter. With that kind of power, you are truly a ruler of your IT-verse.

Private Link

The value of log files is often underestimated given their pedantic recitation of every routine operation of the system or application emitting them. In truth, a log might store trade secrets or competitive opportunities, security risks, or intrusions against the same, performance and reliability data, and so much more. Thus, the logs themselves become a target for theft and malfeasance.

---

[25] https://docs.microsoft.com/en-us/azure/lighthouse/concepts/
cross-tenant-management-experience#enhanced-services-and-scenarios

The idea behind Private Link is that none of your log traffic will travel on the public Internet. Instead, it will travel on Azure's internal backbone, and when it crosses a boundary outside of that network, it will run through a protected tunnel everywhere else (e.g., ExpressRoute). This sounds ideal and combined with encryption is a near-impenetrable solution; however, there are some caveats.

A severe constraint on any solution, not only those pertaining to security, is that it must integrate with existing systems. Microsoft describes Private Link as "constellation of different interconnected services that work together to monitor your workloads." To translate that elegant statement to English, Private Link has been stapled on to Azure in order to provide much needed security enhancement. The impact to an organization wishing to implement Private Link is that an entire existing network topology may be affected.

Microsoft describes the impact as "setting up a Private Link even for a single resource changes the DNS configuration affecting traffic to **all resources**. In other words, traffic to all workspaces or components are affected by a single Private Link setup." Their networking guide for Private link further elaborates, "Some networks are composed of multiple VNets or other connected networks. If these networks share the same DNS, setting up a Private Link on any of them would update the DNS and affect traffic across all networks."[26] Microsoft's suggested resolution is that there should be only one Private Link scope in all of an organization's shared DNS. Clearly, the implementation of Private Link should be treated as a potentially breaking change if there is existing shared DNS.[27] It is worth noting that if you are a commercial or government client, Private Link can be utilized not only in conjunction with monitoring but also as a private

---

[26] https://docs.microsoft.com/en-us/azure/azure-monitor/logs/private-link-design#plan-by-network-topology
[27] www.networkworld.com/article/3268449/what-is-dns-and-how-does-it-work.html

route for Azure Automation. This can offer a greater return on the effort to set up Private Link as will be explained in a later section of the book covering process automation.

Security

Secure Access Service Edge (SASE)

The need for new ways to look at security has been underscored over the past decade's trickle and then rush to the cloud, along with the situation of the very scenario of hybrid and cross-cloud distributed computing that Arc is designed to address. The standard paradigm of establishing a traffic route to the data center, guarding the entrance with a firewall, and piping traffic in and out through a VPN simply doesn't cover the yawning gaps that new infrastructure and application models have opened. For instance, the traditional monolithic app sitting within the data center has changed to massive proliferations of APIs delivering services, each of which needs to be examined from numerous perspectives from the beginning of the application lifecycle when determining the scope of what the API will expose to monitoring queries against it when live. And APIs are just one segment of the "Service Edge" around which "Secure Access" must be constructed.

SASE inverts the traditional model of siloed and sometimes disparate authorization and authentication models by moving those functions out to the perimeter or edge of the computing environment. Companies such as Cloudflare, AWS, Microsoft, Akamai, and others maintain global networks that form an "edge" or perimeter through which all traffic must pass. What this facilitates is the ability to examine requests while they are far away from the actual resources you are protecting. The identity of the requestor can be authenticated and then impersonation attempts blocked by examining the context and other risk signals at the moment of the interaction.

We have already touched on ways Arc facilitates edge computing scenarios, and SASE implementation is implicit in some of what has been discussed in terms of securing individual assets so that request traffic can only travel on paths where specific access has been granted (e.g., permission to the results of a specific query but not to its data source). To zoom out to the big picture though, SASE enhances security by simplifying traffic patterns and management. SASE is an architectural paradigm that may dictate a change to network traffic patterns. Instead of protecting each co-location with its own authentication providers and authorization controls, those functions move up to the cloud, and a key benefit is that an entire distributed architecture can benefit from a single sign-on whether accessing corporate systems, retail locations, edge compute functions, or any other asset.

In addition to industry standard security and compliance frameworks that Azure complies with, it has its own set of standards, the Microsoft Cloud Security Benchmark.[28] The benchmark attempts to address a majority of the functions and services available on Azure, as well as external systems managed using Arc, and map each one to security controls that are "consistent with well-known security benchmarks, such as those described by the Center for Internet Security (CIS) Controls, National Institute of Standards and Technology (NIST), and Payment Card Industry Data Security Standard (PCI-DSS)."[29] This very granular implementation guide can serve as an invaluable security checklist that will ideally be consulted from planning stages forward. The responsibility for implementation will vary with architecture, since some Azure service offerings will remove the need to manually construct security.

A current challenge in SASE implementation, or even distributed applications in general, is performance. SASE vendors heavily compete on this aspect, with Cloudflare currently claiming best performance and

---

[28] https://docs.microsoft.com/en-us/security/benchmark/azure/overview
[29] www.cisecurity.org/cis-benchmarks

Akamai asserting they have more edge locations than any other vendor. Microsoft doesn't limit its customers to their own Front Door offering, but facilitates integration with all of the major vendors (as is the case with AWS and GCP also).

Since the human firewall will always have limitations, and frictionless access to key business resources is key to business operations, building security into every layer of your infrastructure should be a primary objective. Criminals seeking entry into your company's systems are very thoroughly assessing every possible attack vector, and intrusion attempts are often automated so that waiting for a human response to discover and respond to a threat would be a futile exercise. In a future chapter, we will discuss how Arc's monitoring feedback loop can be closed by an automated response to identified threats.

Role-Based Access Control (RBAC)

Role-based access control [RBAC] is not a new concept in IT security. According to the National Institute of Standards and Technology [NIST],[30] instances of RBAC can be found as far back as the 1970s or well before the advent of personal computing. NIST also notes a key point that RBAC differs from simple security groups in that members of a group may have individual security permissions assigned to them, whereas in a true role-based security schema, roles hold only activities, and thus a user or group may only perform an activity if they are assigned to a role which has permissions to perform it. Groups still exist for the aggregation of users, as it is simply not practical to provision thousands of individuals manually, but for RBAC to function correctly, it is important to focus on the roles membership provides.

---

[30] https://csrc.nist.gov/projects/role-based-access-control/faqs

A classic permission problem has been the difficulty of assuring a user who changes to a new position in an organization sheds the privileges belonging to their former assignment. Over time and the user's career advancement, this can lead to organization-wide privileges, a situation diametrically opposed to another key security principle that users have the least privilege required to accomplish their tasks.[31] In order to use RBAC effectively then, a role change must be treated as a new hire, and prior role assignments must be removed before creating new ones. Additionally, the level of privilege a user should have does not necessarily correlate to their authority in the organization since seniority within a company may reflect on a person's business acumen rather than their technical proficiency. Thus, an executive may have few limits on information access, but severe restrictions on the ability to unhook policy controls or change infrastructure – all in the interests of their own and the company's protection from liability.

Today's authentication and authorization tools are many leagues better than those available even a decade ago. Today, Microsoft Entra[32] (formerly Azure Active Directory) can effectively manage business-to-business [B2B] relationships and allow partners access to resources internal to your organization without allowing them to federate their Active Directory with yours or requiring you to create an account in your organization for them. This can be particularly useful in terms of vendor management so that, for instance, application developers can be given access to development environments but be completely restricted from areas like quality assurance or production environments for the safety of the company's internal data. You can also put additional authentication controls on B2B accounts, such as requiring an additional multifactor authentication step (e.g., entering a code received via text message or through an

---

[31] www.onelogin.com/learn/least-privilege-polp
[32] https://learn.microsoft.com/en-us/entra/identity/role-based-access-control/custom-overview

authentication application) which can be particularly valuable if their home organization's security controls do not meet internal standards. A particularly egregious example of that was the infamous Target breach of 2013, wherein an HVAC contractor fell victim to a phishing scam and their access to Target's vendor systems (which were not well protected in terms of network segmentation from the rest of Target's infrastructure) was misused by hackers to install software to steal customer's credit card data directly from point-of-sale systems at checkout.[33] That HVAC vendor was using a free version of an anti-virus product that did not perform real-time detection and hence did not detect the attack. Target paid some of the highest regulatory fines ever assessed to that point in time for compromising PID (personally identifying information) data as punishment for lax security controls.

Entra also allows you to time-box authorization to resources for any user, internal or external, for periods as brief as five minutes.[34] You might think it would be advantageous to frequently have users reenter passwords, but many security experts do not favor this approach since it offers more opportunities for users to be compromised while entering their credentials and is not particularly valuable on a device managed by the organization. However, short sessions are of real value when working with external partners to assure they frequently validate their membership in the organization you have contracted for services.

Entra also covers business-to-client [B2C] scenarios elegantly so that users of an application hosted on Azure may use local or external authentication providers such as Facebook or Google to log in to the application (while having zero access to anything else in your organization).

---

[33] www.commerce.senate.gov/services/files/24d3c229-4f2f-405d-b8db-a3a67f183883

[34] https://learn.microsoft.com/en-us/entra/id-governance/privileged-identity-management/pim-how-to-add-role-to-user

With the previous examples of security failures in mind, it becomes apparent that security personnel should be viewed as "special forces" among the "citizen army" protecting your organization. Hiring and retaining talent that understands the modern security landscape along with promoting a culture of integrity throughout the organization is an indispensable aspect of IT security for the business. Further, it's important to minimize the destructive impact that any one failure in the human fabric of the organization can accomplish.

In the space of server management, a few individuals may manage very large portions of the IT landscape. Even if there is proper network segmentation and other controls protecting against external threats when an administrative group has permission to cross those boundaries, there is inherent risk that can only be mitigated somewhat by centralized management and appropriate monitoring.

Azure has comprehensive server management solutions that Arc is designed to extend beyond the boundaries of the Azure platform. This is a special boon in terms of security for large distributed server installations which can now be managed as Azure resources. For actively connected servers, it allows you to use Azure RBAC across all of your organization's assets, be that Kubernetes clusters living in AWS, web servers running Linux, or on-premise SQL Servers in your data center. All of these can have the same access policies and role assignments. Local accounts on servers need only be used to onboard the server to Arc initially by installing the agent, and from that point forward, the agent serves as proxy to execute administrative actions on the machine that is under Arc's purview. If there were only one "killer app" feature that stands out as justification for the cost of running Arc in an organization, the ability to unify server security administration under Arc's umbrella might be it.

Security Risks Resulting from Arc

While Arc can contribute greatly to the security posture of an organization, it's worth noting that Arc itself can be an attack vector. The security principal used by Arc agents could be compromised as described in a June 2021 blog by Matt Felton.[35] While, as Felton concludes in his article, this security risk is a trade-off that is "leagues better" than common industry practice, it is not one to be ignored. Organizations implementing Arc will want to apply appropriate security controls and monitoring to this portion of the infrastructure as any other, assuring that the service account running an agent has only required privilege for the jobs it is assigned and that credentials for these accounts are rotated regularly.[36]

In truth, the risks highlighted for Arc's agents are common to using agents on a server in general for tasks like virus scanning, backup, and more. There are also management issues such as the risk of missing or gaps due to agent incompatibility with various operating systems and legacy hardware, while agentless approaches such as using network scans may miss disconnected devices. As management platforms have become a requirement to run operations at scale, I think you can expect the development of new protocols to facilitate running administrative controls in a secure and friction-free manner.

Myriad Risk Factors Require Thoughtful Design

In terms of security, changes to application protocols have also posed new challenges. Cloud-native development relies heavily on APIs to interact with application models, and ways of exposing those interfaces

---

[35] https://journeyofthegeek.com/2021/06/12/experimenting-with-azure-arc/

[36] https://docs.microsoft.com/en-us/azure/active-directory/fundamentals/service-accounts-governing-azure

vary from classic REST to modern GraphQL. As the move to cloud-hosted applications has accelerated, the popularity of APIs as an attack vector has also grown. An F5 Labs security article notes, "some of the largest and well-known companies—Facebook, Google, Equifax, Instagram, T-Mobile, Panera Bread, Uber, Verizon, and others—have suffered significant data breaches as a result of API attacks."[37] One Gartner webinar[38] cited research indicating that organizations using an external API management solution had more robust security profiles in terms of API protection, highlighting the value of objectivity in assessing risk profiles.

API protection starts left at the design phase of the application lifecycle as discussed earlier in this book. Application design must carefully consider exactly what information is required from the data source behind the API and strictly limit the ability of the application to make API calls to only the required scope of data (avoiding what OWASP calls "Excessive Data Exposure"[39]). Consideration must also be given to how even that limited access could be misused by manipulation of the query language used, and when the API is under development, it should be evaluated for security flaws of this nature. Protection of the data source itself is also key, and this highlights the importance of data stores being an integral part of the DevOps pipeline. There are many ways to surface data for application use without allowing an API access to the actual database. Applications should be designed to enumerate queries, so that simple replay attacks cannot succeed. Finally, carelessness or malfeasance can put APIs at risk when encryption keys and other secrets are stored in the codebase. It is

---

[37] www.f5.com/labs/articles/education/securing-apis--10-best-practices-for-keeping-your-data-and-infra see footnotes directly in article for company scenarios listed

[38] www.gartner.com/en/webinars/4002323/api-security-protect-your-apis-from-attacks-and-data-breaches

[39] https://owasp.org/www-project-api-security/

helpful to remember that a single application may draw and update data from or even circulate it among multiple APIs, thereby broadening the attack surface in even a small application.

If left solely to an internal development team, security could be compromised by delivery pressure, individual skill profiles, and even a lack of corporate enthusiasm for updating software where later versions benefit from updated security. No organization should ever consider their applications to be protected without a deliberate security strategy (the "Sec" in DevSecOps) that can provide continuous feedback to the development team creating an application. Simply discovering the number of APIs present can be a significant challenge, since API calls are part of the core development paradigm for many development frameworks. Scanning for internal and externally facing APIs so that they can be registered with an API protection platform is the critical mitigation step to assure that undocumented APIs do not put the organization at risk.

What processes exist in Azure for API protection, and how do they integrate with Arc? Azure's API Management service offers full lifecycle management of APIs and includes the ability to apply policies, perform API discovery, manage API gateways, and more.[40] Azure also offers an API gateway within Azure as a managed service and the ability to use a self-managed API gateway on non-Microsoft and other on-premise API hosts.[41]

A gateway provides many features that enhance API security, but should not be considered a stand-alone security solution. Advantages include avoiding direct connections to API endpoints (instead, the gateway provides a proxy connection), HTTPS traffic, and certificate management. Gateways can also accomplish request routing to numerous APIs to improve an application's responsiveness, sometimes reducing the complexity of the application itself by offloading these features onto the

---

[40] https://azure.microsoft.com/en-us/services/api-management/#overview
[41] https://docs.microsoft.com/en-us/azure/api-management/
self-hosted-gateway-overview

gateway. Gateways can also manage authentication to the application and improve performance with cached response data. However, the gateway alone is not a comprehensive API security solution and must be combined with policies governing API usage, targeted monitoring, and appropriate safeguards against abuse when it is detected.

An API gateway is not to be thought of as a singular effort. Multiple gateways prevent performance bottlenecks and are a standard in large organizations. For a self-hosted gateway, it will be important to link distributed systems to Arc management controls, for instance, Azure Monitor is not automatically available in a self-hosted gateway, but the gateway can be configured to export its logs so that they can be consumed by Azure Monitor.

Arc provides the ability to apply policies to protect APIs across a hybrid server landscape. A few examples of the type of policies that might be employed for API protection include tracking where a request to the API originates and blocking suspicious origins, limiting the rate and number of requests allowed, rejecting requests where the data contained in the response does not match predefined parameters, as well as specifying what type of authentication is required and the length of time an authorization for data will exist. Additionally, when using a gateway, policies can be used to assure internal application URLs are never exposed, but are instead replaced by gateway URLs. With the ability to deploy some Azure services through Arc-enabled Kubernetes cluster extensions, you can now run Azure's API Management Gateway on clusters in your own DC[42] or on a competitor's cloud (in preview as of this writing). For companies with many API-first workloads, that feature alone is likely to motivate adoption of Arc.

In summary, neither this chapter nor this book is sufficient to cover every aspect of enterprise security controls, but can hopefully highlight key areas on which to focus attention and the need for rigorous attention to security management. Next, we'll take a look at Arc-enabled data services.

---

[42] https://learn.microsoft.com/en-us/azure/api-management/
how-to-deploy-self-hosted-gateway-azure-arc

CHAPTER 5

Enterprise DBS Management and Arc

Introduction

Before discussing the scenario of a SQL Server migration, it will be helpful to understand the data services Arc provides, both in how they underpin activities like migration and other benefits that are gained with Arc as the control plane for SQL Server installations.

If you look at the history of Microsoft, it's fair to say their dominance was shaped not only by the market for business and computer operating systems that rivaled Linux on the server side but also by the astounding success of SQL Server. In 2001, Microsoft published its own summary of the struggle to compete in the enterprise database arena against behemoth Oracle and its excitement as a company when SQL Server reached a billion dollars in sales.[1] Early iterations of SQL Server entered the Microsoft family via partnerships with Ashton/Tate and Sybase, but as Microsoft began to diverge in order to create a version of SQL Server that was compatible with their Windows NT operating system, the Microsoft flavor of SQL Server came into its own. Technologically, the growth of SQL Server became

---

[1] https://news.microsoft.com/2001/06/28/building-the-billion-dollar-database-microsoft-sql-server-climbs-to-new-heights/

© Ramona Maxwell 2024
R. Maxwell, *Azure Arc Systems Management*,
https://doi.org/10.1007/978-1-4842-9480-2_5

very interesting after the release of SQL Server 2008 R2 when Master Data Services,[2] essentially a tool to discover and remediate inconsistent versions of the same data across large enterprise data stores,[3] was introduced.[4] For SQL geeks, this was great stuff, and at the PASS[5] launch event I attended at the Marriott in Santa Clara, California, the excitement was so high you could have been excused for mistaking it for a wedding party.

Ubiquitous and powerful as SQL Server is, its reputation for being expensive and difficult to administer persists. From a voracious appetite for system memory[6] and a perennial home on the OWASP site describing SQL injection attacks to the rarity and expense of finding a top-tier database administrator [DBA], SQL Server is not an easy keeper. A recent glance at DBA salaries in the San Francisco Bay area on glassdoor.com showed the top of "likely" salaries at around $350k but allowed for a range of almost $800k – meaning someone reported salary data to the site in that stratospheric range. In popularity surveys,[7] SQL Server consistently hovers around number three behind Oracle SQL and MySQL despite ranking above Oracle in its cloud offering per Gartner's Magic Quadrant.[8]

The real problem though, facing not just SQL Server but any enterprise data store, is an ever-ballooning corpus. It's quite tempting to riff off the second definition of corpus on dictionary.com referring to a dead body.[9] One of my

---

[2] https://cloudblogs.microsoft.com/sqlserver/2009/05/13/master-data-services-whats-the-big-deal/

[3] www.dnb.com/perspectives/master-data/june-2020-tei-master-data-study.html

[4] https://en.wikipedia.org/wiki/History_of_Microsoft_SQL_Server

[5] https://passdatacommunitysummit.com/

[6] www.brentozar.com/blitz/max-memory/

[7] https://db-engines.com/en/ranking and www.statista.com/statistics/809750/worldwide-popularity-ranking-database-management-systems/

[8] https://azure.microsoft.com/en-us/blog/microsoft-named-a-leader-in-2021-gartner-magic-quadrant-for-cloud-dbms-platforms/

[9] www.dictionary.com/browse/corpus

favorite quotes is from Brian Tuemmler, Information Governance Solution Architect at Infotechtion Inc., "Collaboration is a high value component of cloud-based solutions, yet most of our content in large organizations is never touched once it is created." In a technical survey at a Fortune 100 client, he found, "80% of the content that had been modified was active for less than 3 weeks." Data storage hardware provider Seagate reached similar conclusions in a 2020 report estimating more than two-thirds of data collected "lies fallow" per Phil Goodwin, research director at IDC.[10] Seagate also teamed with IDC in an earlier 2018 estimate that the world's data stores would inflate 61% by 2025 according to a short summary in Network World that does a great job of translating what a number like 175 zettabytes actually means.[11]

Data Proliferation and Our Planet

Taken out of the realm of unfathomably massive numbers though, data bloat has a genuine impact on our physical earth. Corporations around the globe now list their ESG [Environmental, Social, and Governance] initiatives as part of their prospectus, but as yet, there is no standard being applied to the accuracy of what is claimed[12] in terms of environmental stewardship. A 2021 ABC News story about the impact of data centers [DCs] on precious water supplies[13] showed some creative mitigation of

---

[10] www.seagate.com/news/news-archive/seagates-rethink-data-report-reveals-that-68-percent-of-data-available-to-businesses-goes-unleveraged-pr-master/

[11] www.networkworld.com/article/3325397/idc-expect-175-zettabytes-of-data-worldwide-by-2025.html

[12] www.benefitspro.com/2022/02/24/when-it-comes-to-esg-investing-prospectus-language-often-can-be-misleading-report/?slreturn=20220221013553

[13] https://abcnews.go.com/Technology/wireStory/big-tech-data-centers-spark-worry-scarce-western-80730977

the environmental impact of the enormous need for water cooling and power, such as placing DCs in naturally frigid locations – however, such mitigations cannot keep up with ceaseless failures to curb the perdurable expansion of data.

A 2022 McKinsey article on ESG[14] highlighted disagreement over whether environmental and social goals being gunny-sacked together in a three-legged race along with governance will really be beneficial in the long term to ESG as a factor in corporate profits. Other caveats listed were that it is difficult to measure the success of ESG initiatives in a way that ties to financial performance of a company or in some cases even to find a metric to gauge whether the ESG activities themselves were beneficial. Those are interesting objections that do have some validity; nonetheless, we all need a healthy environment to live in if we are to enjoy the fruits of the labor we spend in the continuous and fairly miraculous evolution of technology.

A practical approach that is aligned with the subject of this book is to use the administrative tools at our disposal to combat the overproduction and storage of unneeded data. Storage costs are measurable, and a model that charges more to keep data past typical retention periods could discourage hoarding and encourage data housekeeping. Many companies are sharply restricting email retention for security reasons alone, having been bitten by outdated missives for which they could still be held accountable for. An article in Business Law Today[15] correctly states that a rules-based approach to purging data is bound to be more successful than individual discretion as to what is preserved. In the chapter on policy, information is presented on the value of consistent, organization-wide rulesets that will reduce not only the cost of excessive data retention but also its impact on the beautiful world we inhabit.

---

[14] www.mckinsey.com/capabilities/sustainability/our-insights/does-esg-really-matter-and-why

[15] https://businesslawtoday.org/2022/11/data-retention-growing-risks/

Data Integrity

Another database issue facing enterprises trying to migrate data and applications to the cloud is that as database engines developed proficiency at not just storing but calculating data, programmers began splitting application code between the database and the application modules. As noted previously, this practice blocks DevOps initiatives by burying unknown hooks in the database code that create unexpected risks when updating the application itself. Operating on the database becomes akin to a surgery in which no one knows where the bullet is, and everyone gathered around the victim is concerned the most delicate touch might send it straight through an artery. A long-lived database might also grow to such a size that even a simple "lift-and shift" move to the cloud or a new DC becomes daunting, again complicating not only the migration of the database but also applications that rely upon it.

SQL Server backup and disaster recovery are simple topics that quickly become complex in the face of real-world application to enterprise-scale databases.

Another challenge endemic to managing SQL Servers is backup and disaster recovery. SQL backups are easy to set up if the database size and traffic are within manageable limits, but a common lesson often learned painfully by new DBAs is that untested backups are worthless.[16] About a decade ago, I worked at a government-sponsored affordable housing agency to redesign and upgrade their failure prone SharePoint farm. They had hired a prominent records archival and disposal company to take daily differential and weekly full backups of the SQL database for the farm.

---

[16] www.sentryone.com/blog/your-disaster-recovery-strategy-is-useless-if-your-sql-server-backups-havent-been-tested

Eventually, database corruption took down all of their systems residing in SharePoint, both public facing and internal. They paid the archival company to overnight a disk containing their latest backups only to find that they were corrupt and a restore was not possible. Further efforts and testing revealed that their untested backups had been corrupt for a number of months, leaving them in the same situation as if they'd not taken backups at all for that entire duration. The organization was greatly impacted financially as well as handicapped in their daily operations (which also rippled out to affect those served for a short period of time).

PaaS [Platform as a Service] database offerings promise to relieve some of the pain and uncertainty around database maintenance and availability but still require thoughtful implementation. There is a tendency to trust that cloud-hosted systems are automatically redundant when in fact, if lightning strikes your data center, you may be toast if you've not set up a replica in a second region for purposes of disaster recovery. A SQL Server Managed Instance or SQL Azure also won't protect you from racking up huge bills if your database is not well architected. Poorly designed queries will eat up processing power, while unmanaged data can cause storage requirements to grow exponentially. Each of these can dramatically affect operational costs.

Azure has a healthy suite of database offerings and with its flagship Cosmos DB, a NoSQL approach that ironically uses a SQL-like language for queries. Cosmos friendliness to the application stacks developers already know extends to its APIs which include not only SQL but MongoDB, Cassandra, Gremlin, and .NET applications (even Java). This makes Cosmos an easy entry onto a primarily PaaS offering for development teams managing a diversiform application stack, yet despite Cosmos ranking well in Gartner's Magic Quadrant for cloud DBMS,[17] Amazon's DynamoDB remains the leader. They each offer endless horizontal scaling (with the caveat that you must either allow this to happen automatically and accept the associated charges or the requests from your application

---

[17] www.gartner.com/doc/reprints?id=1-28G8D49N&ct=211216&st=sb

to the database may fail when you have exceeded the amount of capacity you have agreed to purchase); however, there are some differences in the way they scale, as with DynamoDB you can choose whether to scale for reads or writes depending on the type of traffic you expect, while Cosmos DB considers either a read or write as a single unit of traffic. Both emit a stream of database activity that allows for event-driven programming, but they take slightly different approaches that may recommend one over the other in specific use cases. For instance, Cosmos DB has a very good rewind feature so that you could reuse its stream from a certain point in time to rehydrate a cache, for example. DynamoDB uses a lot of verbiage to create a JSON document record in comparison to Cosmos trim list of attributes, but also betters its rival by including a sort key in the record. The winner, in the end, will depend on which company is able to evolve features without creating fragility in the product or unneeded security risks. Google cannot be ignored in this NoSQL comparison, considering that its Cloud Bigtable[18] underpins everything from Google Maps to Gmail. Both Amazon and Google have a long history of integrating with the open source community, a strategy that Cosmos DB illustrates Microsoft is beginning to align to.

The relationship between Arc and Cosmos DB is not obvious as would be the case for a SQL or PostgreSQL database directly managed via Arc's control plane, but Cosmos is key to Arc's internal operations. For instance, Arc uses Cosmos DB to securely store internal configurations (such as for Kubernetes clusters that are attached to Azure via the Arc agent). Thus, Cosmos serves as a facilitator for Arc operations.

Azure, at the time of this writing, is offering seven managed database services including Apache Cassandra, Redis, PostgreSQL, Azure SQL, MySQL, MariaDB, and of course Cosmos. All three of PostgreSQL, MariaDB, and MySQL are now eligible to be protected by Microsoft

---

[18] https://cloud.google.com/bigtable

Defender for Cloud. Since they are managed databases, they are not shown in the Azure Arc dashboard; however, in the reverse view, Defender will show instances of those database types you may have running in other clouds or on-premises via the Arc agent.

At Build 2022, Microsoft upped the ante for managed relational databases by releasing the Business Critical version of Azure SQL Managed Instances. As they sweeten the pot for enterprise customers, they are including goodies like two free replicas (one active for extra read capacity and one passive for failover) and a free Developer Edition. Giving away or selling a developer edition at a minuscule price has long been a Microsoft strategy for boosting SQL Server adoption. If a company's IT professionals are skilled on a platform, that factor alone can inhibit the ability to jump to a cheaper or more full-featured competitor. Whether it's Redis University or the extensive free training offerings from the big cloud vendors, the point of these offerings (which often offer certification in addition to courseware) is directly supportive of the vendors' sales efforts. It takes much of the burden off corporations to offer specialized training (indeed, many expect engineers to pursue external training and certifications on their own time in order to qualify for better roles within the company) and assures them that if they choose a specific product, there will be qualified people to implement it.

Distributed Computing and Your Data

Chief among the problems facing both the consumers and creators of today's massive, distributed computing platforms is data consistency. What was once a typical deployment scenario of a commercial database running in an enterprise data center with an application hosted from servers in the same network and likely at the same physical location is becoming rare. In that legacy model, tight coupling often existed between the database and the application. This allowed developers to rely on known patterns to assure that items stored in a transactional database system met ACID[19] criteria assuring that only a single, correct copy of the transaction appeared in the database record. With the advent of mega-scale enterprise cloud computing also came challenges in meeting that basic requirement in assuring data would consistently reflect the actual transaction that had occurred. The issue arises when disparate processes operating in various parts of a distributed network contend for writes on the same transaction. If a process writes out of order, then the concluding process may fail.[20] You may have experienced the impacts of this, perhaps shopping online when you attempt to check out and the application seems to forget where you are in the process (which you now must repeat to acquire your item).

One of the problems opposing the resolution of this issue by distributed computing providers is that latency is also a chief concern on their platforms. What the term distributed describes is physical separation of computing resources, for example, processing of either application routines or data may not occur on the same computer, the same rack of computers served by a single network switch, the same data center, or even within the same geographic region (major cloud providers attempt to collocate processing, but actual scenarios for global distribution, failover, and other factors impact the degree to which this is possible). Further network routes over which transactional processing happens have their own set of complexities and rules that heavily impact how much optimization is possible (this hard barrier is one of the three components of the CAP[21] or Brewer's[22] Theorem which states you can achieve at most

---

[19] www.ibm.com/docs/en/cics-ts/5.4?topic=processing-acid-properties-transactions

[20] www.linkedin.com/pulse/data-consistency-distributed-computing-platforms-ramona-maxwell

[21] https://en.wikipedia.org/wiki/CAP_theorem

[22] https://en.wikipedia.org/wiki/Eric_Brewer_(scientist)

two out of three of consistency, availability, and tolerance for network issues). Coordination strategies which assure consistency then necessarily require processing delays *which increase latency in order to guarantee consistency.*

Given the foregoing classic strategies for assuring ACID transactions are simply not suitable for distributed computing scenarios. Determined and innovative efforts to solve this problem by everyone from the Amazon's CTO Dr. Werner Vogels[23] to teams of researchers the Berkeley Computer Science lab have been underway for literally decades with encouraging results. Microsoft claims ACID transactions in a NoSQL database are achievable only within a partition and that is born out by their service-level agreement(s) [SLA] around Cosmos Consistency[24] which is described as a "single read operation scoped within a logical partition."[25] DynamoDB now claims ACID capabilities using a combination of a transaction coordinator and an immutable ledger. Its transactions are one-shot, go or no go commits, and a lock to wait for related transactional data is not possible.[26] They are also limited to a single region, and replications to additional regions must wait until the region processing the transaction has fully committed it.

What does the preceding dichotomy of performance vs. consistency adduce for enterprises owning applications with absolute consistency requirements? That on-premise hosting is still a valid, if not optimal, choice for certain types of data. This is a core rationale for Arc and for

---

[23] A 2008 summary of the challenges meeting consistency objectives in distributed computing systems by Dr. Werner Vogels: www.allthingsdistributed.com/2008/12/eventually_consistent.html

[24] https://docs.microsoft.com/en-us/azure/cosmos-db/consistency-levels#guarantees-associated-with-consistency-levels

[25] https://docs.microsoft.com/en-us/azure/cosmos-db/consistency-levels#scope-of-the-read-consistency

[26] www.mydistributed.systems/2021/12/dynamodb.html *and* https://docs.aws.amazon.com/amazondynamodb/latest/developerguide/transaction-apis.html

Azure Stack HCI and other private cloud systems. The promise of Arc is that it will make hybrid hosting scenarios both manageable and easier to secure.

Data sovereignty often creates constraints that require an edge computing solution. Governmental or other regulatory bodies may set boundaries that prohibit colocating data in the cloud or outside of a specific geographic area, dramatically affecting how systems operating within their borders must be engineered. The data may need to be fully processed and stored in its edge location, including application of machine learning models, even if the insights gained become the intellectual property of a company with a broader geographic reach as the consequences of failing to comply could mean a loss of revenue if a company incurred a fine or, worse, restrictions on profit-making activities. In order to benefit from primary cloud service offerings, there has to be some intermittent connectivity, if only for billing usage, but systems must be designed so that data residency can be validated. In a practical sense, even if regulatory oversight is not a concern, localizing data makes it readily available and reduces transaction latency.

A 2022 Gartner whitepaper[27] divides submarkets of the edge computing industry vertical into eight categories that range from setting up a CDN that will be accessible at the edge to data management and IoT platforms. The potential surface area and complexity of an edge computing solution makes Arc a great lever toward success, as it enables consumption of many Azure platform services such as IoT and machine learning anywhere along with centralized management.

Some business models particularly require or lend themselves to edge computing solutions such as remote mining operations, farming, cinematography, mobile medical services, factory operations, digital gaming, and many others. Edge computing is about proximity, whether

---

[27] www.gartner.com/doc/reprints?id=1-2BTD6JNA&ct=221128&st=sb

that is to a user or a process. If a movie can be produced with real-time editing collaboration as scenes are being filmed, a customer can make a purchase without waiting for back-end accounting and fulfillment systems, or someone on a tractor can work with real-time data regarding which fertilizer they should apply, then the potential ROI of setting up an edge solution becomes apparent as the ease with which each of these things can be accomplished ties directly to revenue.

The aspect of security is another primary driver. Banks were easily the last enterprises to hop on the cloud bandwagon with understandable reluctance to rent space on someone else's computers for information they already had strong procedures in place to defend. It is not lost on corporate leadership of financial institutions that in June of 2022 an AWS Systems Engineer working in cloud storage was convicted of stealing the financial data of more than 100M Capital One customers in 2019, along with breaching the accounts of 30 additional companies. AWS absolved itself of all responsibility, saying it was Capital One's misconfiguration of a third-party firewall that facilitated the intrusion; however, many security researchers didn't accept that explanation since the attack used a well-known technique (Server-Side Request Forgery or SSRF) that AWS did not at that time[28] provide mitigation for, while Azure and GCP were already blocking SSRF attacks.[29]

To the dismay of many who have long considered Microsoft as a leader in cloud security, they do not come out of the battle for secure distributed computing models[30] unscathed. During 2021 and 2022, they've had a

---

[28] https://aws.amazon.com/blogs/security/defense-in-depth-open-firewalls-reverse-proxies-ssrf-vulnerabilities-ec2-instance-metadata-service/

[29] https://attackware.com/index.php/2022/06/06/thoughts-on-the-capital-one-security-breach/security-world-news/admin/ and https://krebsonsecurity.com/2019/08/what-we-can-learn-from-the-capital-one-hack/

[30] https://github.com/SummitRoute/csp_security_mistakes

string of unexploited (meaning they felt the wind of the train that almost hit them but were saved at the last possible second by an ethical research team) vulnerabilities aimed at multi-tenant services.[31] The most horrifying of these was discovered by Orca Security researchers who demonstrated how an Azure Synapse (Microsoft's flagship analytics platform) workspace was lacking basic multi-tenant isolation so that workspaces could easily be broken into and controlled by an attacker.[32] This was extremely surprising to me as multi-tenant security is something Microsoft has had an excellent grasp of since their first commercially successful multi-tenant collaboration solution SharePoint Server, where tenant isolation consisted of individual database instances. When this vulnerability was exposed, Microsoft was uncharacteristically slow to respond, and Orca published its opinion that this was due to larger infrastructure issues that had to be solved in order to make the platform truly hardened against this type of hijacking.[33] When you consider that Microsoft advertises Synapse as able to ingest data from more than 90 sources and companies typically use it together with a data lake, the magnitude of this vulnerability was incalculable. I'd like to stop there, but in April 2022 Wiz Research called out another unexploited vulnerability with Microsoft's PostgreSQL offering (again resulting from incomplete tenant isolation) that could have allowed tenants at minimum read access to databases owned by other Microsoft customers.[34] Are you feeling like your old-school SQL Servers at your corporate DC are looking pretty good?

---

[31] www.protocol.com/enterprise/microsoft-azure-vulnerabilities-cloud-security

[32] https://orca.security/resources/blog/synlapse-critical-azure-synapse-analytics-service-vulnerability/

[33] https://orca.security/resources/blog/synlapse-critical-azure-synapse-analytics-service-vulnerability/

[34] www.wiz.io/blog/wiz-research-discovers-extrareplica-cross-account-database-vulnerability-in-azure-postgresql/

In fact, you can continue to run that beloved SQL Server 2012 antique in your own DC and still benefit from Arc as a management plane and to wrap your database with additional layers of security. SQL Server running on OS versions clears back to Windows Server 2012 R2, Ubuntu 16.04, as well as SUSE, and Red Hat Linux distros can benefit from Azure Defender and Azure Sentinel protection when connected to Azure Arc. Key to remember with this approach is that unless your company has invested heavily in geo-redundant data centers, or your SQL Server hosts run on the infrastructure of a cloud provider that allows you to set up regional failover, your data is still at risk in case of a natural or man-made disaster. Currently, you can have up to 800 instances of a single resource type in an Azure Resource Group [RG], allowing you to manage a good-sized cadre of SQL Servers in a single RG. You can also now view the databases living on those servers,[35] including their individual properties, although Microsoft's documentation states there could be a period of latency (up to an hour) before modifications to an existing database or the creation or deletion of a database are visible. Still in preview as of this writing is the ability to query your database catalog with Azure Resource Graph, a feature that should prove to be incredibly useful for operations since it will allow you to quickly determine facts like version, encryption status, compatibility level, and more no matter where you are hosting an Arc-enabled SQL Server.

Companies often have dual objectives of both modernizing legacy applications and getting out of the corporate DC. In this case, one approach is to lift and shift servers onto cloud infrastructure before beginning the analysis that will support the sometimes massive effort of modernizing legacy applications. A significant drawback to this approach is the latency an older application will experience communicating over a distributed network as compared to when it was collocated in a DC. When

---

[35] https://learn.microsoft.com/en-us/sql/sql-server/azure-arc/
view-databases?view=sql-server-ver16

this latency is tolerable, companies often choose this approach anyway because of the simpler billing model and the opportunity to reconfigure applications with the difficulty of the migration itself in the rearview.

If you decide to deploy SQL Server on Azure hardware, you do gain some significant advantages from Arc akin to purchasing a managed instance but without the significant limitations imposed by a less customizable managed instance.[36] The differences may prove significant if you have database administrators who are experienced with advanced management features within SQL Server, or if your use case relies heavily on interactions with the Windows file system (which SQL Managed Instances do not support). When you deploy SQL Server in an Azure VM, you can use the Windows SQL Server IaaS Agent extension to facilitate features like automated patching and backups if running in single instance mode, thus relieving some pain around repetitive tasks while continuing to maintain control of some of the intricate tuning details that are possible with in-house administration of SQL Server. However, the primary rationale for deploying this way would be things like Independent Software Vendor [ISV] certification (validating compatibility of software with specific hardware), legacy application support pending a modernization effort, or a requirement to use advanced features of SQL Server.

A managed SQL Server instance is billed by usage and is advantageous in terms of disaster recovery and high availability. It is simple to deploy and particularly beneficial in a modern microservice environment where new database instances may be created frequently. It can utilize dedicated storage, or multiple database instances can share a storage pool for both cost savings and improved performance. There are query tuning features available which can impact performance, as well as some logging data to show what your instance is consuming in terms of memory and CPU. All of the administration chores such as upgrades and backups are Microsoft's

---

[36] https://docs.microsoft.com/en-us/azure/azure-sql/managed-instance/
transact-sql-tsql-differences-sql-server?view=azuresql

responsibility, and you are guaranteed 99.99% uptime along with high availability and even some compliance controls for standards such as SOC and HIPAA. The core-based licensing model means you can purchase instances with the compute, memory, and storage you think you'll need by making a rough comparison with your on-premise SQL Server. There is an additional (no feature trade-offs and consequently expensive) business-critical performance tier available as well.

One interesting use case for managed instances is a "get out of jail free" card for SQL Server customers who are still running on the 2008 version which has reached the end of its lifespan and will no longer be supported by upgrades. If a customer migrates their legacy SQL Servers to Azure's SQL Server Managed Instances, Microsoft notes that application code changes will not be required and that existing licenses may cover more than half of the cost to operate in a modern and secure cloud instance.[37]

For Arc-enabled SQL Managed Instances, the benefit provided by Arc is primarily around the incredible fact that you can run a SQL Managed Instance on your own hardware with full data sovereignty. This is the point at which I think the term hybrid should be thrown out in favor of describing the amalgam of Azure control plane architecture with customer-owned hardware as a "Unified Computing Platform." At Microsoft Build 2022, it was announced that the Business Critical tier had been added to Arc-Enabled Managed SQL with *unlimited* (except by the hardware and OS it's run on) memory, compute, and storage. The default max memory setting in SQL Server is a bit over 2,000 terabytes (basically specifying that it won't stop consuming memory until it runs out of 32-bit integers), while Windows Server 2022 "only" supports up to 48TB RAM. It's unlikely that even if you are limited to a measly 48TB of memory, that

---

[37] https://azure.microsoft.com/en-us/blog/announcing-new-options-for-sql-server-2008-and-windows-server-2008-end-of-support/

heavy pressure from enterprise OLTP or analytics workloads will put much of a brake on performance, and if you string a few of these together, your setup might qualify to run the next NASA mission.

Another advance in capabilities is the ability to run a SQL Managed Instance in indirect or disconnected mode. Businesses that by their nature will have only intermittent connection to the Azure cloud (cruise ships, commercial fishing operations, oil rigs, or mining operations, for example) can have a PaaS-like experience of automated backups and monitoring even without full connectivity. Even the installation of container images needed in these edge scenarios can be adapted to use a local repository of images previously downloaded from Microsoft. Just because you're floating in the Bering Sea or at the bottom of a mine shaft, Microsoft doesn't think you should be deprived of the opportunity to run a modern software stack. Of course, Microsoft wants to be paid for this luxury, so if your installation is stuck on the tennis shoe network in the long term, you'll be asked to export the usage of your setup to a file and then upload it to Microsoft, so they can send you a bill. The same methods apply if you wish to, for instance, upload to Azure Log Analytics. While not ideal (and frankly to be avoided if transferring unencrypted or sensitive data), that is the current workaround in disconnected environments.

Security Enhancements for Arc-Enabled Data Services

Aside from the foregoing scenario of trusting a human to walk around with your thumb drive full of logs in their pocket, guarding the data at the heart of your application has never been more challenging than it is today – until tomorrow. As security technology grows, so do the attempts to circumvent it.

A win for managed SQL Server is that it has feature parity in most areas with the version you would run yourself, and this applies also to security.[38] In practical terms, database security still relies heavily on isolation and segregation of workloads; however, there are many features in the database engine itself that also increase safety such as row- and column-level protection.

In preview as of summer 2022 is the ability to set data access policies on Arc-enabled SQL Servers with Microsoft Purview. Management by policy is almost always more thorough and effective than tuning permissions individually; however, it looks like the approach to accomplishing this via the Arc control plane needs refinement. Implementation guidance from Microsoft[39] notes that a server admin can simply turn off Purview policy enforcement and that a "rogue admin" (please don't hire any of those) could tamper with the server path, allowing policies to be misapplied to the wrong server. Despite these early wrinkles, this is the type of enterprise management that needs to be applied in a multilayered approach to securing data, and there are both cost savings and operational advantages to doing so. In a similar vein to how AWS allows administrator to create a Service Catalog[40] of IT resources that can be freely used, Purview delineates access privileges so that access is predictable and further extends automation to allow self-service workflows to request permissions where a need for access might not have been anticipated. So far, Purview governance is able to be applied to Arc-enabled SQL Servers, SQL Managed Instances, and storage.

---

[38] https://docs.microsoft.com/en-us/sql/relational-databases/security/sql-server-security-best-practices?view=sql-server-ver16

[39] https://docs.microsoft.com/en-us/azure/purview/how-to-data-owner-policies-arc-sql-server

[40] https://aws.amazon.com/servicecatalog/?aws-service-catalog.sort-by=item.additionalFields.createdDate&aws-service-catalog.sort-order=desc

If the assets in an Azure resource group are stable, the strictest security approach to protecting not data but the resources themselves is to lock them. The simplest form of lock is cannot-delete, which will assure no critical resources disappear but has quite a few side effects – for instance, it can cause Azure Backup service to fail because it cannot delete old restore points. A draconian read-only lock can hamstring portions of key services like the Log Analytics Service and Application Gateway. While there can be use cases for locks, their impact on functionality needs to be well understood. They can be used to enhance security and prevent deletion of, for example, a Microsoft Purview account, but they will also calcify a dynamically growing resource group.

SQL Server 2022

Worth mentioning because of the significant impact it has on this topic is the General Availability release of SQL Server 2022. This release is a game-changer, particularly in the analytics space, where Azure Synapse Link for SQL allows "near real-time with no ETL or data integration logic".[41] The limitations of this very cool new capability are still plentiful (unsupported column/field types, unsupported DDL operations, limitations on schema other than dbo, etc.[42]), to the point where it might be most suitable to also start with a freshly designed data application. Still, the performance gains of the replication approach along with the immediacy of the analyzed data will likely incentivize a cycle of continuous improvement.

---

[41] https://docs.microsoft.com/en-us/azure/synapse-analytics/
synapse-link/sql-synapse-link-overview
[42] https://docs.microsoft.com/en-us/azure/synapse-analytics/
synapse-link/synapse-link-for-sql-known-issues

Completely in harmony with the purpose of Arc as a bridge to unified hybrid computing models, you can also now leverage "S3 [AWS] compatible" storage with SQL Server for backups and restores.[43] SQL Server cannot reach into your AWS tenancy and create the bucket for you, but if you have it, you are now able to make use of it. It appears that Microsoft is not terribly concerned about where you purchase cheap storage, but they will make every effort to secure your compute business. Many vendors besides AWS also host S3-compatible object stores,[44] so this opens the door to using those storage products also.

SQL Server 2022 will allow you to attach your server to Azure via Arc during the installation process when installing from the command prompt, reflecting an administrator first approach in the way the feature is being released. Further, you will now be able to attach a SQL Server installation to a managed instance for purposes such as offloading read-only workloads to Azure, executing a stepped migration to an Azure Managed Instance that would require little or no downtime, or as part of a disaster recovery strategy. As the line blurs between your SQL instance and theirs, Microsoft hopes you will become attached to the ease of managed SQL. From a cloud provider's standpoint, reliable income combined with global, systemized management operations is a very good thing, but it is also a winning scenario for customers for whom IT operations are incidental to their primary line of business.

---

[43] https://docs.microsoft.com/en-us/sql/relational-databases/backup-restore/sql-server-backup-to-url-s3-compatible-object-storage?view=sql-server-ver16

[44] www.techtarget.com/searchstorage/tip/How-to-use-S3-compatible-storage

PostgreSQL on Azure

PostgreSQL, like other technologies covered in this book, owes its existence to Berkeley being a provenience of new computing technologies fostering solutions to some of the biggest data problems in enterprise computing while adhering to an open source model that let the best minds of the IT community test and enhance things like PostgreSQL and Spark.

While the PostgreSQL docs describe the genesis of the product being created in at Berkeley in 1986 (with both military and National Science Foundation sponsorship[45]), its creator, Michael Stonebraker, recalls the inception as beginning in 1972 when a research project led himself and a colleague to create its predecessor, INGRES.[46] One striking parallel between their team and Spark's is a motivation to simplify in order to foster usage. Stonebraker read a paper from fellow relational database design pioneer Ted Codd[47] which struck him as not workable in real-world implementation scenarios since "Nobody who didn't have a PhD could understand Ted Codd's predicate calculus or his relational algebra... so it was pretty obvious that the right thing to do was to build a relational database system with an accessible query language."[48]

Fast forward nearly a half-century and PostgreSQL has become a developer standard used by small business and major corporations alike. As with the Linux operating system, vendors seek a way to make money from free products by decorating them with features, support contracts, and offers to host and maintain them. All of the major cloud providers offer PostgreSQL options, and some smaller ones such as Heroku do also as well as many low-end providers who flock around these larger companies like seagulls following a fishing boat, making a few dollars

---

[45] www.postgresql.org/docs/current/history.html
[46] https://amturing.acm.org/pdf/StonebrakerTuringTranscript.pdf
[47] https://en.wikipedia.org/wiki/Edgar_F._Codd
[48] www.youtube.com/watch?v=3IW_2dtm3jw

from selling what should be free to the unwary. AWS offers PostgreSQL as one of the flavors available in its Relational Database Service along with other top database engines, and its cost-saving product Aurora claims "full MySQL and PostgreSQL compatibility," while Google (like Azure) began offering a high-performance computing [HPC] version called AlloyDB in 2022. Alloy is a good name to describe how these high-performance products are built since they marry a core PostgreSQL installation with products to accelerate the ability to query and scale. Azure meanwhile offers three flavors of managed PostgreSQL[49] including a Single Server edition which was purported to be ideal for cloud-native applications and providing hot standby should a database instance go down but is now on a retirement path[50] in favor of Flexible Server which is similar but offers greater customization and options for cost control in terms of scalable and burstable workload management. PostgreSQL Hyperscale using the Citus extension[51] (renamed in October of 2022 to CosmosDB for PostgreSQL[52]) distributes data horizontally among nodes which can concurrently process portions of a record (which although using a different implementation is similar to GCP's AlloyDB approach which claims four times the processing power of the underlying PostgreSQL engine by means of "Read connections [that] scale horizontally, backed by low lag, scale-out read replica pools."[53]). In either case, the speed enhancement of distributing the workload can be visualized as a pit crew changing all four tires in an

---

[49] https://docs.microsoft.com/en-us/azure/postgresql/single-server/overview-postgres-choose-server-options

[50] https://learn.microsoft.com/en-us/azure/postgresql/single-server/whats-happening-to-postgresql-single-server

[51] www.citusdata.com/

[52] https://learn.microsoft.com/en-us/azure/postgresql/hyperscale/moved?tabs=direct

[53] https://cloud.google.com/alloydb

automobile race; four well-synchronized mechanics can change four tires much faster than one mechanic is able to, and that is a miniature example of the power of distributed workloads.

Some of the reasons behind PostgreSQL's popularity are its handling of geographic information systems [GIS] data via the PostGIS extension which adds spatial data types and operators.[54] It has plenty of competitors,[55] both commercial and open source, but its presence ties back to Stonebraker's original objective to freely allow data types that made sense for a particular domain rather than constrain the relational database schema to a business paradigm.

Since full-featured enterprise PostgreSQL is free, why do companies pay both time increment and volume charges to cloud vendors for the privilege to use it, as well as potentially incurring licensing costs for customized versions? Protecting enterprise data requires extreme expertise even with managed products, and the risks of rolling one's own product with no vendor SLA to guarantee that the product will meet specific redundancy, high availability, and platform security standards pose too great of a risk to large companies. Additional burdens of upgrade and patch management further discourage unmanaged installations. With PostgreSQL in particular, I have seen companies stranded on outdated versions that exposed them to significant security risk (OWASP identified outdated components as #6 in its top ten list for 2021) simply because the open source guru that set up their system is long gone.

Azure Arc-enabled PostgreSQL server is the sole edition of Azure PostgreSQL products under the Arc umbrella as of Q2 2023. Microsoft describes it as PostgreSQL 14 with "a curated set of available extensions,"[56]

---

[54] https://en.wikipedia.org/wiki/PostGIS

[55] https://en.wikipedia.org/wiki/Spatial_database#List

[56] https://learn.microsoft.com/en-us/azure/azure-arc/data/what-is-azure-arc-enabled-postgresql

including one enabling Active Directory integration. Since it can be consumed as a PaaS service or deployed to your choice of cloud providers, Microsoft is betting that the value proposition of the Arc control plane and Azure enhancements to operations are enough to justify corporate spend for their administration layer.

The Arc-enabled version of PostgreSQL is recommended by Microsoft as an antidote to a couple of common but complex scenarios which are multi-tenant and real-time applications, and they freely admit that if the product is not architected properly, you will not be happy with performance. To implement successfully will require accurate knowledge of the application requirements as well as expertise from the data science and networking teams along with performance testing prior to a production implementation. A final caveat noted by Microsoft is that at the time of this writing, it is not yet possible to configure Arc-enabled PostgreSQL for high availability[57] – a fact that may drive customers with SLAs around uptime to instead use the managed service option, Azure Database for PostgreSQL – Flexible Server.[58]

One of the reasons for having a thorough understanding of your application and its consumption and usage patterns is that when you deploy Arc-enabled PostgreSQL, you must set your storage options during deployment (unlike the PaaS offering which allows you to start with basic storage and then to scale up to standard when needed), which will affect your application's cost and performance throughout its lifecycle. Essentially, the only way out of this conundrum is migration of your data to a new Kubernetes server group. The relationship of your application's data to its domain must also be well understood since the distribution of your database across multiple nodes will only provide a performance increase

---

[57] https://learn.microsoft.com/en-us/azure/azure-arc/data/limitations-postgresql

[58] https://learn.microsoft.com/en-us/azure/postgresql/flexible-server/overview

if you assure that when the data is split into multiple shards related data stays together on the same physical hardware in order to avoid network transversal of data – which would defeat the purpose of speeding up query responses.[59] An assumption that is often made when modernizing an application stack is that data is just data, and reforming the APIs or exiting the monolith will be enough. This is patently untrue, and data structures deserve the same careful inquiry as to whether they need new schema in order to better adhere to the business domain as well as to properly take advantage of modern database technologies.

Azure Data Studio

ETL (*extract* data, *transform* it into a format readable in its destination, and *load* it into that destination) has a history of difficulty, slowness, and sometimes near impossibility to accomplish that makes modern ETL tools seem like they're running to a soundtrack of angels singing – it's that much better than it used to be. Still, the core challenges remain. When data moves from one system to another its core meaning cannot change even if its format does. If it is polluted with irrelevant or duplicate data or needlessly exposes personal information, it must be cleaned as part of its transformation. What standards will be used for validating the data? If the source data corpus is large, then it is also a matter of the time it will take to run the ETL job.

From a governance standpoint, it is very important to protect the business from the dead-end trap of nonstandard data capture and storage systems, unregulated and unmonitored data systems, and all kinds of administrative malefice in between. This can be done by aligning purchasing with industry standard formats and also by employing high-caliber professionals as data stewards.

---

[59] https://docs.microsoft.com/en-us/azure/postgresql/hyperscale/howto-choose-distribution-column

To give just one anonymous example of how badly it can go if proper data governance is not exercised, I was part of an evaluation team troubleshooting data quality problems at the headquarters of the largest firm in the world at that time in a core vertical of the financial industry. Through a series of backup and migration efforts that were not well done, they lost the north star copy of the database on which core business applications were running. Executives and senior IT had versions of the database they personally trusted running on private servers under their own desks. Which one would be served up in case of an audit was a good portion of the reason they sought an outside consultancy to look for a way out of their dilemma.

Less dire but still troubling was a database at the center of a critical architecture that was being ported to microservices in a piecemeal fashion at an international accounting firm. This NoSQL database encouraged building a taxonomy on top of its product to achieve requirements that really should have indicated the use of a relational database from the beginning. The group owning the application had strong sponsorship for moving to a new database platform, but to do so posed an extreme challenge due to the freeform metadata that had grown like a mat of spiderwebs over their entire data store.

Both ADF (not to be confused with the unfortunately similarly named Azure Data Studio [ADS] or Azure Data Explorer [ADE], which are a client for running queries compatible with multiple operating systems and a stand-alone data analysis tool) and Synapse are able to create ingestion pipelines, but ADF holds a strong advantage in the number of connectors and types of data it can process. In comparison to ETL using AWS Glue, ADF is replete with low-code options to connect data sources and set up transformation pipelines while the massive developer playground known as AWS takes the expected approach of letting you approach your analytics projects programmatically using Python or Scala with much less handholding. Microsoft also shows its corporate roots in supporting more compliance frameworks than AWS. Their varying approaches to enterprise-scale data processing and analysis enable a feature-based approach to selecting the platform that is best for your business.

Both AWS and Azure plus GPC underpin several tools with Apache Spark. In a LinkedIn article referenced earlier, I wrote, "Apache Spark for instance (a technology incorporated into managed data solutions from all three major cloud providers) creates Resilient Distributed Data Sets (RDDs) which are read-only partitioned collections of records that can be materialized as needed in a lazy fashion, thus allowing an extremely fast in-memory parallel processing engine to respond to requests for the journaled data." With smashing success over a short dozen years since its first open source release in 2010, Spark was and is a fascinating product to dive into. Like many great discoveries, Spark was created incidental to other research as the progenitor of the massive open source project; Matei Zaharia[60] was fascinated with big data platforms such as those used by Facebook and the granddaddy of social media giants, Yahoo. He imagined an application capable of processing massive amounts of data on a distributed platform could apply to many other industries and use cases if the speed and accessibility of querying the data could be improved. He set out to help a friend, Lester Mackey, who was on a team competing for Facebook's 1M prize for discoveries contributing to the improvement of its algorithm and also to respond to machine learning researchers at Berkeley who wanted a faster and more scalable ML engine. After his first attempt at a new programming model passed the muster with the ML team, it was decided to open

---

[60] www.databricks.com/speaker/matei-zaharia

source the project, and from there new applications in the scientific field began to validate his ideas about the broader capabilities of distributed processing of massive datasets.[61] In terms of its original objectives of benefiting scientific disciplines,[62] making querying accessible to non-engineers as well as the ability to analyze streaming data in near real-time Spark has been wildly successful.

ADF claims over 90 data ingestion connectors,[63] and if you can't find one to your liking, you can use classic ODBC connectors, REST, SOAP APIs for HTTP, or OData. Synapse utilizes some of these via ADF for its own ingestion processes. While ADF is a capable ETL and data migration tool, Azure offers Azure Migrate[64] for moving entire servers, and if you intend to simply host your SQL Server on cloud infrastructure, this "lift and shift" approach may be optimal. If instead you simply wish to move your SQL databases to Azure SQL Server or SQL Managed Instance, you can use the Data Migration Assistant[65] which doesn't transform your data in any way as an ETL tool like ADF would.

A final comment is to know the data surface you are protecting when using any tool, including those approved by your cloud vendor. In May of 2022, the Microsoft Security Response Center published a mitigation to a serious vulnerability in a third-party ODBC connector for Amazon

---

[61] www.youtube.com/watch?v=p4PkA2huzVc

[62] www.databricks.com/session/very-large-data-files-object-stores-and-deep-learning-lessons-learned-while-looking-for-signs-of-extra-terrestrial-life and www.nasa.gov/content/exploring-space-through-streaming-analytics

[63] https://docs.microsoft.com/en-us/azure/data-factory/connector-overview

[64] https://docs.microsoft.com/en-us/azure/migrate/migrate-services-overview#azure-migrate-server-migration-tool

[65] https://docs.microsoft.com/en-us/sql/dma/dma-migrateonpremsqltosqldb?view=sql-server-ver16

Redshift.[66] Their recommendation to securely isolate your network traffic is applicable to the next still-undiscovered security hole not only in ETL tools but across a complex IT estate in general. Dig your moat very deep and be sure to pull up the bridge.[67]

Ease the Challenges of Database Management with Arc

When you subscribe to a PaaS database, you can be confident that replication will not increase the risk of duplication. Nonetheless, when running SQL instances in a VM, there is a very real danger that shadow copies could arise, much like the aforementioned servers under executive desks. A database machine image, like any other, needs a governed deployment pipeline and security controls to prevent unauthorized copies. This can be accomplished with versioning and security controls applied by policy to the container registry and will be covered in more detail in a subsequent chapter on automating policy and governance.

High availability [HA] is another database management concern that has wholly transformed with the maturation of cloud computing. Circa 2008 Microsoft introduced database mirroring for SQL Server – a single database instance mirrored on separate servers and a modestly spec'd witness server to assure they remained in sync. Then clustering appeared providing redundancy at the database server level for however many database instances are running as well as increasing the level of redundancy with additional servers in the cluster. Both of these technologies are present today and have been joined by cloud-friendly

---

[66] https://msrc-blog.microsoft.com/2022/05/09/vulnerability-mitigated-in-the-third-party-data-connector-used-in-azure-synapse-pipelines-and-azure-data-factory-cve-2022-29972/

[67] https://docs.microsoft.com/en-us/azure/data-factory/data-movement-security-considerations

replication strategies that make databases available globally or in different regions and allow for nearly unnoticeable failover strategies as well as great protection from physical disasters at far lower monetary investment than constructing redundant DCs. As the difference between, for example, a PaaS PostgreSQL Flexible Server instance which provides HA and an Arc-enabled PostgreSQL server which does not underscore the need to plan carefully not only in terms of offering costs between the various models but also the ability to support them in the long term. If the database engine is an industry standard with high compatibility, you are not locked in if, for instance, you start with an IaaS solution and later wish to switch to PaaS, but the costs and general stress of the potential for this sort of secondary migration should be accounted for as a risk when selecting an initial hosting approach. Finally, selecting PaaS is not in itself a worry-free guarantee of HA or resilience. An Azure Arc SQL Managed Instance is deployed to containers and relies solely on Kubernetes ability to spin up a new containerized database instance and reattach to resilient storage, a strategy which is far less sturdy than the approach taken for the Business Critical tier of layering a contained availability group using SQL Server Always On capabilities.

Upgrades and updates have also become easier to manage and database servers require minding the health of the underlying server, including updates that strengthen the security of the kernel and operating system, as well as the database engine. Today, even if you choose an IaaS deployment model, calling a weekend outage and staffing a team to supervise each step in an upgrade or patch cycle of your server farm is largely a thing of the past since with distributed systems it's possible to do rolling upgrades that move from server to server and never require downtime. That doesn't mean updates have become trouble-free as was illustrated by Microsoft having to roll back their own Microsoft

365 update recently due to simple actions causing Outlook to crash.[68] If it can happen to Microsoft on a global platform, it can happen to you, but happily when an occasional misstep is made on its gargantuan platform, the remedy transforms into better options for enterprise customers. Generally available since September 2023, Microsoft has released Azure Update Manager which utilizes Arc[69] in order to provide better coverage than Microsoft's previous update offering and is in preview for SQL Server VMs.[70]

This chapter has shown how Kubernetes underpins some of Microsoft's data platform, and in Chapter 6, we'll discuss Arc-enabled Kubernetes and what it offers to multi-cloud and hybrid Kubernetes installations.

---

[68] www.bleepingcomputer.com/news/microsoft/microsoft-365-version-2206-update-pulled-due-to-apps-crashing/

[69] https://techcommunity.microsoft.com/t5/azure-governance-and-management/generally-available-azure-update-manager/ba-p/3928878

[70] https://learn.microsoft.com/en-us/azure/update-manager/guidance-patching-sql-server-azure-vm

CHAPTER 6

Managing Kubernetes Workloads in Hybrid or Multi-cloud Data Centers

Kubernetes is foundational to Arc's capabilities. For instance, extending Azure PaaS services such as Key Vault, App Service, Arc-enabled data services, and more to edge or on-premise locations relies on the Kubernetes runtime. Once your clusters are Arc enabled and running stably, wherever they are located, all of these services can be pushed to the cluster where it is most advantageous to have them running – you are no longer constrained to run your infra on Microsoft's cloud to take advantage of Azure PaaS.

Before diving into control plane technologies that can be utilized to manage Kubernetes clusters, both those provided by Arc and Kubernetes-specific products like Istio, it's helpful to take a look at what Kubernetes is and why it so rapidly became such a pervasive technology.

The genesis of Kubernetes was not a single stroke of genius by a small development team, but rather the mammoth effort of continuous improvement at no less than Google as they sought ways to improve their

© Ramona Maxwell 2024
R. Maxwell, *Azure Arc Systems Management*,
https://doi.org/10.1007/978-1-4842-9480-2_6

original container management system (aptly called Borg).[1] Borg was
built at a time when container isolation was just becoming available in the
Linux kernel, and thus Google also contributed heavily to the development
of Linux's containerization approach. While a fantastic advancement over
prior workflow and batch execution tools in terms of resource utilization,
the "result was a somewhat heterogeneous, ad-hoc collection of systems
that Borg's users had to configure and interact with, using several
different configuration languages and processes," and these irregularities
precipitated the next-generation product named Omega.

Omega is described by the Kubernetes development team as
being "built from the ground up to have a more consistent, principled
architecture" than Borg. To accomplish Omega's design goals Google
pursued a greenfield build of a product that allowed for concurrent
processing and, while using many of Borg's design patterns, avoided
"funneling every change through a monolithic, centralized master."

By the time Google began to develop Kubernetes as its third attempt
at a container management platform prior to its 2014 initial open source
release, their experience with distributed computing challenges and
opportunities met or exceeded any team worldwide. Microsoft was
concurrently developing Service Fabric to meet the challenges of running
the Azure Platform, with it underpinning major service offerings from
Event Hubs to Cosmos DB and Cortana. A major difference between the
two was the ability of Service Fabric to support stateful applications,[2]
something Kubernetes wasn't designed to do as a distributed stateless
platform although the massive community support for Kubernetes

---

[1] https://static.googleusercontent.com/media/research.google.com/en//
pubs/archive/44843.pdf

[2] https://techcommunity.microsoft.com/t5/azure-developer-community-
blog/service-fabric-and-kubernetes-community-comparison-part-1-8211/
ba-p/337421

has engendered effective strategies in this regard[3] (usually by backing workloads with storage solutions designed to preserve state). Kubernetes brought fundamental changes in approach designed to make it both more accessible and concurrently more secure in allowing access solely through its REST API over which all Kubernetes management communications take place whether by users or internally.[4]

I think my favorite point in the whitepaper around the evolution of control planes at Google cited earlier is the fact that with Kubernetes the focus changed from machine management to application management, for example, "application-oriented infrastructure." A Kubernetes pod is a container which encapsulates one or more application containers nested within it. The pod container provides operating system level services required by the application container(s) nested within it. When we refer to an application being designed to be cloud native, one of its core attributes is being to a great extent agnostic as to the operating system of the underlying host. There are numerous benefits to this approach. From an operational standpoint, monitoring can be focused on the needs of the particular application and return workload-specific metrics. A natural feedback loop is created when monitoring a pod is providing application usage metrics, which in turn can inform how to scale the application. CPU utilization or memory consumption become traceable to the application itself, what it does and how it was designed – allowing the possibility to iterate toward improvements in how the application manages resources. The benefits can be substantial in terms of manageability and cost savings also.

If you think of a traditional application that was designed as a Windows Desktop application, it has extended another application – the operating system GUI – and thus will have a hard dependency on that operating

---

[3] www.techtarget.com/searchitoperations/tip/How-to-manage-
stateful-containers-with-Kubernetes
[4] https://kubernetes.io/docs/concepts/overview/kubernetes-api/

system. It is possible to have more than one operating system on a physical
server by means of virtualization, which allows a "virtual" or software-
defined machine to run with a completely different operating system
complete with the OS kernel while accessing storage, memory, networking
devices, and other connected peripherals as if it were installed directly
on the machine. This differs mightily from containers which isolate their
workloads only by running in separate processes on the host's primary
operating system. The OS layer you may bake into your containerized
image is not a full virtualized OS as would be required for a virtual
machine; rather, it provides just the necessary pieces for your application
to utilize just a slice of the host's operating system kernel. This reliance on
the host's OS kernel is why an image might be designated as appropriate
to run on a Linux or Windows host in particular; however, well-designed
cloud-native applications could, for instance, move from Windows
containers to Linux containers on Azure with few modifications and reap
cost savings as a result.[5] The performance and capacity improvements
offered by containerization over virtualization are a key driver in the
modernization of languages, as is very evident in the evolution of classic
.NET programming with its specific reliance on the Windows OS to today's
.NET which Microsoft says supports "Android, Apple, Linux, and Windows
operating systems."[6]

The usage of the term container is ubiquitous and nonspecific. Some
may use it to refer to a virtualized operating system (e.g., a Windows or
Linux container), while others use it to loosely describe what container
images are, that is, containers with both an operating system as a base
layer along with additional application layers. The minimal operating

---

[5] Scott Hanselman's POC of moving an application from its Windows container
to Linux for cost savings: www.hanselman.com/blog/moving-an-aspnet-core-
from-azure-app-service-on-windows-to-linux-by-testing-in-wsl-and-
docker-first

[6] https://docs.microsoft.com/en-us/dotnet/core/introduction#support and
also see www.mono-project.com/

system layer in a container could almost be thought of as an interface, as it still relies on a virtual or physical machine's operating system and provides a facade of a host machine that is indistinguishable from running directly on the host to the containerized application. This chapter will follow the official Kubernetes definition which states that "A container image represents binary data that encapsulates an application and all its software dependencies."[7]

Kubernetes documentation summarizes what it does and does not do in its introduction of the product,[8] and the following table paraphrases and highlights key points from the documentation.

Summary of Kubernetes Capabilities per Their Docs

Kubernetes IS	Kubernetes is NOT
Service discovery and load balancing: Kubernetes can expose a container using the DNS name or using the IP address. Kubernetes can load balance and distribute the network traffic	A limiter of the types of applications supported. Kubernetes supports stateless, stateful, and data-processing workloads. If an application can run in a container, it should run great on Kubernetes
Storage orchestration: Kubernetes allows you to automatically mount a storage system of your choice	A tool to deploy source code and/or build your application

---

[7] https://kubernetes.io/docs/concepts/containers/images/
[8] https://kubernetes.io/docs/concepts/overview/

Kubernetes IS	Kubernetes is NOT
Automated rollouts and rollbacks: You can describe the desired state for your deployed containers using Kubernetes, and it can change the actual state to the desired state at a controlled rate	It does not provide application-level services, such as middleware (e.g., message buses), data-processing frameworks (e.g., Spark), databases (e.g., MySQL), caches, nor cluster storage systems (e.g., Ceph)
Automatic bin packing: You provide Kubernetes with a cluster of nodes that it can use to run containerized tasks. You tell Kubernetes how much CPU and memory (RAM) each container needs. Kubernetes can intelligently fit containers onto your nodes	Does not dictate logging, monitoring, or alerting solutions
Self-healing: Kubernetes restarts containers that fail, replaces containers, kills containers that don't respond to your user-defined health check, and doesn't advertise them to clients until they are ready to serve	Does not provide nor mandate a configuration language/system
Secret and configuration management: Kubernetes lets you store and manage sensitive information, such as passwords, OAuth tokens, and SSH keys. You can deploy and update secrets and application configuration without rebuilding your container images and without exposing secrets	Does not provide any comprehensive machine configuration, maintenance, management, or self-healing systems

Kubernetes IS	Kubernetes is NOT
	Additionally, Kubernetes is not a mere orchestration system. In fact, it eliminates the need for orchestration. Kubernetes comprises a set of independent, composable control processes that continuously drive the current state toward the provided desired state

With all the good that Kubernetes brings to containers, it has weaknesses around management and security that were not easily solved in the product itself without adding complexity that worked at cross-purpose with the intent for the product to make container management straightforward. What could possibly make this incredible control plane engineering masterpiece better? Another control plane, this one accompanied by a data plane (this is probably a good time to inject a new IT acronym, YACP, Yet Another Control Plane).

Although Istio provides a control plane as part of its architecture, its function is to provide a service mesh. Istio, another brainchild of Google along with IBM and Lyft,[9] is one among products like AWS App Mesh, Azure Service Fabric, Linkerd,[10] and others that as the AWS docs explain, "provide… application-level networking."[11] The benefit to this approach is that instead of trying to facilitate communication directly between an application's services that each reside in an ephemeral container using a classic networking overlay, the mesh identifies containers by the application they host and directs their coordination. Many of these products, like Istio, incorporate Envoy[12] to facilitate management at

---

[9] Google repeated its initial generous move of donating Kubernetes to the CNCF by also donating the Istio service mesh which serves as a management control plane over large Kubernetes installations to CNCF in 2020. Today, Istio underpins Google's service mesh offering for Kubernetes.

[10] https://linkerd.io/

[11] https://aws.amazon.com/app-mesh/

[12] www.envoyproxy.io/

the application level. Envoy runs a sidecar container alongside your application container which performs a plethora of useful tasks to enable the service mesh such as communication between services mentioned earlier, monitoring, load balancing, circuit breaking when a container is down and can't respond to requests, and more.

Sidecars are a great way to provide for nonfunctional requirements like those noted earlier without modifying the code of the application itself and also add security by not exposing core application code in order to achieve those tasks. However, they also consume cluster resources, and Istio has released a sidecar-less approach called Ambient Mesh[13] which can provide some of the most advantageous features of a service mesh, for instance, mutual TLS authentication between application components without the burden of sidecar resource consumption. Linkerd, another mesh noted for being lean and performant, still prefers sidecars but doesn't use Envoy in order to stay consistent with their minimalist approach.[14]

Kubernetes is not standing still either, for instance, its API recently offered an alternative to conventional endpoints called EndpointSlice(s) that perform service discovery by means of a tag belonging to every container labeled with a selector (tag) identifying the service it belongs to. If your application were named mybiz.com, the EndpointSlice for the billing service would live on a DNS subdomain such as billing.mybiz.com.

Arc-Enabled Kubernetes

So where does Arc fit in all this and what does it add to Kubernetes operations? Microsoft labels its offering "Azure Arc-enabled Kubernetes," and the title aptly communicates that Arc layers on some special sauce that

---

[13]www.cncf.io/blog/2023/03/14/istio-ambient-service-mesh-merged-to-istios-main-branch/

[14]https://linkerd.io/

no competitor really has a recipe for yet. For Kubernetes operators with large clusters (a single cluster can hold up to 300,000 container instances) running on multiple cloud platforms, the fact that Arc provides the ability to manage core aspects of disaster recovery, security policy, and more from a single vantage point is remarkable.

Before these benefits can be realized, there first have to be Kubernetes installations to enable Arc upon. These can be greenfield or net new at the time of implementing Arc, but are more commonly existing clusters. Some organizations have an architectural design supporting how their Kubernetes installations were done, and some suffered from organic growth. The former is of course preferable and will allow a similarly orderly adoption of Arc, but if your existing architectures resemble a Jackson Pollock painting,[15] then the ability to treat them all as Azure resources will be transformational – bringing immediate cost savings and the ability to leverage existing assets more effectively.

Running a Successful Production Trial

Although not as directive and detailed as, for example, Azure Landing Zones[16] (which provide comprehensive architectural guidance on multiple facets of a large Arc-enabled Kubernetes[17] installation), Microsoft does offer suggestions for how to start down this happy path of successfully managing huge swaths of Kubernetes infra. Their proffered approach is to have you build a test environment that you will put under load and run for at least 30 days before placing actual business assets under Arc's control plane. Taken alone that period of time for a trial is fairly meaningless. It needs

---

[15] www.guggenheim.org/artwork/3482

[16] https://learn.microsoft.com/en-us/azure/cloud-adoption-framework/ready/landing-zone/

[17] https://learn.microsoft.com/en-us/azure/cloud-adoption-framework/scenarios/hybrid/enterprise-scale-landing-zone#azure-arc-enabled-kubernetes-design-guidelines

to be combined with knowledge of what's required to run Kubernetes at scale so that you can estimate the right amount of people from various IT disciplines to run the trial in a way that the proof of concept has meaningful application to the real-world implementation. A trial run should produce a template that aligns with your change management process and provides GitOps artifacts (or as a secondary option integrates with your existing CI/CD system) that will be used in the subsequent rollout. Whether that could occur in 30 days will depend on the resources and people you devote to it. With qualified leadership and engineering expertise, running an Arc trial can be straightforward and is worth the initial effort in order to reap the exponential benefits of centralized management.

To successfully compare other options to Azure Arc, an organization could decide to set parameters and trial their Kubernetes installation on more than one platform (mindful that running even a single trial will be a significant investment of both time and money). A better approach might be to look at the suitability of a home platform for IT operations and make the decisions about control plane technology dependent upon that. For those already invested deeply in AWS or GCP, the choice may not be as clear-cut, and a dual trial may be the only mechanism to discover the effectiveness of the approach a provider takes.

Kubernetes Deployment Paths for EKS, GKS, and On-Premise Clusters

If you were to set up AKS on Azure[18] (obviating the need for Arc unless you deploy to multiple clouds), you would capture all of the advantages of the Azure platform that Arc extends to additional locations. Using AKS makes the operational aspects of deploying and running a large Kubernetes installation less daunting, but initial configuration can still be a substantial

---

[18] https://learn.microsoft.com/en-us/azure/aks/

endeavor as you map clusters to VNets, choose an appropriate networking
overlay for your workloads, set up deployment pipelines, configure secrets
management, RBAC, enable monitoring, select a service mesh, and more.
In all of these, Microsoft provides what they describe as sensible defaults,
but when there is a use case for an enterprise-scale Kubernetes installation,
it is likely that there are also some unique requirements. Qualified
networking and security teams need to lay the groundwork, and if it's done
well, on any of the major cloud platforms, it should be frictionless from the
standpoint of the developers who will eventually deploy workloads to it.

Amazon's Elastic Kubernetes Service [EKS]

If you compare AWS approach to deployment on EKS, it is far more
directive and simpler, but in conjunction also less flexible. If you opt in
to EKS, benefits include having a managed platform with few concerns
around the control plane or updates and full integration with other AWS
services such as Identity and Access Management [IAM]. The other option
is a full-on build of your own Kubernetes platform using IaaS, really not
much simpler than running in your own DC, and as in Azure, you must
fully understand AWS networking landscape, how to achieve scaling,
manage upgrades, and provide HA and DR. On the data plane, you can
choose to manage your own nodes, but then you become responsible for
security and updates to them as well. Fargate is sometimes described as
a Kubernetes option on AWS, but it is much more akin to the Azure App
Service as it is PaaS, and workloads can be deployed to it directly. Its back
end is not Kubernetes but AWS's own container management system
ECS. Its interesting aspect is that you can deploy EKS *pods* to it,[19] and Azure
AKS has an equivalent feature of *virtual nodes* that are hosted by Azure
Container Instances [ACI].[20]

---

[19] https://docs.aws.amazon.com/eks/latest/userguide/fargate.html
[20] https://learn.microsoft.com/en-us/azure/aks/virtual-nodes

AWS has always been a platform for and by engineers. While
Microsoft's written materials hold your hand with not only reference
docs but long explanatory journeys through their products and features
via Microsoft Learn, AWS docs run rapid-fire through the products and
steps you'll need to configure an EKS cluster[21] using the AWS CLI, AWS
Management Console, or a third-party CLI eksctl.[22] If you choose to
deploy a cluster from within the AWS Management Console, you must
still understand the implications and caveats of each choice made there.
Because of the "for engineers" culture, eksctl lives as an open source
project outside of AWS and accepts contributions that advance the goal of
this product-specific CLI, automating some of the steps that must be taken
manually if using the AWS CLI.

Google Kubernetes Engine [GKE]

Google's documentation for their Google Kubernetes Service [GKS]
offering is frequently sprinkled with the word "opinionated" reflecting their
long experience of not only inventing much of the technology that is now a
core offering among cloud providers but also that they've long "eaten their
own dog food" in terms of using these technologies and their predecessors
to run Google itself. It is to their credit that they have become versatile,
platform-agnostic tools that can not only be utilized but also enhanced
by other providers to the great benefit of the enterprise computing
community as a whole.

When setting up clusters with GKE, the service offers an initial fork
in the road between a fully preconfigured GKE instance called Autopilot
and a configurable option labeled as Standard. Standard can be thought
of as setting the standard, rather than barely meeting it as it's designed
with enterprise workloads in mind. Setting up clusters is ridiculously

---

[21] https://eksctl.io/

[22] https://docs.aws.amazon.com/eks/latest/userguide/create-cluster.html

simple, but you still must understand how to manage your installation, for instance, Google's documentation warns that if large clusters exceed CKE limits on resources, you may experience "degradation of cluster performance," and in fact if your etcd database gets too fat, you may lose access to your cluster's control plane and need the Google Cloud support team to help you get it back.[23]

Interestingly, Google encourages the use of Kubernetes native RBAC simply because this limits users assigned to a role to cluster operations only, whereas if they were assigned a Google Cloud user role with privileges on the cluster, it may also entitle them to perform activities on other Google Cloud Resources.[24] This is quite opposite Microsoft's approach of distilling permissions management down to a single paradigm of Entra (formerly Azure Active Directory).

On-Premise Kubernetes

Since Kubernetes is a cloud-native project, running it on-premise is not the most natural fit, and yet many organizations do choose to make the effort for reasons such as cost savings, data isolation, and others. Yet AKS and other providers of managed Kubernetes services may begin to look very appealing when you begin to consider a few of the operational tasks involved in configuring and running a large Kubernetes installation such as

- Hardware provisioning

  - Multiple servers including 3–7 per cluster for
    master nodes and others for HAProxy load

---

[23] https://cloud.google.com/kubernetes-engine/docs/concepts/
planning-large-clusters#limits-best-practices-large-scale-clusters
[24] https://cloud.google.com/kubernetes-engine/docs/concepts/
security-overview#authentication_and_authorization

balancing and automation. Whether physical
or virtual, for production Kubernetes servers
it's advisable to have fat specs. Platform9[25]
recommends "two CPUs with 32 cores each, 2TB of
error-correcting RAM and at least four SSDs, eight
SATA SSDs, and a couple of 10G network cards"
as typical

- A fleet of fast SSDs since Etcd (Kubernetes primary
  datastore, it retains service discovery, scheduling
  and shared configuration information in a
  consistent key-
  value store) is continuously writing to disk

- Management and operations tasks

  - Configure a load-balancing solution

  - Network design and integration

  - Monitoring solutions

  - Securing clusters and their workloads

  - Frequent upgrades to remain aligned to Kubernetes
    release cycle[26]

In addition to the preceding list, Kubernetes is complex, and CNCF
offers multiple certifications for topics such as administration, security,
development, and more. Hiring and retaining people with these skills is a
hardline requirement of an on-premise installation of Kubernetes.

---

[25] https://platform9.com/

[26] https://kubernetes.io/releases/release/

124

Conclusion

While all of the previously discussed platforms have suitable approaches
for running Kubernetes, each also has limitations that impact scale, cost,
and operational complexity that can be improved by the multi-cloud or
hybrid approach that industrial strength control plane products like Azure
Arc or Google Anthos and the next portion of this chapter will examine
exactly what they provide.

What About Google Anthos?

If any Kubernetes control plane product could be hot on the heels of Azure
Arc, it would be Google Anthos. Anthos also claims to cover multi-cloud
and edge computing scenarios and now competes with Arc's ability to
manage on-premise bare metal and virtual servers by extending KubeVirt[27]
(which was designed to allow the integration of VMs into Kubernetes) to
provide features such as virtual network switches, predefined VM profiles
to assign memory and CPU, as well as storage management using the
Anthos VM runtime.

Anthos prioritizes sameness over singularity with the goal
of simplifying the management of large multi-cloud Kubernetes
installations[28] and refers to a logical group of clusters as a fleet. If a security
action or policy should apply to objects in multiple clusters, Anthos will
execute it against every identical namespace no matter which cluster in
the fleet it resides in. Anthos extends GKE to run on competitor clouds
and on-premise, but its approach to AKS and EKS differs from how Arc
makes foreign cloud resources appear as if they were native to Azure. In
Anthos, foreign cloud clusters are called "attached clusters," and Anthos

---

[27] https://kubevirt.io/

[28] https://cloud.google.com/anthos/docs/concepts/overview

only manages its own services running on attached clusters. Anthos and Arc share the significant benefit of being able to configure clusters through GitOps and to monitor clusters for conformance with their desired state.

Anthos also provides authentication using a Google identity or other identity providers such as those from Microsoft and Okta. It does not attempt to integrate authorization in the way that Arc does by mapping Kubernetes RBAC to built-in Azure roles and simply assumes you will use Kubernetes own RBAC system except when granting access to a service hosted by Google. The workloads running on clusters inside of a Google fleet also have an identity that is consistent for that workload across the fleet, allowing it to be targeted for specific actions and services. As with Arc, there is a policy engine, the Policy Controller,[29] which comes with a library of prebuilt policies and supports custom templates as well as groups of related policies referred to as bundles. The status of policy application is shown in the Policy Controller dashboard which will reflect how well your clusters align to best practice for Kubernetes as well as industry standards. Like Arc, Anthos promises extensive monitoring capabilities observable in a central dashboard as well as monitoring and configuration control including self-healing configurations.[30]

Reaping the Benefits of Kubernetes Running Under Arc

Completing a trial of Arc will be enough to expose operational challenges and knowledge gaps and compare that to what the ROI on a successful Arc implementation may be; however, the full scope of benefits doesn't become as obvious until you actually do match the tool up against large-

---

[29] https://cloud.google.com/anthos-config-management/docs/concepts/policy-controller
[30] https://cloud.google.com/anthos/config-management

126

scale hybrid Kubernetes installations. Then the benefits of being able
to automate deployments and governance as if multi-cloud were one
cloud will surface. The landscape of what is available from various cloud
providers is constantly changing. For example, in May of 2023, AWS
announced a new version of their Aurora serverless database (Aurora I/O-
Optimized[31]) offering that doesn't charge fees on a per request/response
basis, claiming it offers 40% up to a potential 90% cost reduction for high-
traffic workloads. Being able to manage clusters on any platform allows
you to choose where your workloads will run if new innovations around
cost, security, or performance make a particular platform advantageous.

GitOps with Arc

GitOps can move an organization from a culture of blame where an
operations team insists the application developers are incompetent,
and the developers in turn insist the ops team can't string two servers
together to support them, to one where both teams work under the
same framework. Like DevOps, GitOps promotes a single source of truth
using Infrastructure as Code [IaC] stored in a Git repository that must be
changed via a classic merge process that includes approval. This approach
limits the tendency to rely on system gurus to "make it run" with ad hoc
and undocumented changes that can pose great risk to systems when
those individuals are no longer available. It provides a documented system
naturally and facilitates a CI/CD (continuous integration and deployment)
approach to systems management that greatly accelerates the pace of
infrastructure management improvements.

---

[31] https://aws.amazon.com/blogs/aws/new-amazon-aurora-i-o-optimized-
cluster-configuration-with-up-to-40-cost-savings-for-i-o-intensive-
applications/

Kubernetes out of the box is designed to have its configuration declared as code and thus is a natural fit for a GitOps workflow. When applied consistently, GitOps provides similar benefits to the DevOps principles governing application development it inherits from including

- A single source of truth for the desired and actual configuration of the Kubernetes installation in a Git repository

- The ability to audit both the current configuration and the change history within the version-controlled repository

- Automation of deployment steps reducing human intervention and error

GitOps itself adds more benefits that are specific to operations such as

- Least privilege access to the Kubernetes cluster in that deployments must go through automated approval flows and cannot be executed by individuals

- The ability to apply policy as a configurable setting prior to deployment

- Self-healing without deploying a new instance as a Kubernetes controller continuously maps the desired cluster state stored in Git to the running cluster state and reconfigures a cluster that has fallen out of alignment to match the desired state

Each managed Kubernetes provider has a different approach to implementing GitOps and CNCF open source projects from Crossplane,[32] Argo,[33] and Flux[34] rule here. Each of these projects relies on underlying projects to extend their functionality such as Kustomize,[35] a configuration management tool able to *generate* new cluster configurations or *transform* (override) existing ones. Azure is all in with Flux for both Arc-enabled Kubernetes installations and AKS.

Another project core to using Flux or native Kubernetes is Helm.[36] Like templates used by Azure Resource Manager or AWS CloudFormation, Helm charts (written in YAML) contain the metadata describing elements of a Kubernetes ecosystem and can be combined to define a complete deployment of the same. Helm's structure underscores the mini me relationship of GitOps to DevOps. Like Maven, Gradle, or any other application manifest, a Helm chart contains a dependencies section in which you can create dynamic links to other Helm charts on which the current chart depends. These dependencies can be made conditional, such as by a tag which must be present for the dependency to be included at runtime. In an application manifest, you would specify dependencies on other application modules, environmental constraints, or software packages, but Helm charts focus on describing the platform those applications will run on. Helm is also sometimes described as a package manager for Kubernetes,[37] and that description also echoes GitOps developer roots as instead of the packages being software modules, they are configuration metadata. Technically, Kubernetes is middleware, since it sits between the functionality provided by the operating system and

---

[32] www.crossplane.io/

[33] https://argo-cd.readthedocs.io/en/stable/

[34] https://fluxcd.io/blog/2022/11/flux-is-a-cncf-graduated-project/

[35] https://kustomize.io/

[36] https://helm.sh/

[37] www.youtube.com/watch?v=Zzwq9FmZdsU&t=2s

the workloads it facilitates. Helm provides yet another translation layer
so that Kubernetes (the job of which is simply to facilitate the running
of containers while remaining indifferent to their workloads) can be
equipped to dress those containers with needed plug-ins to participate in
network traffic, enable monitoring solutions, attach to storage, and much
more. Regardless of which flavor of database you wish to deploy, how
you want your containers to communicate, or myriad other configuration
choices affecting your workload, there's a Helm chart for that (which will
become an artifact in your IaC repo).

As Flux needed to run within the Azure Resource Manager
ecosystem, Microsoft built the Flux (GitOps) cluster extension[38]
specifically to accomplish this. Cluster extensions live in the `Microsoft.`
`KubernetesConfiguration` namespace and accomplish a variety of
integration tasks that make AKS and Arc identifiable as Azure products.
These extensions allow Kubernetes clusters running in AKS or Arc-enabled
Kubernetes to use key Azure services for monitoring, data services,
security, machine learning, and more as listed by Microsoft[39] and shown as
follows:

- Azure Monitor Container Insights

- Azure Policy

- Azure Key Vault Secrets Provider

- Microsoft Defender for Containers

- Azure Arc-enabled Open Service Mesh

- Azure Arc-enabled Data Services

- Azure App Service on Azure Arc

---

[38] https://learn.microsoft.com/en-us/azure/azure-arc/kubernetes/
extensions-release#flux-gitops

[39] https://learn.microsoft.com/en-us/azure/azure-arc/kubernetes/
extensions-release

- Azure Event Grid on Kubernetes

- Azure API Management on Azure Arc

- Azure Arc-enabled Machine Learning

- Flux (GitOps)

- Dapr extension for Azure Kubernetes Service (AKS) and Arc-enabled Kubernetes

If you look at the definition of the Flux (GitOps) cluster extension, you see it is composed of the six controllers listed in Flux own documentation, which describes Flux as a microservice application that runs on the cluster it is managing. Each controller manages its own concerns in support of Flux's objective to utilize a version-controlled immutable definition of the cluster to both create and maintain it according to that definition. The Source controller has read-only access to the Git repository (or of late even an AWS S3 bucket) containing that definition in the form of Helm charts and other configuration metadata. Prior to packaging the resources for use by the other Flux components, it validates their authenticity and version as well as the chart contents defining the deployment. The Helm controller works hand in hand with the Source controller to publish the desired state of the cluster as the `HelmRelease` resource which feeds into the Kustomize controller that as noted earlier has the ability to create or transform artifacts in the Kubernetes cluster in order to reconcile the actual state of the cluster to the one that is desired. The Notifications controller is able to consume notifications about changes to source definitions, as well as to emit notifications to popular collaboration tools such as Slack or Teams. Finally, Image controllers assure that policies governing which version of an image will be used are respected and can also perform automated commits to update a container image. When using the `Microsoft.Flux` extension, the image components are optional.

For a project that started internally at Weaveworks in 2016 (before Kubernetes itself became predominant) and was then donated to the open source community, Flux is an impressive example of combining assets like Kustomize and Helm into a powerful superset of Kubernetes management tools. If you look at the timeline chart of Flux development on Weaveworks "What is GitOps" page,[40] you can see that they're very proud of Microsoft picking up their product for the Azure platform following their graduation as a CNCF project.

Remember that to use the Flux extension, the Kubernetes clusters must first be connected to Arc[41] and permissions granted to roles that you will use both to manage the cluster[42] and deploy applications.[43] For uniformity of deployments, cluster definitions can be applied to entire subscriptions or resource groups, rather than cluster by cluster. These definitions will include everything from network traffic and scaling to authorization and RBAC.

There are times when deployments and the services they require will differ, particularly if the workloads being run are multi-tenant. One option to assure that a service like Azure Arc-enabled SQL Managed Instance or an Azure Arc-enabled PostgreSQL server only exists for a specific tenant is to use custom locations. You can create a custom location using the Azure CLI and bind it to a namespace in your cluster where you want the tenant resources to be located.

---

[40] www.weave.works/technologies/gitops/#what-is-gitops

[41] https://learn.microsoft.com/en-us/azure/azure-arc/kubernetes/
quickstart-connect-cluster?tabs=azure-cli%2Cazure-cloud

[42] https://learn.microsoft.com/en-us/azure/aks/hybrid/connect-to-arc

[43] https://learn.microsoft.com/en-us/azure/azure-arc/kubernetes/
tutorial-use-gitops-flux2?tabs=azure-cli

Utilizing GitOps is a security control, as cluster configurations that begin to deviate from their desired state can be an indicator of a breach, and the continuous monitoring coupled with automated restoration can effectively block rogue configurations. The next subheading will offer more information on how Arc-enabled Kubernetes installations can be secured.

Proactive Security for Arc-Enabled Kubernetes

By this point in our discussion, it is well apparent that there are many facets to operating Kubernetes that require security controls be effectively applied. From network configuration and security controls to managing intra-pod communication, a zero trust approach requires methodically cataloging potential vulnerabilities and protecting each potential attack vector while still assuring clusters host their workloads effectively. According to Red Hat's 2022 State of Kubernetes security report,[44] a little over half of their survey respondents said they had delayed or canceled application deployments due to security concerns. Fully 30% stated they'd experienced a security incident relating to their Kubernetes installation. Interesting and also alarming is the fact that another 22% failed security audits, which might be a particular area of concern for entities that undergo security audits by regulatory agencies. According to an ISACA (a professional organization serving auditors) blog post, the more complex an IT landscape the less likely it is to be audited regularly.[45] An enterprise-scale Kubernetes installation is both dynamic and incredibly complex, yet the need to monitor and inspect its security posture is something that warrants more frequent attention – not less. DevOps and GitOps labels are changing to reflect that security is an integral, ne *central* part of either

---

[44] www.redhat.com/rhdc/managed-files/cl-state-of-kubernetes-security-report-2022-ebook-f31209-202205-en.pdf

[45] www.isaca.org/resources/news-and-trends/industry-news/2022/an-integrated-approach-to-security-audits

process – thus, DevSecOps and GitSecOps are entirely proper terms for the overall process of managing operations with security in focus every step of the way.

Whether looking at Kubernetes clusters or the workloads that reside on them, a primary step to provide security is the proper use of role-based access control [RBAC]. For Arc-enabled Kubernetes clusters, both Kubernetes native RBAC system for granular control of its operations and Entra come into play. While you can manage your Kubernetes cluster solely with Kubernetes authorization, it is necessary for the two authorization systems to work in tandem in order for the Kubernetes cluster to benefit from the services provided by the Azure platform such as Network Security Groups, load balancing, Log Analytics and monitoring, storage, and more. You can do this either by using native Kubernetes to manage the cluster (requiring an administrative user to have an identity in that system) and using system-assigned managed identities[46] to allow access to Azure platform services *or* by utilizing Azure RBAC roles that are specifically mapped to Kubernetes management roles (meaning you do not have to directly configure Kubernetes RBAC).[47]

If the authorization strategy is not clearly delineated, there is a risk of duplicating permissions and one or the other permission store drifting into an unmanaged state, which can be prevented by determining which RBAC system is the source of truth and then excluding alternate approaches. Correctly configuring security should be undertaken at the outset of an initial AKS or Arc-enabled Kubernetes trial since misconfiguration not only escalates the risk of a security breach, it can result in authorized users being unable to access or administer the cluster. As we discuss Kubernetes

---

[46] https://learn.microsoft.com/en-us/azure/azure-arc/servers/
managed-identity-authentication

[47] https://learn.microsoft.com/en-us/azure/azure-arc/kubernetes/
identity-access-overview

Native vs. Azure RBAC,[48] it will become apparent that the value of setting up a sole authorization system in Azure is well worth the effort. Having a single source of truth for authorization is as or even more important than maintaining a single source of truth for data since it impacts security. Microsoft learned this the hard way with legacy versions of SharePoint Server, as it was possible to have privileges coming from a classic Active Directory group and then also be assigned to privileges directly within SharePoint. Many times, this resulted in someone who'd been removed from an AD group still having access as privileges granted directly in SharePoint were more difficult to audit and relied on individual site administrators, many of whom were business users with friendly ties to former colleagues, to maintain.

Kubernetes RBAC controls access to the cluster itself. There are no deny rules, so precedence does not affect access. The Kubernetes RBAC API targets four objects including roles and role binding at the cluster and namespace level. They function in pairs to identify a scoped role and then bind that role to an identity.

---

[48] Still in preview as of Q1 2024 – see https://learn.microsoft.com/en-us/azure/azure-arc/kubernetes/conceptual-azure-rbac

Kubernetes RBAC

RBAC API objects

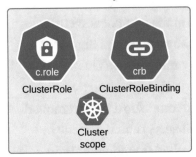

RBAC API object scopes

1. Cluster scope includes:
   a. All cluster resources
   b. Non-resource endpoints
   c. All namespaces
2. Namespace scope includes:
   a. Namespace resources
3. Binding
   a. Attach scope object to identity

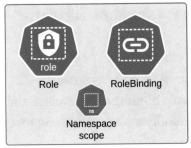

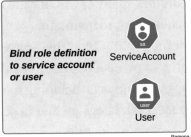

Figure 6-1. *Kubernetes RBAC, Ramona Maxwell @2023*

Just as the Arc control plane offers a familiar Azure interface for managing Kubernetes clusters hosted elsewhere, integrating Azure Active Directory [AAD] abstracts away Kubernetes own RBAC implementation and allows administrators to effectively manage their clusters using familiar Azure role designations such as contributor. This is accomplished by means of the webhook capabilities of Kubernetes own API.[49] Microsoft uses a webhook server called Guard (the repository for which is public but not accepting contributions[50]) in order to process a request made by a user, for instance, a kubectl command. On the first request of a kubectl session,

---

[49] https://kubernetes.io/docs/reference/access-authn-authz/webhook/
[50] https://github.com/kubeguard/guard

the user will be prompted for their Microsoft credentials, even if they have
already logged in to Azure, since the Kubernetes API needs the user's
authentication context in order to send a request to Guard to validate the
Java Web Token representing that user and also to return which Azure roles
the user has been granted.

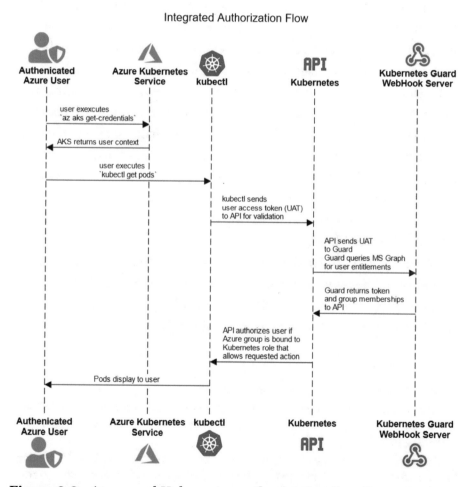

Figure 6-2. *Azure and Kubernetes authorization flow, Ramona
Maxwell @2023*

Aside from the ease provided by the aforementioned workflow around authorization, Microsoft earns another blue ribbon in security for the ability of Microsoft Defender for Containers to protect both managed and IaaS Kubernetes deployments on all three major clouds plus any OCI-compliant[51] installation elsewhere when they are connected to Arc (where they effectively become Azure resources). Announced in December 2021, this container-specific product rolled out just after the announcement that Azure Security Center and Azure Defender were being renamed as Microsoft Defender for Cloud in November of that year.[52] A key advantage to the Defender product for containers is that it runs natively within the Kubernetes cluster. It is recommended the `microsoft.azuredefender.kubernetes` extension be installed during cluster deployment so that there is no initial gap in protection. The Defender for Cloud suite has a much broader view in terms of monitoring everything from network traffic and SQL to Key Vault, storage, and DNS[53] in order to create a composite view of your security posture, including the Kubernetes-specific alerts[54] flowing in from Defender for Cloud.

Defender for Cloud implements Cloud Security Posture Management [CPSM] principles as well as Microsoft's own recent release of its Microsoft Cloud Security Benchmark[55] [MCSB] which rolls up standards such as the US Department of Commerce National Institute of Standards and

---

[51] https://opencontainers.org/about/overview/

[52] https://techcommunity.microsoft.com/t5/microsoft-defender-for-cloud/a-new-name-for-multi-cloud-security-microsoft-defender-for-cloud/ba-p/2943020

[53] https://learn.microsoft.com/en-us/azure/defender-for-cloud/defender-for-cloud-introduction#extend-defender-for-cloud-with-defender-plans-and-external-monitoring

[54] https://learn.microsoft.com/en-us/azure/defender-for-cloud/alerts-reference#alerts-k8scluster

[55] https://learn.microsoft.com/en-us/security/benchmark/azure/introduction

Technology[56] [NIST] and more into guides for every service area it covers on its own and other clouds. Defender for Cloud continuously samples the environments it's protecting in order to provide

- An initial evaluation of security posture along with analysis and recommended actions

- Ongoing threat monitoring and remediation suggestions which can be executed automatically

- A choice of security standards by which you may want to evaluate your workloads, including those published by The Center for Threat-Informed Defense[57] detailing container-specific attack modes, as well as whether your installation meets the standards of the cloud it runs on

Defender for Cloud creates a metric called Secure Score which is a composite on a collection of best security practices.[58] They have in a sense gamified the scoring algorithm, as you must follow rules as to remediation that do not allow you to cherry-pick the easy items to raise your score; you must thoroughly address the areas identified for improvement.

IT administrators have been known to bemoan the massive surface area over which they must respond to alerts and remediate issues. Since the capabilities of technology are unlikely to shrink, effective responses are limited. The old saw about an ounce of prevention being better than a pound of cure was never truer than when managing enterprise systems. Some basic proactive steps include

---

[56] www.nist.gov/

[57] https://mitre-engenuity.org/blog/2020/12/15/ctid-releases-security-control-mappings-to-attck/ and www.microsoft.com/en-us/security/blog/2021/04/29/center-for-threat-informed-defense-teams-up-with-microsoft-partners-to-build-the-attck-for-containers-matrix/

[58] https://learn.microsoft.com/en-us/azure/defender-for-cloud/secure-score-security-controls#security-controls-and-their-recommendations

- Guard images by controlling the repository in terms of access and requiring strict standards for versioning

- Use Flux features to prevent the proliferation of unicorns and automate the reversion to the desired state of your deployment if any are found

- Make use of Azure Private Link[59] to keep cluster traffic off the public Internet

- Remember that security is a wholistic endeavor and aim your reticle at every layer of your ecosystem from the firewall encircling its perimeter down through clusters, nodes, pods, and workloads

Custom Locations for Arc-Enabled Kubernetes

Not all of the advantages offered by colocating related workloads are lost in cloud computing scenarios. Azure offers a feature called Custom Locations that is especially powerful in the context of Arc-enabled Kubernetes. Custom Locations correlate one to one with a namespace within your cluster, and since you can use multiple namespaces within a single cluster which can each be a target RBAC, they are an enabler of effective security controls. Kubernetes provides four namespaces initially[60] for system, public, and node operations as well as the one you will see less of if you have a properly defined namespace schema and that is "default," for example, the dumping ground for anything that doesn't fit in the other three. While you could not duplicate a namespace within a cluster, you

---

[59] https://learn.microsoft.com/en-us/azure/azure-arc/kubernetes/
private-link

[60] https://kubernetes.io/docs/concepts/overview/working-with-objects/
namespaces/#initial-namespaces

could across multiple clusters, potentially causing confusion, and thus it will be helpful to incorporate a hierarchical schema that identifies the cluster and standardizes the way resources are referred to.

If your namespaces are meaningful, their relationships to workloads, security roles, and other unique characteristics will be apparent.[61] Since you can apply unique RBAC to each namespace, they're ideal for multi-tenant scenarios. You can deploy portions of a workload to their own namespace, for instance, namespacename-myapp-messaging, namespacename-myapp-functions, or whatever your workload consists of, and then apply network policies so that whichever services within those discrete namespaces need to communicate with one another are able to do so. As Kubernetes is Linux based, no camel casing is allowed in namespace names, and this simplicity contributes to readability. Aside from security, namespaces allow you to target a specific namespace for the application of policy, cost control quotas, service provisioning, and more. This ability to manage a namespace as a group extends all the way to the ability to delete multiple pods using the namespace they reside in as the target, an important reason to consider how roles accessing the namespace should be crafted in terms of permissions. Utilizing namespaces effectively requires a certain amount of discretion. It's important to remember the cluster itself has capacity limits that creating additional namespaces won't expand. The complexity of your namespace schema should be nothing more than is required to match the workloads that need to be identified.

Azure Custom Locations employs Kubernetes namespaces to create custom resources. The Custom Locations resource provider can create role bindings that are required to use additional resource providers within a namespace. Which resource providers can be authorized is dependent upon whether they have first been installed on the cluster.

---

[61] Chapter 2 of Robert C. Martin's *Clean Code* provides a back to basics discussion of what makes a good name in the world of software development. Similar principles apply to namespaces.

Thus, if you think you'll require, for instance, Arc-enabled data services on some Custom Locations, that extension is installed to the cluster. Later, after you have created Custom Locations, you can achieve desired state configuration for a specific Custom Location (namespace) and actually deploy data services only to the namespaces you specify (even though they are technically available to the entire cluster).

As with Azure AD, Microsoft has strengthened part of the Kubernetes ecosystem and made it familiar to operators accustomed to Azure conventions by creating a powerful Custom Locations feature that maps to underlying Kubernetes namespaces.[62]

As we look at policy in the next chapter, we will examine how it is a cornerstone of security and how to use it effectively to govern large IT estates with minimal steering required.

---

[62] https://learn.microsoft.com/en-us/azure/azure-arc/kubernetes/
conceptual-custom-locations

CHAPTER 7

Policy and Governance of Hybrid and Multi-cloud Infrastructure

Introduction

One way to think about policy is as an enforced objective. To be useful, a technology estate must be shaped to suit its purpose. It is constantly subjected to disruptive forces and requires not only that the initial design targets be met but constant tuning to ensure it continually aligns to its desired state.

Chief among the disruptors threatening an IT system's stability, security, and productivity for its intended use are the human beings that interact with it. Flaws are inherent in every physical and logical component of which an IT system is constructed, in the construction process itself, and the tendency to misuse or take expedient shortcuts will be present in those who ultimately use it.

© Ramona Maxwell 2024
R. Maxwell, *Azure Arc Systems Management*,
https://doi.org/10.1007/978-1-4842-9480-2_7

The innumerable theories as to why things devolve into chaos are the topic of some other book; this one is going to focus on how to fend it off, and the superhero saving the day is policy.

As noted in the close of the prior chapter, policy directly impacts security. This is true across the IT estate and from many perspectives. Operational policies can define how the infrastructure layer functions and when automated assure that best-practice security controls are implemented. Enterprise Content Management [ECM] policies can serve to protect business data and are a significant contributor to cost control efforts, as well as a tool to meet regulatory compliance standards. Policies can even serve as a training tool, as the guardrails they set make the organization's standards visible to users.

This chapter will look at several functional areas across the lifecycle of IT systems and their workloads and discuss their governance through the creation and application of policy. In each area, it will call out the opportunities to enhance security through correct policy management practices and will consider how Arc can extend Azure's policy engine across large hybrid IT estates.

Policy Scopes in Azure

The first obvious benefit is that the schema which you will hopefully have already applied to existing resources in Azure is now also available to Arc-enabled assets. An application running on Kubernetes in AWS is contained in a resource group you've designated for it in Microsoft Azure. If you have followed Microsoft's Cloud Foundations guidance for Azure, you will be familiar with the building blocks Microsoft provides to facilitate domain-driven architecture. The root of this architecture is always an Entra (formerly Azure Active Directory) tenant.[1] Underneath this tenant

---

[1] https://learn.microsoft.com/en-us/azure/cloud-adoption-framework/ready/landing-zone/design-area/azure-ad-define

is the first conceptual container of Management Groups. Imagine you are a large healthcare conglomerate with ownership of several health management organizations (HMOs), a few hospitals outside of those HMOs, pharmacy services, and a research facility in collaboration with a pharma company. With Management Groups, you can list out the factors for security, compliance, governance, resources, and so on that are common or disparate and arrange them under a Management Group that will be tuned to the correct requirements. For example, a research arm might need to integrate data feeds from other facilities or to manage the output of instrumentation used in research so that it can be analyzed. It might also have publishing requirements requiring submission workflows and access controls. That is a very different use case than a group focused on treating patients which might engage through remote visits or have heavy Enterprise Resource Planning [ERP] needs around clinic management. While commonalities like HIPAA regulations might show in the intersection of a Venn diagram describing those two use cases, there would also be large areas that do not overlap despite their similar industry, and placing them each in their own Management Group facilitates giving each group what it needs to be successful. Another example might be a multinational accounting firm. In many cases, the clients served are enormous and complex industries themselves, and placing the services relating to the client in a Management Group [MG] allows for a white glove approach to servicing that customer beginning with the fact that you can limit access to their MG to only personnel assigned to that client and their internal users. MGs are an extremely flat structure. Although the root MG has a one-to-one relationship with an Active Directory tenant beneath the root, the next level could consist of up to 10,000 sibling MGs. In contrast, the nesting ability for MGs is limited to six levels (excluding root). It's advisable to use MGs sparingly as very large buckets for key organizational divisions, as dividing by function is more appropriate at the subscription level. Policies or security controls applied at this level will cascade through the entire organization and cannot be reversed at lower levels in the hierarchy, so only those few that are essential to security and operations but do not block normal activities lower in the hierarchy should be implemented at or near the root of the hierarchy. This is true not only for native Azure resources but also for those under Arc's control plane (with some discretionary selectivity using Resource Manager modes).

An Azure subscription is another confusing reference as it rather sounds like your entire purchase of cloud services but instead refers to a logical grouping below both the tenancy and the MG (if you don't create MGs, then all subscriptions automatically belong to the root MG). Continuing with the imaginary healthcare conglomerate, you could imagine two of the HMOs, each in their own MG and within that MG having multiple subscriptions to manage security and track costs for departmental functions such as patient records, appointments, ERP, marketing, consumer-facing applications, third-party integrations, and more. Subscriptions are discrete in terms of billing and policy and because they have a top limit on consumed resources close attention should be paid to subscription design for large workloads. Subscriptions cannot be in the same VNet, but can communicate over ExpressRoute or using virtual network peering (typically with a subscription dedicated to connectivity). Subscriptions can sometimes be moved to a new tenancy, a use case that can occur when spinning off a new business group, but only when created directly in your existing tenant vs. by a Cloud Solution Provider.

Within subscriptions live resource groups [RGs], which are the most common and familiar unit of organization within Azure. Resource groups are a way to organize groups of services, virtual networks, storage, and other artifacts that relate to one another in a logical or functional way (a dedicated RG is one of the first prerequisites to your trial deployment of Arc-enabled Kubernetes). Azure has physical data centers in regions around the globe, and since RGs are again a logical construct, they can contain resources from more than one region. They are a product lifecycle tool and tend to be applied to groups of things that are managed together whether that be a single application, a particular process, or a cost center.

If a business model evolves to place ownership of assets under another department, an RG can, with effort, be moved to a different subscription. Resources inside an RG can also generally be moved to another one if needed, but redeployment to the new RG would be more typical since moving an RG requires migration planning. For instance, a public IP address used by the RG cannot move and has to be disassociated, and then all of the artifacts depending on the IP address in the RG will have to be associated to a new public IP, which will have downstream effects anywhere that IP address is referenced. Overall, there are consequences in cost and complexity to creating more subscriptions than are truly needed, while RGs are a primary tool for organizing assets inside a subscription.

As we will dive into in the next chapter, policies present in the Resource Group, Subscription or Management Group are also applied to the foreign resources as if they were native by means of the Arc agent. Every server you enable (by installing a virtual machine extension) benefits not only from policy-based administration but also the ability to standardize machine configuration. The two features work hand in hand, for example, applying the policy Deploy prerequisites to enable machine configuration policies on virtual machines is a prerequisite to installing the virtual machine extension across groups of servers, as is also having a managed identity with the authority to execute the desired configuration changes. Even without the VM extension installed, you can apply policies to servers visible in the Arc dashboard as Azure objects (and at no cost), but the extension will be required for internal management of the VM and its operating system and will incur subscription charges. Since your servers are Arc enabled, they are now under the purview of Azure Resource Manager, and this means examining your server inventory, tagging, installation of extensions, and other common ARM tasks are free.[2] When

---

[2] https://learn.microsoft.com/en-us/azure/cloud-adoption-framework/ scenarios/hybrid/arc-enabled-servers/eslz-cost-governance#how-much- does-azure-arc-enabled-servers-cost

you utilize an installed extension to perform activities on an Arc-enabled server using its OS, you will be charged as the screenshot from the Azure Pricing Calculator[3] illustrates (Figure 7-1).

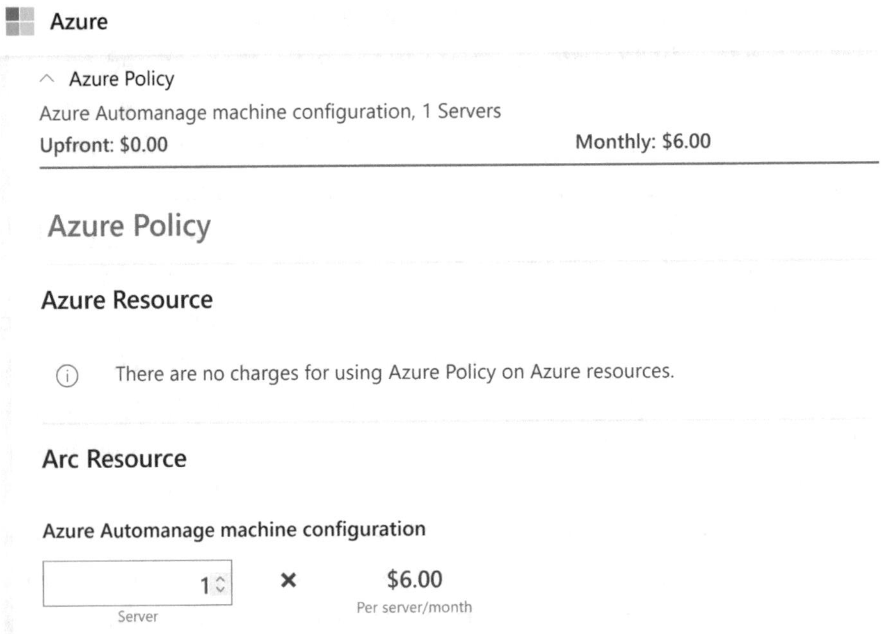

Figure 7-1. *Calculate cost of Azure Policy for Arc-enabled servers*

Azure Automanage Machine Configuration costs are offset by additional administration capabilities, for instance, you could assure that all of your servers, whether native to Azure or Arc enabled, use TLS.

---

[3] https://azure.microsoft.com/en-in/pricing/calculator/

Policy Baselines for Kubernetes

The ability to structure an environment through the implementation of policy is one of the most compelling advantages to a GitOps approach to Kubernetes deployments. You aren't limited to governing your GitOps pipeline at the time you first deploy clusters; rather, you can begin to apply policies anywhere in the lifecycle to begin reaping the benefit of having your installations automatically remediate deviation from policy.

There are built-in policy definitions for a number of scenarios[4] that Microsoft imagines will be useful in a large enterprise with a variety of implementations that address how rigid authorization standards should be or which git repository you will deploy from. Thus, you could have a cluster that allows for storing of secrets locally to facilitate rapid development cycles, but require certificates or the use of a private repository for high-value production assets. The Kubernetes API server is a primary attack vector, and protecting it correctly requires policies that provide the appropriate level of security to prevent inconsistencies and gaps.

As Kubernetes is entirely API driven, controlling and limiting who can access the cluster and what actions they are allowed to perform is the first line of defense.

—Kubernetes Documentation

The API server needs to be thoroughly hardened, thus simply applying RBAC will not be enough to assure its safety. An article on Akami's security blog[5] discussing proposed OWASP changes for 2023 points out

---

[4] https://learn.microsoft.com/en-us/azure/azure-arc/kubernetes/use-azure-policy-flux-2
[5] www.akamai.com/blog/security/proposed-new-changes-in-owasp-api-security

that injection attacks may soon be outranked as a top-tier risk in that authoritative list by Server-Side Request Forgery [SSRF] due to technologies like Kubernetes which pass URLs over APIs. Further basic controls include encryption and hardening network communications. The Shadowserver Foundation offers an interesting set of visualizations on their website showing unprotected Kubernetes API servers to which you can apply various geographic and time series filters, my favorite of which is the world view.[6] The count in some countries, including the United States, is in the hundreds of thousands. While some may not be high-value targets, the large number of exposed servers points to either a lack of awareness of the risks or unskilled teams overlooking basic security controls. Either way, it underscores the value of policy in creating immutable security controls.

Kubernetes' wide adoption has both surfaced its vulnerabilities and encouraged a set of best practices for protecting against them. Victims of crypto mining, ransomware, data breaches, and insider threats have shared hard lessons around the need for a consistent approach to repelling attackers. An article in the Sysdig blog discussing detection and multilayered policies to prevent crypto mining[7] attacks points out that the cost of cloud services to conduct a mining operation exceeds the return on the crypto itself manyfold, providing a powerful motivation for miners to operate on your cloud rather than buying their own (not to mention major cloud providers, including Microsoft as of December 2022,[8] updated their online services agreement to prohibit crypto mining on their platforms without specific permission).

Utilizing the Azure Policy engine is an advanced usage of the Azure ecosystem which is not limited to Arc-enabled resources; in fact, most of the items under discussion for securing Kubernetes clusters will apply

---

[6] https://dashboard.shadowserver.org/statistics/combined/map/comparison/

[7] https://sysdig.com/blog/detecting-cryptomining-attacks-in-the-wild/

[8] www.microsoft.com/licensing/terms/en-US/product/changes/MCA

equally to AKS and even the easy-entry Azure Container Apps service.[9]
Most common Kubernetes distros which are CNCF certified can also benefit
when they have the Arc extension installed.[10] It's important to have a holistic
view of the elements which make policies effective, such as consistent
tagging of resources and determining appropriate actions in response to
policy violations. Policy is an important control plane element that must
be combined with other facets such as GitOps deployments designed to
restore a cluster to its desired state, logging of policy violations to discern
whether they represent a security risk, and monitoring to assure policies
enable profitable workstreams while protecting the organization's resources.
It is this membership in the Azure ecosystem that makes the Azure Policy
engine so powerful in comparison to stand-alone products which may have
well-thought-out policy rulesets (such as the Falco Rules[11] used by Sysdig
and others) but lack the automatic integration with the appropriate Azure
services to respond to them. Microsoft's Zero Trust platform landed them
an impressive top-tier spot in Forrester's Trust Platform Providers, Q3 2023
report,[12] which cites a centralized control plane and support of "diverse
hybrid architectures" as selection criteria. Microsoft itself notes in touting its
inclusion that it "delivers end-to-end cross-cloud, cross-platform security
solutions, which integrate more than 50 different categories across security,
compliance, identity, device management, and privacy, informed by more
than 65 trillion threat signals … each day,"[13] a volume unmatched by most
competitors across an also largely unmatched suite of platform capabilities.

---

[9] https://techcommunity.microsoft.com/t5/fasttrack-for-azure/
azure-policy-for-azure-container-apps-yes-please/ba-p/3775200
[10] https://learn.microsoft.com/en-us/azure/azure-arc/kubernetes/
validation-program#validated-distributions
[11] https://falco.org/docs/rules/basic-elements/
[12] https://reprints2.forrester.com/#/assets/2/108/RES179872/report
[13] www.microsoft.com/en-us/security/blog/2023/09/19/forrester-names-
microsoft-a-leader-in-the-2023-zero-trust-platform-providers-
wave-report/

Arc-enabled Kubernetes takes a proactive approach to policy implementation with a variety of built-in policies[14] intended to assure a uniform application of best practices for securing the clusters it deploys and manages. Security recommendations from the Kubernetes documentation highlight key surface areas to examine such controlling access to the API as previously mentioned and also to secure the network, kubelet endpoints, runtime users, and workloads, as well as cluster components, and we will explore how those surface areas are protected by correct policy implementation. While policy can and should be used to remediate existing installations,[15] it is important to view policy as an essential component of the initial configuration of Arc-enabled Kubernetes and data resources. Building large enterprise systems without initial policy controls is akin to manufacturing a powerful vehicle with no steering capability.

Policy files are written JSON notation and are simple to read and update. In the opening stanza of a policy, typical key-value pairs such as name and description are present, as well as the `policyType` key which defines whether the policy is `BuiltIn` (e.g., supplied by Azure) or `Custom`. This is also where the Resource Manager mode of either `all` or `indexed` is set for the policy. The default and typical value is to apply the policy to all resources. If you specify indexed, then the policy will be applied only to resources that support tag and location identifiers.[16] This could be useful for policies intended for a specific region or cost center but could fail to have the desired result if applied to unsupported resource types.

---

[14] https://learn.microsoft.com/en-us/azure/azure-arc/kubernetes/policy-reference

[15] https://learn.microsoft.com/en-us/azure/governance/policy/how-to/remediate-resources?tabs=azure-portal

[16] https://learn.microsoft.com/en-us/azure/governance/policy/concepts/definition-structure#resource-manager-modes

As with any Azure service, the policy engine has capacity limits as to the number of policies, initiatives (sets of related policies), and lines per policy that are allowed.[17] The policy engine provides functions[18] derived from ARM template functions[19] to perform the necessary calculations to apply a policy, conditions for value matching, as well as logical operators (not, allof, and anyof). The ability to manipulate policy in this way is advantageous only if it's not used to cobble together workarounds for policy structure that was not well designed to begin with. Ideally, policy schema will be intrinsic to the architectural design of your systems from their genesis to enable their remaining compliant and consistent with their performance and security objectives. From your first Cloud Foundations baby step up onto the Azure platform to the installation of the Azure Policy extension,[20] you should know what you intend to govern with policy and how it will be defined in your deployments.

Selecting the correct scope and context for the application of policy should be viewed not just through the lens of a particular problem that a policy might prevent or remediate but also from a high-level observation of how the individual policy fits the policy schema for your organization as a whole. The Azure Policy engine is well organized for this approach, for instance, allowing policies with related objectives to be grouped into a policy initiative. It would be typical to have policy initiatives representing service areas or functional objectives (such as the governance of different

---

[17] https://learn.microsoft.com/en-us/azure/governance/policy/overview#maximum-count-of-azure-policy-objects

[18] https://learn.microsoft.com/en-us/azure/governance/policy/concepts/definition-structure#policy-functions

[19] https://learn.microsoft.com/en-us/azure/azure-resource-manager/templates/template-functions

[20] https://learn.microsoft.com/en-us/azure/governance/policy/concepts/policy-for-kubernetes#install-azure-policy-extension-for-azure-arc-enabled-kubernetes

types of environments). It's important to remember that if a resource is subject to an initiative, it must pass the muster for *all* of the policy definitions contained within that initiative, so if a policy should only be applied under atypical conditions, it is better not to include it in an initiative.

The outcome of the application of a particular policy is simply referred to as its effect. Effects[21] are not random, but rather specify what the policy will accomplish such as to modify an artifact, deny access, audit only, or audit and deploy. If multiple effects are implemented in the same policy, their order of precedence must be considered; otherwise, they may not work as intended.[22]

Manual effects are a new type of effect to allow interactive response to compliance policies. They[23] are particularly suitable for meeting compliance regulations in financial and healthcare fields that require a human being to confirm some action has been performed. The JSON structure of a manual effect specifies the objective and sets its initial status to "unknown." The response to the policy is provided through a separate resource, the Azure Policy attestation structure,[24] which is basically a mini workflow engine that captures metadata regarding the task owner and details of the response, including its updated compliance status, commentary, and evidentiary links to supporting documentation.

---

[21] https://learn.microsoft.com/en-us/azure/governance/policy/concepts/effects

[22] https://learn.microsoft.com/en-us/azure/governance/policy/concepts/effects#order-of-evaluation

[23] https://learn.microsoft.com/en-us/azure/governance/policy/concepts/effects#manual *and* https://learn.microsoft.com/en-us/azure/governance/policy/concepts/attestation-structure

[24] https://learn.microsoft.com/en-us/azure/governance/policy/concepts/attestation-structure

Figure 7-2. *Sometimes, policies require a human touch*

Microsoft defines Policy as Code [PaC[25]] as the intersection of IaC and DevOps, but then takes it a step and an acronym further with EPaC, or Enterprise Platform as Code,[26] which is designed for organizations that must maintain extensive policy libraries and includes approaches for integrating policy with Azure Landing Zones deployments as part of the Cloud Adoption Framework [CAF].

In the Azure portal's Policy ➤ Definitions section, there are search tools for the library of policies and the ability to sort by the platform area you are targeting, whether you are looking for a policy or an initiative, and to filter by keyword (which brings up just under 20 built-in policies containing the phrase "Arc-enabled"). While Microsoft has at the time of this writing disabled the ability to directly export a policy to GitHub, the JSON policy

---

[25] https://learn.microsoft.com/en-us/azure/governance/policy/concepts/policy-as-code
[26] https://azure.github.io/enterprise-azure-policy-as-code/

definition is able to be pasted into an editor and subsequently committed to the repository in which you will manage the PaC. In whatever manner you accomplish it, this will be a necessary step as every policy will need customization to run under the correct service principals and target the actual resources existing in your organization. People with command-line expertise are likely to appreciate the ability to search for policy definitions using a PowerShell cmdlet piped to a where clause and the extensive policy descriptions provided in the shell, allowing for an entirely scripted approach to policy selection and implementation. Policy can also be described and implemented using Terraform or REST calls – all part of the ease and usability of living in an ARM world.

With a Policy as Code[27] approach, testing or validating policies is as important as it would be in preparing the production release of any other type of code. Policies can be designed to execute enforcement actions; therefore, you must assure that your policy doesn't return false positives, and new policies should have their enforcement mode set to disabled until their veraciousness is established.

Network Policies

If you could only choose one target for the policy engine, the network would be the bullseye for which to aim. Motor through a slew of recent published breaches and the network as the communications infrastructure providing required functionality for your workloads is also the roadway used by those with criminal intent. As the seventh item on the 2022 OWASP Top 10 list of Kubernetes security vulnerabilities highlights, with Kubernetes flat networking structure, "when no additional controls are in place any workload can communicate to another without constraint.

---

[27] https://learn.microsoft.com/en-us/azure/governance/policy/concepts/
policy-as-code

Attackers who exploit a running workload can leverage this default behavior to probe the internal network, traverse to other running containers, or invoke private APIs." What does this mean in practice?

Port scanners use a brute-force approach to find either open ports or ports of specific interest because they belong to an asset that has a known path for intrusion. One common example would be a manually installed instance of PostgreSQL that utilizes trust authentication to allow database access for any user able to connect (PaaS offerings of PostgreSQL from Azure, AWS, Google, and others do not allow this setting). Over the past couple of years, this has given the old-school cryptomining malware Kinsing a new playground in the form of Kubernetes clusters. In terms of policy, if you run large Kubernetes installations, you should be assuring that none of your PostgreSQL servers allow trust authentication.

Older versions of Oracle WebLogic, a popular Java application host, are also vulnerable to Kinsing, and Microsoft security researchers note attackers start out searching for WebLogic's default port.[28] Although minimizing the amount of protection changing SQL Server's default port actually provides, since TCP/IP connections allow port scanning as a matter of course, Microsoft to this day provides guidance on how to change it.[29] The problem with ports is not limited to those known to be vulnerable, just having too many open can provide potential routes to your systems. Does the creation of a VNet in your org automatically include a public IP? Why? Turn off or limit that capability via policy.

With a chief advantage of Arc being access to the Microsoft ecosystem of products, the aforementioned built-in policy requiring it be turned on is particularly applicable in the face of known threats like Kinsing, the attack

---

[28] http://techcommunity.microsoft.com/t5/microsoft-defender-for-cloud/initial-access-techniques-in-kubernetes-environments-used-by/ba-p/3697975

[29] https://learn.microsoft.com/en-us/sql/database-engine/configure-windows/configure-a-server-to-listen-on-a-specific-tcp-port?view=sql-server-ver16

vectors for which are already shielded when using Defender. But further than that, whomever you rely upon for additional layers of security has to have a laser focus on the ever-changing threat landscape so that gaps can be filled the moment they are anticipated. Security is very much an activity on which having partnerships matters, so that your company doesn't have to review each CVE and response solo. Manual defense strategies are simply not an option in the age of automated threats.

While Kubernetes natively provides protective ingress and egress policies that can, for example, restrict incoming traffic to a known range of IP addresses or forbid outgoing calls, a significant advantage to Azure Arc is the ability to use Azure Private Link[30] which provides a connection to the resources in your cluster that does not travel over the public Internet, thus greatly reducing the exposure of your traffic to both human and automated threats. Further, Private Link offers control over who connects to services and the scope of services available limiting the potential for data leakage.

Policies governing traffic between pods are a baseline safety configuration to prevent infection or intrusion spreading throughout your cluster by taking advantage of Kubernetes natively open structure. It's important to remember that pod policies are aggregate, meaning that if you have one policy stating that ingress traffic is allowed to pods with the label `customer-address-db` from pods labeled `web-front-end1` and a second policy allowing ingress traffic from `web-request-api`, *both* ingress paths will be allowed, not just the API request. Thus, security again becomes a matter of both appropriate design and testing to assure that traffic follows the path you intend. Likewise, you need policies on both ends of the pipe. If you have no egress policy permitting the pod hosting the API to connect to the database, the communication will fail.

---

[30] https://learn.microsoft.com/en-us/azure/azure-arc/servers/
private-link-security

Policies Governing Containers

Containers are a core policy objective in securing and managing your Kubernetes installation. They are in fact the treasure you guard with Microsoft Defender for Arc-enabled Kubernetes installations. Key considerations in protecting your containers are their source repository, preventing privilege escalation via their operating systems and controlling network access.

A new attack hijacking RBAC controls was caught in a honeypot set up by Aqua[31] (a firm that sells a cloud-native security platform specializing in protections against supply chain and Kubernetes attacks). Unless your clusters are antique or were set up poorly to begin with and grant anonymous access requests to a cluster admin role (or malformed third-party tools have done so), you are likely safe from this particular intrusion,[32] but the two things that are interesting about it are that it escapes typical monitoring by creating a service account with a name mimicking the kube-controller so that role binding that accounts to cluster admin privileges doesn't necessarily raise alarms, and when the hack gains admin privilege and pulls the containers contaminated with the cryptomining software, they are sourced from a public Docker registry. An image pull policy[33] restricting which image registries can be used to populate your clusters is a vital part of both DevOps and GitOps pipelines.

---

[31] https://blog.aquasec.com/leveraging-kubernetes-rbac-to-backdoor-clusters

[32] https://access.redhat.com/articles/7009182

[33] https://portal.azure.com/#view/Microsoft_Azure_Policy/PolicyDetailBlade/definitionId/%2Fproviders%2FMicrosoft.Authorizatio n%2FpolicyDefinitions%2F50c83470-d2f0-4dda-a716-1938a4825f62

Public registries should *not* be used in the enterprise, even for development, since they introduce the risk of unmanaged images into your ecosystem. While you can build a private registry, they are readily available from all major cloud vendors from Red Hat and AWS to Microsoft and Docker and can be configured to integrate with your own RBAC systems.

For a private registry to serve its purpose, what is allowed to be pushed into it and who is allowed to place assets there are the factors that will determine its effectiveness; thus, images should conform to security and performance specifications as well as be digitally signed by contributors. Even with safeguards in place, containers within your registry should also be regularly scanned for vulnerabilities[34] either with Microsoft Defender's Qualys scanner if you are using the Azure Registry or any one of a number of quality tools from vendors like Aqua. An Azure Container Registry policy to assure the scanner is run before a container can be digitally signed and uploaded should be enabled when using Defender.[35] Policy is not the only avenue to assure containers are scanned as many scanning tools integrate with DevOps pipelines so that running a scan is part of a build. On GitHub, a container vulnerability scan is available as an action. A policy engine is not governance, but a governance implementation tool, so you are free to implement the governing standards of your organization in the most expedient way. The advantage of policy is that it is declarative, auditable, can be versioned, and is very easy to reference from a governance document in order to demonstrate compliance. In the case of Azure, built-in policy templates exist for every important service providing a baseline

---

[34] https://learn.microsoft.com/en-us/azure/container-instances/container-instances-image-security#monitor-and-scan-container-images

[35] https://portal.azure.com/#view/Microsoft_Azure_Policy/PolicyDetailBlade/definitionId/%2Fproviders%2FMicrosoft.Authorization%2FpolicyDefinitions%2F090c7b07-b4ed-4561-ad20-e9075f3ccaff

for operational efficiency and security so that you can start in a good spot and grow from there as you develop more sophisticated policies aligned to your business model.

Microsoft advises collocating your registry as close as possible to the containers will be deployed to cut down on egress fees, which can be substantial. Imagine you have thousands of images whose base layer must be updated (perhaps due to an upgraded release or newly identified vulnerability), and you have automated a rebuild and redeployment of all images built on that base. A retailer for whom I worked specifically negotiated reduced egress fees when their cloud provider pushed a mandatory upgrade to its most popular Linux base image. When Cloudflare recently began offering S3-compatible storage with no egress fees,[36] one company actually saw that as an opportunity to build a new container registry,[37] and organizations who run their own registries are likely paying attention.

When securing your enterprise against threats, you could understandably go into CVE overload at the relentless onslaught of new threats. If you focus instead on ranking the criticality of your own assets in terms of what you want to protect and also realize that many "new" CVEs are really recycling the same techniques, you will be able to design a hardened infrastructure and will be able to limit damage or prevent it altogether (however, if you do want to feed the worry monster, visit the official Kubernetes CVE feed[38] which refreshes daily).

Sometimes, it's a combination of Kubernetes design and its platform that causes issues. Palo Alto Networks published a succinct summary[39] of how Kubernetes native design lent itself to "node-to-admin privilege

[36] https://tinyurl.com/cakpbyk2

[37] www.wired.com/story/container-registry-security-chainguard/

[38] https://kubernetes.io/docs/reference/issues-security/official-cve-feed/

[39] https://unit42.paloaltonetworks.com/kubernetes-privilege-escalation/#acc5816d-8466-4eaa-8349-e7855919a873

escalation" by replacing DaemonSets[40] (a type of administrative controller that can facilitate activities like logging and monitoring on a node and ensures the node is running a pod) with an evil version that operated like a cuckoo bird chick, knocking all the other nodes out of the cluster nest by tainting them as `NoSchedule` and then using a `NoExecute` taint on the node containing the pods it wishes to consume, forcing the cluster to recreate them on the only bird left in the nest – the imposter. The article is retrospective and so was able to share how both AKS and EKS now prevent this scenario using validating admission controllers,[41] and understanding their usage is also essential to securing the clusters you deploy that are not part of a managed service like AKS.

Much of what has been discussed in terms of protecting Kubernetes deployments via policy is simplified by using Defender for Containers,[42] which will suggest where the policy extension can be added to Arc-enabled servers and then continuously monitor policy compliance wherever it is enabled. This is active monitoring in that admission requests to the Kubernetes API must pass a Gatekeeper webhook that checks whether policy constraints are met before the request can proceed. These policy checks are in addition to the set of best-practice rules originating in Defender itself and the resulting suggestions it will offer in terms of policy

---

[40] https://kubernetes.io/docs/concepts/workloads/controllers/daemonset/

[41] https://kubernetes.io/docs/reference/access-authn-authz/admission-controllers/#validatingadmissionwebhook

[42] https://techcommunity.microsoft.com/t5/microsoft-defender-for-cloud/leveraging-defender-for-containers-to-simplify-policy-management/ba-p/3755757

and general security management. Defender for Containers[43] is a core value-added provided by Arc-enabled Kubernetes and can be enabled for containers in all three commercial clouds.

When discussing protective policies for containers, it's noteworthy that many of the built-in policy definitions in Azure aim to protect against the ability to run any container's operating system in administrative mode for Windows or as Linux root. A CrowdStrike blog[44] discussing the mechanics of a particular CVE makes this elucidating comment, "Linux kernel exploits are an alternative method to escape container environments to the host in case no mistakes in the container configuration were made. They can be used because containers share the host's kernel and therefore its vulnerabilities, regardless of the Linux distribution the container is based on." Thus, after you have correctly set up your GitOps pipelines, are protecting your supply chain, and have remediating policies to assure your configuration remains pristine, you still must consider hardening the container OS. Cloud vendors are absolutely paying attention to these risks, which threaten not only your workloads but theirs as well. As Google explains in an update to their Vulnerability Reward Program (which has been paying bounties relating to GKE since 2020), they wish to "support researchers evaluating the security of Google Kubernetes Engine (GKE) and the underlying Linux kernel. As the Linux kernel is a key component not just for Google, but for the Internet…"; they have redirected the program toward hardening the kernel itself.

Microsoft has devoted similar energy for a number of years, and the result is the release of Azure Linux, a hardened distribution that was another great fruitage of the Avanade and Microsoft collaboration on

---

[43] https://learn.microsoft.com/en-us/azure/defender-for-cloud/defender-for-containers-introduction?toc=https%3A%2F%2Flearn.microsoft.com%2Fen-us%2Fazure%2Faks%2Ftoc.json&bc=https%3A%2F%2Flearn.microsoft.com%2Fen-us%2Fazure%2Fbread%2Ftoc.json

[44] www.crowdstrike.com/blog/exploiting-cve-2021-3490-for-container-escapes/

behalf of mutual customers. Mike DeLuca explains that Avanade put in special requests in terms of security that Microsoft met and exceeded, asking "we want to know what's open and what's closed" in a new hardened distro that could protect the massive asset base running on Azure. Commercial releases each have their vagaries, for instance, the June 2023 Ubuntu Linux kernel update[45] lists fixes to their distribution that impacted all three major cloud providers. Becoming the responsible party for the Linux distro underlying major services like AKS and Edge gives Microsoft the opportunity to resolve essential security and performance obstacles with a direct line of site into a core platform OS. DeLuca expressed satisfaction with the outcome, commenting, "It's their own Microsoft opinionated distribution – *secure*, everything turned off until you turn it on."

CBL-Mariner Linux was a fresh build from the ground up (with small exceptions related to "borrowing specs" from distros like Fedora and CentOS) rather than a customization of an existing Linux distro. This approach avoids derivative patching cycles and shared vulnerabilities that could have resulted from choosing to modify even an admirable published Linux distribution. While a discussion of the history of Azure Linux might seem out of place in a policy discussion, it is relevant since hardening the OS fills a gap that *both* monitoring and policy have trouble reaching. Kernel exploits often take extreme measures to make their operations look normal until their assault on vulnerable systems is complete, and by the time such exploits are underway, policy gates have already failed or were insufficient. Microsoft starts its Azure Linux distro with a compact core of around 400MB with, as of Microsoft Build 2023,[46] about 300 additional packages available that have been thoroughly tested for compatibility and safety. The distinction between the CBL-Mariner Linux project and Azure

---

[45] https://ubuntu.com/security/notices/USN-6171-1

[46] https://build.microsoft.com/en-US/sessions/e84dd80a-f3bb-4d3d-978e-ffd811e3bfe1?source=sessions

Linux is that Azure Linux distro is the commercially supported version and is already in use internally at Microsoft for products such as AKS, Azure Stack Edge, Azure Arc, and more.

Data Policies

If there was ever an argument for well-crafted policies, Azure's 2023 ten-hour plus outage of SQL databases in their South Brazil DC[47] provides it. While upgrading legacy packages in the Azure supply chain, a "typo" caused the unintended deletion of entire database servers, triggered by a condition having to do with the age of database snapshots. Arguably, the role with access to manage snapshots should not also be able to delete the database server itself, which could indicate one missed opportunity for the application of policy. To restore all 17 production databases wiped out by the accidental deletion of their host, a new SQL Server had to be set up and the databases restored from backup. At this point, a second major delay was caused by inconsistent DR approaches, with some of the databases having been "... created before Geo-zone-redundant backup was available." This meant when using Geo-zone-redundant restoration for the legacy databases, additional hours waiting for the database to be copied into a secondary zone[48] greatly extended the recovery time. This scenario appears to beg for a GitOps policy that would have audited the DR strategy for each database and offered a path to remediate any legacy databases not using Geo-zone-redundant backup. This is especially true since long-standing database instances may have not have been initially created via a GitOps pipeline, but perhaps by an administrator using T-SQL in which case even if policies existed, they would not have been applied. Even as the databases were restored and brought back online, an overwhelming

---

[47] https://status.dev.azure.com/_event/392143683/post-mortem
[48] https://learn.microsoft.com/en-us/azure/storage/common/redundancy-migration?source=recommendations&tabs=portal

number of customer requests forced Microsoft to "[block] all ... to allow all web servers to warm-up and successfully enter the load balancer," thus extending the outage even further, severely impacting business workloads running in that location.

None of the takeaways Microsoft listed in their mea culpa on the outage were innovative or new strategies, all could potentially have been implemented in the normal course of operations. The real object lesson here is not just preparation but having the sort of creative imagination that would fuel a great Hollywood disaster flick. The more adverse scenarios affecting your systems your most vociferous Murphy's Law advocates can come up with, the better you will be able to design a policy strategy to protect them. The principles of RBAC and least privilege are well known, but discovering every opportunity to apply them will require a thorough understanding of your systems and their workloads. While Azure Arc gives you the reach to apply policies to your systems running anywhere, what to apply will be a primary concern.

Arc in and of itself is not auto-magical. For instance, installing the Arc agent on a group of SQL Servers does not enable backup – in fact, because there are potentially already backup routines in place on the servers being onboarded, automated backup is explicitly *disabled*, and you must specifically enable it in order to benefit from Arc's consolidated management of routine operations. If your SQL Servers are part of an Always On availability group, you will only be able to automate backup on the primary replica, and servers that have more than one database instance require you to instantiate automated backup on each individual instance; however, the SQL Server extension that facilitates these management tasks only has to be installed once per server, and that task can be accomplished by a `DeployIfNotExists` policy that requires its installation on every Arc-enabled machine running SQL Server.

Once the SQL extension is installed, the first built-in policy you may want to execute against SQL Servers running anywhere under Arc may be to enable a SQL best practice assessment[49] for those servers (keeping in mind that running the assessment will subtract from the server's ability to run its customary workload), which applies several hundred rules[50] to assess a wide range of configurations from indexes and backup compression to whether you have properly set up OLTP resource pools on your Windows-hosted SQL Servers. The data collected is saved to a Log Analytics workspace where you can perform further analysis as desired and determine candidates for remediation steps that can be performed as part of the policy execution or as separate administration tasks.

Policy is governance applied, and nowhere is this more credible than in the management of data platforms and data. Which data, if compromised, could threaten your business model? Which data offers new or underutilized revenue opportunities? What are the operational blockers to accessing the data you own and extracting full value from it? How close are you to real-time processing of data if you are in an industry where there is a constant flow of new information? Policy is a subset of overall systems architecture that must be continuously evaluated in the light of current business conditions and objectives for as long as the business or organization continues to operate an information technology platform.

Remediating Existing Resources via Policy

One of the most powerful aspects of Azure's policy engine is that it is not limited to reporting policy exceptions, but has the ability to remediate them. Keeping in mind the risks of system changes in general, a well-vetted policy is an excellent foundation for automated systems administration.

---

[49] https://learn.microsoft.com/en-us/sql/sql-server/azure-arc/assess?view=sql-server-ver16

[50] https://github.com/microsoft/sql-server-samples/blob/master/samples/manage/sql-assessment-api/DefaultRuleset.csv

Policy remediation can occur at several junctures. For instance, you might have a policy feedback loop (methods of approaching this are discussed in the next chapter) that informs of new threats and vulnerabilities requiring either audits or changes to various policies, essentially reactive policy implementation procedures. You can also set up proactive policies that automatically remediate any out of compliance resources to assure that key policies remain in compliance. Additionally, policy remediation can flow from the normal architecture of system lifecycles which may indicate some policies can be deprecated and also suggest policy additions or refinements that can require you to remediate an existing policy.

When crafting a remediation task triggered by a policy exception, it's important to remember that the identity executing the remediation must have the appropriate role privileges to perform whatever that particular remediation action consists of. There is a slight advantage to creating a managed identity through the Azure portal, as permissions to the task contextual to the identity creation are automatically granted,[51] but you may wish to grant them specifically in accordance with how you have designed your RBAC controls.

GitOps and Policy Development for Kubernetes

The GitOps workflow for Arc-enabled Kubernetes is an industry standard inner loop pattern,[52] meaning the first iteration of coding and testing is performed on the developer's workstation before it moves to the outer loop of the cloud ecosystem where it can be trialed on development servers that mimic production, undergo various further refinements

---

[51] https://learn.microsoft.com/en-us/azure/governance/policy/how-to/remediate-resources?tabs=azure-portal#grant-permissions-to-the-managed-identity-through-defined-roles

[52] https://developers.redhat.com/articles/2022/12/12/kubernetes-native-inner-loop-development-quarkus#container_based_inner_loop_solutions

such as integration or security testing, and then finally be published to production servers. To achieve consistency, security, and compliance with development patterns and practices, some companies (Google, for example[53]) sometimes use a cloud workstation as the developer machine. Microsoft's DevSpace framework approach to the inner loop pattern[54] allows for coding on the developer's local machine but provides hooks into the cloud for remote debugging and also automates container provisioning so that the developer can sink into code authoring with adjacent deployment tasks abstracted away. When ready, the framework then provides a transition to the outer loop.

Once the development pipeline is set up, your devs are ready to author policies, as well as implement and test them programmatically.[55] While a good workflow as recommended in the docs will contribute to success as it would in any other development project, the most important thing to call out here is that *it is* a major development project and as such should have a solid architectural runway, business oversight that includes program management, and an everlasting CI/CD pipeline that assures the policies used to govern your IT assets remain equal to constantly changing technology stacks, security threats, and business objectives. Effective policy administration is part of an overall architecture for your systems and should never be viewed as "set it and forget it" because like an aging dam it will develop cracks and fail if neglected with perhaps disastrous consequences.

Illustrating the value of a continuous integration approach to policy, in October of 2022 Microsoft reported a vulnerability affecting Arc-enabled Kubernetes clusters and potentially any Azure Stack Edge or

---

[53] https://codelabs.developers.google.com/innerloop-dev-cloud-workstations-nodejs#0

[54] https://learn.microsoft.com/en-us/azure/azure-arc/kubernetes/conceptual-inner-loop-gitops

[55] https://learn.microsoft.com/en-us/azure/governance/policy/how-to/programmatically-create

AKS installations connected via Arc.[56] If an attacker were able to sniff the DNS endpoint for a cluster, they could potentially take administrative control of the entire cluster. Both Azure Arc-enabled Kubernetes agents and Azure Stack Edge require version upgrades to fortify clusters against this attack vector. Although it's possible to set the agent to poll for updates hourly and automatically upgrade using Helm, situations like this provide an opportunity to use the policy engine advantageously when you have large Kubernetes farms and must assure there are no outliers that remain exposed.

If you consider that best practice for Test-Driven Development [TDD] is to write tests prior to writing code, that principle translates well to policy development in that anticipating effect of policy not only as to content but also in terms of the scope it will best be applied to and any other consideration that will assure the policy is effective and not easily circumvented is important.

---

[56] https://msrc.microsoft.com/update-guide/en-US/vulnerability/ CVE-2022-37968

Policy for IT Consumers

Figure 7-3. *Policies should enable worker safety and productivity*

At the time of this writing, a worldwide data breach caused by a SQL injection vulnerability in a file transfer utility, MOVEit,[57] which improves upon antiquated FTP protocols with the intention of ensuring the safety of data like bank records and personal health information by utilizing encrypted transit protocols is underway. The CIOp ransomware group believed to be responsible for the breach may have been executing trial runs for this large-scale attack years in advance according to SecurityWeek.[58] The Federal News Network[59] lists the US Energy Department and Veterans Administration among those targeted and also

---

[57] www.progress.com/security/moveit-transfer-and-moveit-cloud-vulnerability

[58] www.securityweek.com/evidence-suggests-ransomware-group-knew-about-moveit-zero-day-since-2021/

[59] https://federalnewsnetwork.com/cybersecurity/2023/06/energy-department-among-several-federal-agencies-hit-by-moveit-breach/

notes that universities and private businesses including Shell are believed to be affected. The State of Oregon's Department of Motor Vehicles couldn't identify exactly which assets were stolen in the MOVEit hack and so informed everyone who has a driver's license in that state to consider their identity at risk,[60] while the UK payroll provider Zellis use of the software has impacted many of their customers.[61]

While the MOVEit breaches are *not* impacting Kubernetes clusters directly, Mandiant[62] and other security research firms do state that Azure Storage is impacted with Baker Donelson claiming, "The vulnerability allows for unauthorized data access and control, including access to Azure Storage Blob credentials, providing the attackers with the means to steal data directly from a victim's Azure Blob Storage containers. This situation is particularly alarming because, with a copy of the database, threat actors can continuously attempt to access even encrypted data, posing a severe threat to organizational security."[63]

I mention them here because they illustrate the risks inherent in a mixed stack that includes third-party tools, custom applications that may be affected by supply chain vulnerabilities, internal and external connectivity, and the oftentimes sensitive data on which all of these rely. Additionally, the greater the potential damage from an insecure implementation in any of these areas, the louder the clamor to hold someone accountable will be. In March of 2023, the current administration

---

[60] www.oregonlive.com/commuting/2023/06/massive-hack-of-oregon-dmv-system-puts-estimated-35-million-driver-license-and-id-card-info-at-risk-officials-say.html

[61] https://techmonitor.ai/technology/cybersecurity/zellis-cyberattack-british-airways-boots-bbc

[62] www.mandiant.com/resources/blog/zero-day-moveit-data-theft

[63] www.bakerdonelson.com/moveit-transfer-zero-day-vulnerability-what-companies-need-to-know

of the United States published a National Cybersecurity Strategy[64] which commented in part, "We must begin to shift liability onto those entities that fail to take reasonable precautions to secure their software" and also notes that "end-users... often bear the consequences of insecure software," which will be painfully true for large groups of people in this particular case.

As organizations provide the tools, their users need to effectively do business the pace at which change happens is incredibly rapid. Arc particularly shines in the area of accidental hybrid IT estates, where the need for uniformity of governance was never more apparent than it is today. As companies move toward the cloud, consolidate and acquire new lines of business, or even repatriate some assets to privately owned DCs, the need for effective policy to manage disparate resources is readily apparent. Yet if you took only the case of acquisitions, a misapplication of needed controls could leave users feeling unsupported or worse resentful of the changes being made to familiar work routines amid their companies' transition to new ownership.

Policy controls become more palatable when they are framed as an opportunity to contribute meaningfully to the security of the company to which the user subject to the policy is devoting their efforts. Policy guardrails are not intended to prohibit a user from reaching what they need in an efficient manner. To craft policy that enables productivity, the policy designer has to understand the user's workflow while remaining aware of the greater risks posed by potential gaps in security or process. In the case where a policy needs further tuning to meet these objectives, IT must not be reactive – disabling an important policy due to a user complaint – but rather incorporate user acceptance testing into the policy's development lifecycle in a process of continuous improvement.

---

[64] www.whitehouse.gov/wp-content/uploads/2023/03/National-Cybersecurity-Strategy-2023.pdf

If you think about the number and type of policies impacting end users such as eDiscovery, document retention and classification, permission to assets associated with their own role, and more, many of them will live within content management, financial, and document processing systems that already have defined governance controls for working with typical business process flows. But if you start to delve into the infrastructure that supports many of the same tools – the file transfer product mentioned in the introduction of this heading being an excellent example – then policy reverts back to being a platform governance issue most of the time. Whatever useful tool is facing the user, if there is a data store behind it or network traffic exiting the boundaries of your organization, it will need to be governed and secured, with enterprise-wide application of policy being a core tool to accomplish those objectives.

Policy and FinOps

FinOps,[65] or the application of DevOps principles to cost control efforts, is a key use case for the policy engine and one that it is specifically designed to address. Large enterprises require hefty budgets to continue to produce income in their vertical, but leakage of resources reduces a company's velocity and in extreme cases can lead to failure. Technology assets are notoriously difficult to catalog and maintain in such a way that their expense can be mapped directly to the profits they generate, and this challenge only becomes more complex when running in a multi-cloud or hybrid environment. Providing a true accounting of what is in use and assuring usage is trimmed to avoid waste is an area where policy controls shine. Per Tarun Sood,[66] FinOps encourages a culture of accountability

---

[65] https://learn.microsoft.com/en-us/azure/cost-management-billing/finops/overview-finops

[66] www.linkedin.com/pulse/demystifying-azure-cloud-finops-best-practices-optimizing-tarun-sood/

through "clear cost allocation policies that outline the responsibilities and expectations of different teams or departments in managing their Azure costs."

Policies can govern the type of resource or service that can be created and by whom; they can enforce tagging to ensure that costs are easily segregated by department or workload, they can specify which product licenses are available, they can enforce scaling limits, and much more. Key cost management risks include not only overspending but underutilization of capacity blocks that may have been purchased for a discounted cloud spend, and policy can help you control these risks by either remediating policy exceptions or providing timely and actionable audit information. Utilization also matters as companies pursue ESG objectives, and providing sufficient capacity for client-facing workloads to perform well demonstrates that FinOps policy can be used not only to control costs but to increase profits. Every Arc-enabled Kubernetes cluster in Azure has a unique Azure Resource Manager ID and is contained within a subscription and Resource Group, enabling you to both monitor and proscribe how those resources are used with policy.

Effective Policy

Policy is the most effective tool available to assure your governance intentions become reality in your systems. Its design and implementation are as important as the design of the systems and workloads themselves in order to assure the latter two remain operational. We could coin YAOT [Yet Another Ops Term] such as PolSecOps, and it might stick, but the better approach is to simply view policy as the natural approach to governance and then practice governance faithfully starting far left.

A 2022 Trend Micro blog post[67] addresses a perhaps overlooked aspect of policy management and security – finding Open Policy Agent servers open to the Internet – and comments, "If OPA servers are left unsecured, their policies can reveal sensitive application information, including user profiles and services being used. These exposed policies can also unwittingly disclose information on how the system should behave to bypass restrictions on implemented policies, which malicious actors can use to wage attacks." As you would secure any other part of your supply chain, lock down your policies.

If you are a policy geek, you will enjoy digging into the personal project site[68] of a Microsoft employee that attempts to index and update all of the built-in policies that are available. Next, we'll look at process automation underpinned by a monitoring feedback loop and what's possible in terms of automated response.

---

[67] www.trendmicro.com/en_fi/research/22/h/what-exposed-opa-servers-can-tell-you-about-your-applications-.html
[68] www.azadvertizer.net/index.html

CHAPTER 8

Monitoring and Process Automation via the Arc Control Plane

We touched on process automation in the Kubernetes chapter when discussing GitOps. As we take a closer look at what can be achieved, it will become apparent that the surface area to which it can be applied is much broader than operations and that Azure Arc has unique features that can assist in our journey to actively administer large IT estates that are governed, implemented, and managed by automation. Process automation is a big topic that deserves its own book, so this chapter will focus on how the reach of the Arc control plane allows you to extend automation across the IT estate and further is instrumental in creating the feedback loop that nourishes your automated processes.

Monitoring for Discovery and Validation

Core to automation is an accurate understanding of what is being controlled by it, and successful automation depends on the output of monitoring. Azure Monitor is Microsoft's powerhouse tool for accomplishing this in conjunction with Arc for multi-cloud and hybrid installations. It would be a much shorter list to try and identify what Monitor cannot do than to list its capabilities. Monitor is a roll-up of three prior stand-alone services, including Azure Monitor, Log Analytics, and Application Insights, into a single monitoring application that can track the whole of your IT estate from the infrastructure to the workloads it carries. With the maturation of its product components over the past few years, it is equipped to cover most monitoring scenarios, but Microsoft hasn't chosen to lock users in. The list of products that integrate with Azure Monitor includes popular options like Datadog, Grafana, ServiceNow, Dynatrace, and many more,[1] which is advantageous if your teams are already working effectively with a different monitoring solution.

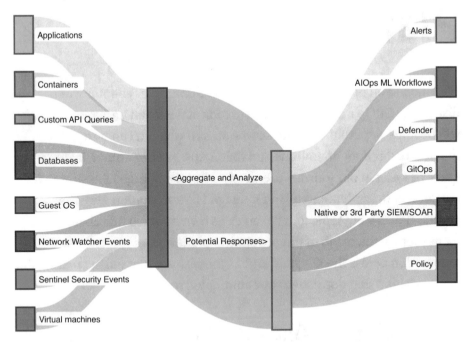

Figure 8-1. *Azure Monitor inputs and potential responses, @2023 Ramona Maxwell*

---

[1] https://learn.microsoft.com/en-us/azure/azure-monitor/partners

Breaking down the components of Monitor starts with the data to be collected. A Log Analytics [LA] workspace is one of Monitor's three key components and will allow you to aggregate logs from many sources and then store them for the time needed to analyze them. Two things that are costly are part of this equation, moving and storing data; therefore, Microsoft recommends you carefully consider how you will design your LA workspace. A single workspace is not constrained as to the amount or type of logs you wish to collect, so a single LA workspace is considered optimal until cross-region data transfer comes into play, at which point it can be evaluated whether multiple workspaces could minimize egress charges.[2] What usually has a bigger impact is the region in which the workspace is hosted, for instance, the per GB price for analytics logs can be more than 25% lower in a more economical region.[3] Further, purchasing a commitment tier beginning at 100GB of data is an immediate 30% cost reduction. When calculating whether this is beneficial, it's important to note some metadata in your logs is not billed as it is simply part of the structural process for the platform and log collection. Some types of security logging utilized by Defender are also not charged up to the 500GB limit included in the Defender product.[4] For very large volumes of log data exceeding 500GB, an Azure Data Explorer cluster containing several LA workspaces and using commitment tier billing by default is the preferred option.[5] Monitoring usage is key to cost control[6] as it is possible to switch to larger commitment tiers during a 31-day commitment period if usage exceeds the original estimate.

---

[2] https://learn.microsoft.com/en-us/azure/azure-monitor/logs/workspace-design#azure-regions

[3] https://azure.microsoft.com/en-us/pricing/details/monitor/

[4] https://learn.microsoft.com/en-us/azure/azure-monitor/logs/cost-logs#workspaces-with-microsoft-defender-for-cloud

[5] https://learn.microsoft.com/en-us/azure/azure-monitor/logs/cost-logs#dedicated-clusters

[6] www.egroup-us.com/how-to-save-on-sentinel-recurring-costs/

An LA workspace serves not only to gather data for analytics but can also be used by Microsoft Sentinel for security analysis, so segregation of sensitive information might be another reason for multiple workspaces, along with other considerations like multi-tenancy or data sovereignty concerns. You are still able to query across up to 100 LA workspaces and Application Insights components in a single request for a more comprehensive view. To the degree possible, it is better to address concerns about log data visibility using RBAC since having multiple workspaces can impact your ability to monitor all of your Arc-enabled resources as a group.

Azure Monitor relies on the Azure Monitor Agent [AMA] (which replaces the deprecated Log Analytics Agent) in order to collect data from monitored resources. As a part of automating configuration, it is good practice to enforce the installation of the AMA via policy[7] on Arc-enabled servers. This is the approach you must take if you are deploying at scale since for this particular task ARM templates or direct command-line deployments are unusually limiting (allowing for reporting to only a single workspace unless you make manual adjustments and targeting a single Arc-enabled server at a time). Enabling the built-in policies for this purpose on either Windows or Linux VMs can also assure that the agent is installed when new VMs are created or restore it on existing VMs if it is not present, but you still face the limitation of a single workspace. You can also use Azure automation to deploy the agent at scale or the portal, but that again is limited to one or a few machines at a time. Multiple Azure services utilize AMA to extend their capabilities, including at this writing VM and Container Insights, Microsoft Defender and Sentinel, Network Watcher, Azure Stack HCI Insights, Change Tracking and Inventory Management, as well as Azure Virtual Desktop Insights. Once installed, the AMA is one of the agents that will be

---

[7] https://learn.microsoft.com/en-us/azure/azure-arc/servers/concept-log-analytics-extension-deployment#use-azure-policy

automatically upgraded for Arc-enabled VMs unless you specifically disable that setting.[8] One of the first priority monitoring tasks you will undertake is to continuously monitor the health of your monitoring solution, for example, Azure Monitor.[9]

Because collecting monitoring data from disparate sources is challenging, Microsoft has looked for a way to improve Monitor's ability to consume data. The result is data collection rules [DCRs]. DCRs are a form of ETL that can be applied specifically to monitoring data to allow for the application of query filters in advance of data import in order to assure that what is consumed is appropriate for the purposes of a monitoring action. This both increases the effectiveness of the monitoring solution and controls the costs of data import and storage. A final step is to reformat the data into a standardized template that can be consumed by AM. This process is now integrated into the API so that if you are using a rest endpoint to send data to AM, you can specify the data collection rule to apply to that incoming data.

If your LA workspace will ingest more than 500GB of data per day, it is a candidate for a dedicated cluster which brings further benefits such as the ability to use customer-owned encryption keys, linking multiple workspaces to the cluster to meet the consumption spend commitment and more – the most beneficial of which appears to be the ability to consume data directly from Event Hubs.

Because of the wide variety of data you may collect with Monitor and the necessity of making it actionable, you may elect to enable and customize continuous export of specific items. For instance, you may want to split information between multiple LA workspaces depending on its

---

[8] https://learn.microsoft.com/en-us/azure/azure-arc/servers/manage-automatic-vm-extension-upgrade?tabs=azure-portal

[9] https://learn.microsoft.com/en-us/azure/azure-arc/servers/manage-automatic-vm-extension-upgrade?tabs=azure-portal

source or to send security alerts directly to your SIEM/SOAR system.[10] Of particular note is the ability to export compliance data, which will be a boon if analysis and reporting of regulated items is also automated.

Application Performance Monitoring[11]

Application Insights is another core piece of AM. Strictly speaking, Application Insights has nothing to do with Azure Arc until you consider that it is a native Azure service that would not be available to your resources on AWS or Google Cloud without Arc.

In Gartner's Magic Quadrant for Application Performance Monitoring and Observability published in July of 2023, Dynatrace is the solid champion among a capable group of application performance monitoring [APM] tools, with both AWS and Microsoft offerings listed only as competitors, and having partnered with Dynatrace in the service of a former employer, I understand why. The capabilities of putting yourself in the user's seat to view an issue in real time and then being able to drill through the application stack all the way to the method facilitating a user's current action with a few clicks are impressive and time efficient. Gartner's evaluation of Application Insights offers commendation of the new DCR ETL strategy for reducing ingestion costs but suggests that determining costs of the product overall might be difficult due to the number of "levers" impacting billing (however, that concern seems overstated for experienced Azure consumers). Gartner also wants Microsoft to ensure compatibility with the CNCF vendor-neutral OpenTelemetry standard for product monitoring,[12] to which Microsoft's response is they are working on it[13]

---

[10] https://learn.microsoft.com/en-us/azure/defender-for-cloud/export-to-siem

[11] www.elastic.co/what-is/application-performance-monitoring

[12] https://opentelemetry.io/

[13] https://learn.microsoft.com/en-us/azure/azure-monitor/app/opentelemetry-overview

while acknowledging that the Application Insight SDKs have historically had a focus on .Net applications. Since Dynatrace and many other products such as SIEM giant ServiceNow are already available as Azure native services in the marketplace, you are not locked to the Microsoft product stack, but may encounter additional integration steps to use them such as the need to install additional third-party agents on Arc-enabled servers or workloads.

What Application Insights can provide is a closed loop of monitoring followed by remediating action. If your workloads are native to Azure, then all of the tools for updating, deploying, securing, and managing them are readily available, but as an enterprise APM, it is suitable for most enterprise workloads no matter where they run, offering you a one-world view of the health of your application portfolio. In terms of application monitoring, it's a satisfactory and comprehensive tool with adequate language and framework coverage[14] beyond the expected support for .NET. While you have more options for auto-instrumentation[15] (which collects telemetry without the installation of an SDK) of workloads running on Azure services (including those in Arc-enabled edge installations as well as in Java workloads running anywhere), the JavaScript client-side SDK facilitates information collection with plug-ins for React and Angular, handily pulling back information for common tasks in those frameworks regardless of where the web application is hosted such as observing router activity and specifically for React being able to track component load and unload events. Click analytics as well as error reporting can be enabled as plug-ins to the SDK, and click activity is customizable based on HTML DOM element IDs.

---

[14] https://learn.microsoft.com/en-us/azure/azure-monitor/app/app-insights-overview?tabs=net#supported-languages

[15] https://learn.microsoft.com/en-us/azure/azure-monitor/app/codeless-overview#supported-environments-languages-and-resource-providers

When properly configured, AM tools offer more than log analysis and can be instrumented to monitor application components in real time in order to identify performance blockers or incorrect dependencies. The Application Insights SDK executes synthetic queries against your application in order to construct a map of its topology, and in a large application, it will take time for the representation of your application to complete. For the application components you have provided coverage for (but not necessarily external systems such as databases to which your application connects), you can examine their performance and diagnose individual component failures. Application Insights distributed tracing enables individual component monitoring even when your application workload is spread across various clouds and on-premise DCs because Arc-enabled resources benefit from Azure Monitor's AM capabilities that are facilitated by Application Insights.

Scaling is not the answer to every performance problem, and AM tools are designed to help you identify errors in application architecture or as well as to quickly respond to failures that may occur only under specific conditions that might be difficult to diagnose from logs alone. Anyone familiar with the challenges of tracing errors using timestamps, call logs, and, if fortunate, a correlation ID for an event will appreciate the value of being able to drill through to the events of a specific erroring component. The monitoring API can in a single test show whether your application's endpoint is available and whether it is properly encrypted as well as its response to typical REST commands. Every workload has a unique identifier, and in some cases, monitoring instrumentation can be automated, eliminating the need to install and maintain an SDK for that purpose.[16] Continuously monitoring availability and then automating response strategies can assure that your workloads remain available.

---

[16] https://learn.microsoft.com/en-us/azure/azure-monitor/app/codeless-overview

The performance of your workloads can have a direct impact on their profitability since downtime can result in lost revenue whether they provide internal functionality supporting your core business or are customer facing. The impact of a particular workload suffering an outage may vary from nearly inconsequential to catastrophic; thus, analysis and then prioritization of which workloads deserve premier treatment in your monitoring strategy is an important part of a business continuity plan. A centralized monitoring strategy raises the visibility of priority workloads and can further be used to assure both the high availability and security of those workloads. But the benefits of centralized monitoring don't stop at operational insights and can be used to optimize commercial strategy as well. As you monitor requests, you might assess the popularity of product offerings or regional sales trends to enable targeted promotions or adjustment of stock levels. The ultimate goal is that no facet of your business model be left out of the cycle of continuous improvement you instantiate with a monitoring feedback loop coupled with automated remediation.

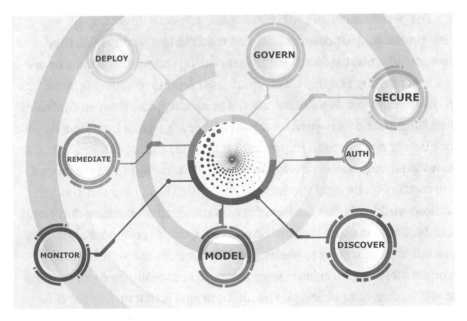

Figure 8-2. *Elements contributing to a continuous cycle of automation, @2023 Ramona Maxwell*

Monitoring for Security

If you are utilizing Defender or Sentinel, much of the automation that you will require is already accomplished for you once you identify the appropriate source data to take action on. For instance, the web application logs might list unsuccessful login attempts indicating an attempt to breach an account. Sentinel will automatically identify those types of log entries and alert as to potential actions, even creating incidents in Sentinel or even another SOAR tool such as ServiceNow.[17] Monitoring points that are unique to your enterprise or workload is where the ability to customize both the query of log analytics data and your response is invaluable.

---

[17] https://docs.servicenow.com/en-US/bundle/vancouver-security-management/page/product/secops-integration-sir/secops-integration-ms-azure-sentinel/concept/microsoft-azure-sentinel-integration.html

Being a large presence in the enterprise compute space, Microsoft tends to get called out if observers think its response to a security issue is not proportionate. A recent incident resulted in a win for customers of the platform that may pressure competitors to also remove financial barriers hindering the acquisition of information that affects security. Wiz documentation of Storm-0558[18] discusses a 2023 token forgery attack in which a signing key for verifying Azure Active Directory keys compromised at least Exchange Online and Outlook.com (per Microsoft) and potentially more areas of the Microsoft ecosystem such as Teams and SharePoint (as postulated by Wiz). As the federal government of the United States had suffered some impact due to the breach of Exchange, its Cybersecurity and Infrastructure Security Agency [CISA] became a collaborator with Microsoft in identifying ways to improve access to log data for cloud customers to enable timely discovery of serious threats.[19] Microsoft's decision to expand free access to certain types of log data[20] and extend access to many previously premium Purview events to standard customers is an impressive example of a leading cloud provider forgoing profit when their customers' ability to defend their IT estates is on the line. Microsoft is certainly not exclusive in having its feet held to the fire over event visibility in logs. Security startup Mitiga recently appealed to Google to make its logging entries more transparent so that customers could put appropriate protections in place depending on the type of activity that had occurred on their stored data,[21] quoting what appears to be a tepid response at best

---

[18] www.wiz.io/blog/storm-0558-compromised-microsoft-key-enables-authentication-of-countless-micr

[19] www.cisa.gov/news-events/news/when-tech-vendors-make-important-logging-info-available-free-everyone-wins

[20] www.microsoft.com/en-us/security/blog/2023/07/19/expanding-cloud-logging-to-give-customers-deeper-security-visibility/

[21] www.mitiga.io/blog/mitiga-security-advisory-insufficient-forensic-visibility-in-gcp-storage

from Google despite the fact that the SANS Institute identifies log visibility as a core defense against ransomware in the cloud.[22] On the whole, cloud vendors do not rejoice in one another's failures, and the big three are de facto stewards for the industry with a keen interest in preserving the reputation and usability of their product.

What this means for enterprise consumers under a shared responsibility model for security is that you must engage a monitoring solution that is prepared to consume security monitoring outputs at scale and also have the proper tools and knowledge to extract actionable data from them. While it's critical to prioritize security alerts in terms of risk, it's not necessary or advantageous to do this manually. It is the opinion of this author that if you are running hybrid or multi-cloud systems on Azure, Microsoft Defender for Cloud is not optional, but is instead foundational to success. Once you have connected Arc-enabled servers and VMs,[23] Kubernetes containers,[24] and endpoints[25] (as well as Azure native services such as Key Vault, APIs, storage, Azure DevOps pipelines, and more including and up to ARM itself[26]) to Defender and begun feeding their data into an LA workspace, you are benefiting from all of Microsoft's aggregated security expertise and that of the security community as a whole. Microsoft's documentation describing how Defender functions[27]

---

[22] www.sans.org/blog/ransomware-in-the-cloud/

[23] https://learn.microsoft.com/en-us/azure/azure-monitor/best-practices-vm#configuration-recommendations

[24] https://learn.microsoft.com/en-us/azure/defender-for-cloud/defender-for-containers-enable?tabs=aks-deploy-portal%2Ck8s-deploy-asc%2Ck8s-verify-asc%2Ck8s-remove-arc%2Caks-removeprofile-api&pivots=defender-for-container-aks

[25] https://learn.microsoft.com/en-us/azure/defender-for-cloud/integration-defender-for-endpoint

[26] https://learn.microsoft.com/en-us/azure/defender-for-cloud/defender-for-resource-manager-introduction

[27] https://learn.microsoft.com/en-us/azure/defender-for-cloud/alerts-overview#how-does-defender-for-cloud-detect-threats

explains that its detection algorithms are based not only on known threat signatures, behavioral analytics, and anomaly detection but also on in-depth research of emerging threats, telemetry collected from all of the systems they manage and are tuned against "real customer datasets" which are in turn used to build ML models for security analytics. Indeed, in a recent blog article "Implementing a Zero Trust Security Model at Microsoft,"[28] *pervasive* telemetry is cited as one of four requirements necessary for a successful implementation of a zero trust model such that "Pervasive data and telemetry are used to understand the current security state, identify gaps in coverage, validate the impact of new controls, and correlate data across all applications and services in the environment." Note that telemetry reflects a *current* security state. Tools such as Microsoft Defender for Storage monitor the telemetry stream even when you have logging turned off in the storage account, offering near-real-time advantage in identifying potential attempts to exfiltrate data as well as immediate scanning of uploaded blobs for malicious payloads.

Crafting and maintaining your organization's strategy for collecting, storing, and processing monitoring data is a major endeavor that will only be worthwhile if followed by effective analysis and response. Discussions of toolsets for managing enterprise infrastructure and workloads become complex simply because there are such a plethora of choices, and products tend to have some overlap in function. A helpful diagram on Microsoft Learn on the topic of security controls that are part of microsoft cloud security benchmark[29] charts the platform tools across four verticals, including "Identity and Access Management, Infrastructure and Network, Data and Application, and Customer Access," aligning everything from WAF and gateway services to API management to its coverage vertical.

---

[28] www.microsoft.com/insidetrack/blog/implementing-a-zero-trust-security-model-at-microsoft/

[29] https://learn.microsoft.com/en-us/azure/security/fundamentals/media/end-to-end/security-diagram.svg

It is noteworthy that only Monitor, Defender, and Sentinel cover all four verticals. Microsoft Defender for Cloud provides coverage across clouds and on-premise assets as well when these are Arc enabled. On-premise servers can now be protected by Defender even without Arc, but the usefulness of this approach is limited to the security benefits and missing all the goodness of GitOps. It also leaves these servers bereft of an Azure Resource Manager ID which makes them instantly recognizable to all services in the Azure ecosystem for benefits such as automatic configuration and updates. Defender has an additional arm to protect Microsoft 365, is integrated with the policy engine, and automates a comprehensive security response even if left uncustomized. At the end of Q4 2023, Microsoft followed up on the explosion of AI-driven workloads that marked the year with the announcement that Defender for Cloud features for cataloging and controlling generative AI-based applications are now generally available.[30] Response types range from completely disallowing any application that isn't internally approved to milder approaches such as monitoring these apps and blocking any that don't meet the bar of the organization's security and compliance standards or that are unknown.

Sentinel is primarily a SIEM/SOAR tool and a next-level option when you are ready to look at patterns across your organization, develop machine learning models, and tackle advanced scenarios such as industry or regulatory compliance. Once connected,[31] events can be streamed from Defender into Sentinel for analysis and across a large enough sample surface patterns of activity that indicate a threat. In

---

[30] https://techcommunity.microsoft.com/t5/microsoft-defender-xdr-blog/discover-monitor-and-protect-the-use-of-generative-ai-apps/ba-p/3999228

[31] https://learn.microsoft.com/en-us/azure/sentinel/microsoft-365-defender-sentinel-integration#connecting-to-microsoft-365-defender

Gartner's 2022 Magic Quadrant for SIEM, the Microsoft dot is floating far atop all competitors in their ability to execute, and this reflects the benefit of a consolidated ecosystem for security. Microsoft intends that both Defender and Sentinel be used together for a comprehensive extended detection and response [XDR] strategy.[32] While Defender provides automated real-time responses and does allow some investigation of detected anomalies, Sentinel is the tool senior security technologists can use to detect hidden malignancies trying to gain a foothold from which to spread through your systems.

In a hybrid or multi-cloud environment, attack surface management [ASM] is particularly germane as a multistage attack may take advantage of different platforms having stronger or weaker defenses in a particular area. If storage or clusters are easier to breach on one platform than another, that might be an entry point through which infection can spread to components elsewhere. Network vulnerabilities in a private DC might also allow for an entry point. Being able to look at an entire workload as if it were native to Azure is a tremendous advantage that is further enhanced by the ability to respond via remediation policies and GitOps. DSC helps to assure that workloads are fortified from every aspect. A key risk of containerization technologies is that if vulnerabilities are not discovered and cleansed, a corrupted container will be deployed numerous times and perhaps in many virtual networks. Fixing the problem in source control and redeploying may be impossible if discovery is not thorough enough to find every instance of an infected container.

As Sentinel is also a SOAR tool, it offers the ability to automate responses to detected threats. Much like the policy engine either has a single policy or a policy initiative aggregating a collection of related policies to be applied as a group, Sentinel has both a rules engine and

---

[32] https://learn.microsoft.com/en-us/security/operations/siem-xdr-overview

playbooks that allow you to combine a set of responses.[33] Rules can range from triage and suppressing log noise to assigning a response task to an analyst, the last of these edging over into the domain of a ticketing system. You can execute a rule based on a trigger or condition, and you can use a rule to kick off a playbook for a more comprehensive response. Playbooks are based on Logic Apps (a low to no-code workflow engine), and analysts will require RBAC permissions to the Logic Apps service as well as Sentinel to be able to create, modify, and run playbooks. When streaming events from Defender to Sentinel, response records are synchronized with only about ten-minute latency, so that if an issue is marked as resolved in Sentinel, it will also be reflected in Defender's dashboard or vice versa.

The key to the foregoing is to utilize every applicable automated response before pursuing customizations as without automation you are continually climbing up a muddy scarp to patch your fortifications. Running hybrid workloads simply increases the number of hills to scale, and without the ability to work from a single control plane, fragmentation of security controls and policy poses significant peril.

Monitoring and Data

The very title of the information technology industry hints at the fact that data is at the core of everything we do in IT operations management. Data Security Posture Management practice [DPSM] is referred to in the Microsoft product stack as data-aware security posture, a useful construct to highlight that it's all about the data all the time.

In the ancient days of monolithic on-premise application stacks, we used to think of data as something that lived in a *database*. If it didn't conform to a relational model, we tried to find ways to trim the edges of

---

[33] https://learn.microsoft.com/en-us/azure/sentinel/tutorial-respond-threats-playbook?tabs=LAC%2Cincidents

our square data peg in order to stuff it into our nice round data silo. That wasn't an accurate perception then, and it very obviously isn't true today. Data is ubiquitous, and not just in terms of descriptive metadata but every event and interaction that occurs with humans and the systems that serve them can be ascribed meaning and converted to data. Data that used to automatically be purged by time may now survive its originators without the efforts of archeologists wielding picks and axes. Data management is a concern of our time and, as will be discussed shortly in the context of AI, the critical foundation we are laying for the future. Data tools like Azure Data Explorer [ADX] aggregate and analyze your data as it exists, whether on an IoT device, an event stream, or data store, and adapt to its structure in order to extract its meaning in accordance with why it was collected, help control costs by identifying superfluous data that shouldn't be gathered or stored, and perform analytics on the paths data takes to provide actionable insights or shore up security defenses. For tools with such powerful capabilities in the areas of monitoring and analysis to be effective, they must reach all of the data they are capable of operating on, and that is a core use case of Azure Arc and its denizens. That in no way minimizes the importance of the relational databases that are still at the core of many enterprise workloads, and Arc-enabled data services are a chief reward of using Arc.

There are two agents involved when a SQL Server is connected to Azure via Arc, the Azure Connected Machine agent (which is not a substitute for Azure Monitor's AMA agent) and the Azure Extension for SQL Server. If your GitOps process doesn't adequately cover the installation of both agents when a server is first registered with Arc, or perhaps you have a post-registration installation of SQL Server on an existing registered Windows or Linux server, Azure iterates over all of your registered server instances, and if an installation of SQL Server is present but no SQL Server Extension is found, it automatically installs it. Both agents communicate using SSL over port 443. Installing the SQL agent enables feature capabilities such as Defender, Purview, and Microsoft

Entra authentication (the updated name of Azure Active Directory) unless you are running SQL with a low-cost SKU such as a CAL[34] or developer edition.

Azure Monitor and Defender for Cloud have their own integration muscle, and you could connect, for instance, an on-premise SQL Server without Arc, so if security is one of your main rationales, why make sure your SQL Servers are Arc enabled? Essentially, it's the necessity of having a unified control plane to enable a consolidated management approach. If your servers are registered with Arc, you can see their security profile in the Arc dashboard along with all the other attributes you are managing for those servers. The roll-up of information is key to making sure it is seen and acted upon as the more dashboards there are to check – even if you have people to monitor each type – the less consolidated your monitoring and security will be with core operations. Further, you're not limited to a portal view as Arc-enabled SQL Servers also can be queried using the Azure Resource Graph,[35] a powerful appurtenance to Azure Resource Manager which makes it possible to query Azure resources by type, identity, and properties for purposes of discovery and management. For SQL Servers, this means not only discovering instances of Arc-enabled resources, but also discovering properties that directly impact their governance and administration such as their distro or whether they are encrypted. The Resource Graph's database is kept current both by ARM updates and continual scans of your resources deployed to Azure, so no matter how you got them there – GitOps, one-off portal adjustment, migration, or any other legitimate means – the Graph will tally them for you. This visibility may also be useful in terms of cost control, as was pointed out by Microsoft in their December 2022 announcement of the public preview of the ability to view databases hosted on Arc-enabled SQL

---

[34] https://www.microsoft.com/en-us/licensing/product-licensing/client-access-license

[35] https://learn.microsoft.com/en-us/azure/governance/resource-graph/overview

Servers (now generally available[36]). Mike DeLuca[37] therein commented that not only does an inventory of individual databases and their usage contribute to migration readiness, it can "directly tie to and drive cost savings."[38] Its usage is included with commercial licensing only similar to the SQL Agent, but queries are throttled[39] on a per-user basis, so if you need to make use of it at industrial scale, you'll have to either reach out to Microsoft with your use case requesting capacity or draft your army of minions to run multitudinous queries.

Another issue with SQL Servers is that they are the diesel engine of the database world, they just run and run making companies and administrators loathe to upgrade if the legacy version they already own is sufficient for their workload. Windows and SQL Servers released a decade ago reached the end of support by Microsoft in late 2023 through the beginning of 2024,[40] placing those instances at risk of missing updates critical for security. While Microsoft would like to pry all the cold dead fingers off of these antiquated versions, they are taking a merciful approach of making Extended Security Updates available for purchase and enabling the application of those updates with Arc.[41]

Of all the operations you will run if you spend your lifetime administering SQL Servers, backup is the most critical and troublesome. Database backups can become corrupted for reasons as mundane as

---

[36] https://learn.microsoft.com/en-us/sql/sql-server/azure-arc/view-databases?view=sql-server-ver16

[37] This book's technical editor and Global Lead for Hybrid Cloud at Avanade

[38] https://techcommunity.microsoft.com/t5/azure-arc-blog/announcing-public-preview-of-viewing-sql-server-databases-azure/ba-p/3698410

[39] https://learn.microsoft.com/en-us/azure/governance/resource-graph/concepts/guidance-for-throttled-requests

[40] www.microsoft.com/en-us/windows-server/extended-security-updates

[41] https://learn.microsoft.com/en-us/windows-server/get-started/extended-security-updates-deploy

version incompatibility or having change management turned on,[42]
and if a backup cannot be restored, it is valueless. Issues around data
safety, consistency, and business continuity tend to be a primary reason
companies engage consultants, so planning and management of data
stores is a chief contributor to both cost control and business continuity.
When you bring your SQL Servers living on-prem and on other clouds
under Arc's umbrella, automatic backup is turned off by default so that
it doesn't pave over whatever backup routines are hopefully already
executing on the server; however, unifying your backup strategy for all
eligible servers under Arc's umbrella will assure you are protected and can
apply policies to assure versions are consistent, backups are tested, and
shadow copies of data are purged.

The processes for SQL Server backups noted earlier are a great example
of the policy feedback loop that Azure enables for most operational tasks.
The monitoring input of a loop aids in discovery of SQL Servers across
your IT landscape, and then once you have the SQL agent installed, more
key details surface that will be needed to effectively automate backups
on Arc-enabled SQL Servers[43] (such as whether the database recovery
model is set to full as is required for automated backups). Unfortunately,
there remains at the time of this writing a significant gap in coverage
for SQL Servers running on Linux which are not yet able to benefit from
automated SQL agent installation, backup, or patching[44] and most notably
absent – Microsoft Defender for Cloud. As Microsoft continues to build
out the SQL Server on Linux offering (a sampling of new features includes

---

[42] https://learn.microsoft.com/en-us/troubleshoot/sql/database-engine/
backup-restore/backup-restore-operations#miscellaneous-issues

[43] https://learn.microsoft.com/en-us/sql/sql-server/azure-arc/
point-in-time-restore?view=sql-server-ver16

[44] https://learn.microsoft.com/en-us/sql/sql-server/azure-arc/
overview?view=sql-server-ver16#feature-availability-by-operating-
system

things like replication, machine learning, and several more), hopefully close attention will be paid to the operational benefits of automation when a Linux-based SQL Server is onboarded to Azure using Arc. Another operational caveat is that of rogue administration. When utilizing Defender, alerts can be responded to in accordance with best practice, or someone could choose to reset the baseline for what triggers the alert – entirely defeating the purpose of setting up a system of controls to align with governance objectives. Likewise, a server admin can turn off Purview policy enforcement on workloads or obfuscate the paths required for correct operation.[45] This is why monitoring should take place from both operational and change management perspectives, and ideally the SecOps team will have the objectivity and authority to insist on proper application of the available controls.

If your application depends on data streams, either internal or external, the health of those streams will be a critical indicator for that application. The LA workspace query engine is based on Azure Data Explorer [ADX], and this combination of toolsets allows you to do not only reactive monitoring of events relating to your data corpus but also proactive health monitoring of the data itself. If you want to work from ADX on Monitor data, you can, but are subject to cross-resource query limits if you approach it that way. ADX utilizes compressed row and column storage along with caching strategies to achieve Microsoft's claimed performance of "Terabytes and petabytes of data can be queried ... with responses arriving in milliseconds to seconds."[46] Despite this capacity, ADX is not intended for training very large ML models or

---

[45] https://learn.microsoft.com/en-us/purview/how-to-policies-devops-arc-sql-server#security-considerations-for-azure-arc-enabled-sql-server

[46] https://azure.microsoft.com/en-us/resources/log-and-telemetry-analytics-with-azure-data-explorer/

other long-running tasks; its advantage is speed together with interfaces, including its native Kusto Query Language [KQL] and classic REST to SDKs in C#, Go, Java, Node.js, Python, and R.

Exercising the extreme vigilance required to assure your data remains safe requires proactive monitoring for threats and inconsistencies. All three major cloud providers can now be scanned for vulnerabilities in both compute and storage. Among the scan technologies in use is agentless scanning, and this is beneficial because the scanner uses only temporary memory to hold your data while scanning, and thus you are not creating a secondary copy of your data on permanent media that must then also be protected. This is the scan type Defender uses when, for example, monitoring through your GCP buckets to see if any of your SSH keys are exposed in a compute instance. When combined with scans of storage for exposed or unhealthy artifacts, Defender is able to provide an analysis of potential paths through which an attacker could travel, and this is accompanied by a visual representation allowing you to drill down at each juncture to examine the particular data or configuration that is at issue. Among the reference list of Defender recommendations for GCP,[47] Microsoft highlights the need to enable Azure Arc auto-provisioning on all projects as well as assuring that VMs and GKE clusters are properly configured with Arc. The same principles will apply to AWS and workloads running elsewhere when enabling Defender for Cloud.[48]

---

[47] https://learn.microsoft.com/en-us/azure/defender-for-cloud/recommendations-reference-gcp

[48] https://learn.microsoft.com/en-us/azure/defender-for-cloud/auto-deploy-azure-monitoring-agent#prerequisites

Monitoring the Internet of Things [IoT]

In a complex scenario such as the monitoring of IoT devices, log analysis objectives cannot be reached without consistently reliable monitoring, and in some cases this means monitoring of devices that are at least partially disconnected. Examining just one vertical, healthcare, demonstrates how reliant we are on these almost invisible pieces of networked compute hardware. An operating room might have not just expected monitoring devices for things like oxygen, heart rate, glucose levels, and blood pressure but innovative uses such as the pill that is able to perform a colonoscopy on its way through the body[49] or sponges equipped with tracking so that a surgical team doesn't accidentally leave one in the patient's body, risking infection and death.[50] Every day when I step on the bathroom scale, the result appears in my electronic medical record [EMR], and if my doctor chooses, they can review a timeline of both weight and blood pressure entries if I consistently use the monitored devices. If this information were being correlated with geospatial and activity information from a wearable fitness device, it could answer the question of whether walking a few thousand steps could cancel the effect of stopping at the coffee shop that serves homemade carrot cake (my nontechnical conclusion on that is a solid no). My IoT sensor–equipped device likely has an IoT Device Hub twin in the cloud that allows the scale to represent its data in the office where it will be reviewed, but Azure Digital Twins is a more sophisticated sibling technology that can actually build an entire model of what you are trying to represent. It is capable of combining the output of physical sensors with additional modeling data so that you

---

[49] www.mdpi.com/2075-4418/12/9/2093
[50] www.theweek.in/news/health/2023/04/11/how-iot-enabled-surgical-sponge-tracking-can-improve-patient-saf.html

can create a representation of whatever is important to your use case, for instance, a 3D model on which to practice brain surgery or the impact of various material selections on an object that is not yet physically built. It has even been used for tele-mentoring of surgical interns performing live procedures.[51]

The personal nature of medical information and the possibilities around its collection and correlation in a way that jeopardizes privacy make careless data handling a grave concern. Not only PID metadata such as birthdate or national identity number are stored, but often biometric PID such as fingerprints or facial scans. Healthcare analytics firm Arcadia cites a 2018 whitepaper claiming that the healthcare industry is responsible for more than 30% of the growing volume of data being produced worldwide, as well as claiming that nearly 60% of that data is not being correctly utilized.[52] Combining those startling estimates with reports of massive breaches in healthcare information systems in both the United States[53] and the UK,[54] it becomes obvious that it is essential to adequately monitor, process, and protect healthcare data. All of the problems just referenced are resolved when integrated monitoring and automated remediation tools are applied throughout the lifecycles of infrastructure and workloads. For example, if a medical facility decides to implement the Azure Health Bot, the ability to capture its telemetry with Application Insights, a core component of Monitor, is already present along with all sorts of customizable automation for governance and compliance.

---

[51] www.ncbi.nlm.nih.gov/pmc/articles/PMC9231158/

[52] https://arcadia.io/resources/market-insights-from-himss-and-arcadia

[53] www.chiefhealthcareexecutive.com/view/the-11-biggest-health-data-breaches-in-2022 and www.beckershospitalreview.com/cybersecurity/prospect-medical-hit-with-lawsuit-over-patient-data-breach.html

[54] https://heimdalsecurity.com/blog/massive-data-breach-affects-uk-hospital-group/

To understand how Arc enables IoT infrastructure, we can continue with a healthcare industry analogy examining just a few areas sensor data might be present, how it could be utilized, and concerns around its management.

Facilities Management/ ERP	Climate control I fire suppression I environmental controls such as heating and cooling, air quality, and seismic monitoring I traffic control and parking I entry systems I security I lighting I inventory controls I grounds I transportation	Mischievous or malicious hacking to disrupt normal operations I network intrusion I theft of inventory I inaccurate or incomplete data
Patient Monitoring and Care	Biometrics I pacemakers I EKG I breathalyzer I cameras I body scans I robotic surgical instruments I pharmaceutical administration, tracking, and storage	Patient privacy I faulty operation I incomplete data I incompatibility with existing systems
Administration	RFID tagging of physical records I scanners I printers I inventory	Patient privacy I network intrusion

When you instantiate an IoT device, security should be the first concern. Azure Arc will authenticate your edge device to the IoT hub at its initial connection, but many devices live partially offline if they are reliant on battery power and cellular networks or have other reasons for intermittent connectivity. Arc creates a shadow copy of the IoT hub local to the devices so that they continue to send data, unaware of the proxy target. They send this data through compact messaging protocols since the compute and memory capacity of an IoT device is typically very small. In Azure, since devices are sending data, this disconnected state makes them vulnerable if data encryption is not enforced. While a managed service (e.g., AWS Greengrass) enforces encryption and closes inactive connections automatically, the best protection for IoT farms you build is to enforce the same GitOps routines you do with Kubernetes. Assure that your supply chain is secure, encrypt data at rest and in transit, and practice proper network segmentation so that IoT devices are not on the same VNet as IT devices such as servers. As of a December 2023 update,[55] Microsoft enhanced its IoT security architecture for offline and air-gapped devices to better support local processing of monitoring data and changed a default role for operations as well.

Albeit IoT is automation, it is nevertheless a field where you'll need people to build and run it across several disciplines. The field of IoT is a hacker's paradise (using that term in a complimentary way). There is plenty of hands-on bench work to be had for engineers that like to build what they program. Just reading the Microsoft Docs specs of how to select equipment for POC work[56] is enough to kick off a serious gearhead spending spree. Azure IoT utilizes the Digital Twins Definition Language,[57] which is extended from JSON-LD (a flavor of JSON better equipped to describe related or unstructured data), to develop models representing the desired operational attributes and data to be extracted from a particular IoT device. Just the downloadable PDF provided by Microsoft as an IoT manual runs a thousand pages, and its status as a core technology is further emphasized by the fact that Microsoft for some time offered certification for IoT specifically,[58] and with some of the technical intricacies that come with managing large cadres of IoT devices, it will not be surprising if the future brings other opportunities to credential for this specialty.

---

[55] https://learn.microsoft.com/en-us/azure/defender-for-iot/organizations/whats-new#december-2023

[56] https://learn.microsoft.com/en-us/azure/iot-develop/iot-device-selection

[57] https://github.com/Azure/opendigitaltwins-dtdl

[58] https://learn.microsoft.com/en-us/certifications/azure-iot-developer-specialty/

As with many large platform products, it is likely that you will purchase complete IoT solutions for your use case rather than build the hardware in house since fleets of IoT devices, for instance, in manufacturing or agriculture, can number in the millions or billions, and items such as medical equipment are preconfigured with both hardware and software interfaces. Because of the inherent risks of distributed data platform management that bridges physical devices, your network, and software, unusual care must be taken to select a vendor with appropriate experience and security credentials. A well-researched article appearing on the US National Institutes of Health website[59] discussing cybersecurity in healthcare states, "the exponential adoption of Internet of Things (IoT) devices... has increased the threat surface presented for cyberattack" and also remarks, "the Internet of Medical Things (IoMT); ventilators, anaesthetic machines, infusion pumps, pacing devices, organ support and a plethora of monitoring modalities. All of these devices, once connected to a hospital network, present another opportunity for a malevolent party to access the hospital systems" while labeling the risks of deliberate miscalibration of medical instruments a danger to patient safety. With so much at stake, the criticality of properly monitoring and securing IoT workloads is evident.

Microsoft provides a simple reference article for a healthcare IoT implementation utilizing Arc[60] that is provisioned with either Azure Stack Edge or an Arc-enabled Edge Server. The diagram for that architecture is pictured in Figure 8-3, followed by a second in Figure 8-4 where I have overlaid more possibilities for monitoring and processing the telemetry from your IoT installations.

---

[59] Contributed to NIH by Springer Nature, the publishers of this book: www.ncbi.nlm.nih.gov/pmc/articles/PMC10123010/

[60] https://learn.microsoft.com/en-us/azure/architecture/solution-ideas/articles/healthcare-network

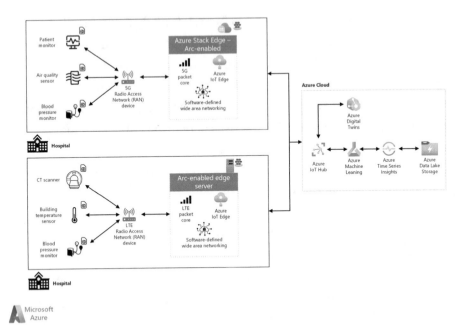

Figure 8-3. *Microsoft reference architecture for IoT in healthcare[61]*

Within the IoT hub, device data is available for seven days and by nature ephemeral, reflecting the state recorded by the device the moment the message is sent. Once it leaves the hub, it can be processed in ways that take advantage of the time series inherent in the travel of messages through the queue, for instance, to be consumed by Cosmos DB as the data source for a tracking application. Operational data might be sent to a SQL database or server as well. Telemetry and device data can be sent to Azure Monitor and stored in an LA workspace to query against. The Event Grid (also a message queue) presents limitless possibilities for ways to forward event messages, and its particularly favorable use case is to be

---

[61] https://learn.microsoft.com/en-us/azure/architecture/solution-ideas/articles/healthcare-network

able to use the data in Logic Apps. Most important to the security issues previously mentioned, Microsoft Defender for IoT can protect your device data workloads and then forward them to Sentinel[62] (or another SIEM) for processing.

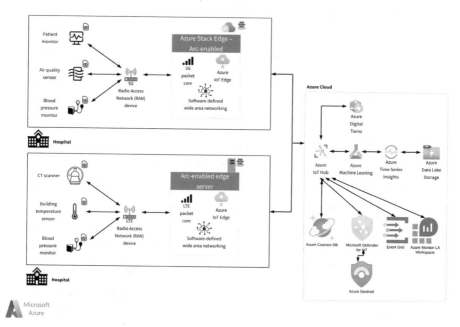

Figure 8-4. *Additional potential consumers of IoT hub data*

Although the illustrations show just two entry points for IoT data provisioned by Arc, the same applies to IoT workloads running on any server or Kubernetes cluster, as long as that server or cluster is registered with Arc as an Azure resource. Interestingly, one of the threats repeatedly cited regarding IoT devices contributing to security breaches in healthcare and other industries is the impact of outdated SDKs or OS on the devices themselves, a problem that monitoring will give you the insights to

---

[62] https://learn.microsoft.com/en-us/azure/defender-for-iot/ organizations/iot-solution

prevent and solve. As to what's possible with Azure IoT, including more monitoring scenarios and many more potential industry verticals for which Microsoft has specialized offers (for instance, agriculture), we've only gotten the tourist's view from a fast-moving car in this section, and an IoT architecture specifically tailored to the business rules of your industry is vital to extract the intended value.

The programmatic elements of how utilizing Azure IoT Hub enables edge computing in a disconnected environment are fascinating. Microsoft calls the Azure IoT Edge Runtime "a collection of programs that turn a device into an IoT Edge device,"[63] and these programs (as well as your own workloads or many other Azure and third-party offerings) are distributed as Azure IoT modules which are in fact containers. The core components of the runtime, the IoT Edge agent and the IoT Edge hub, are each containerized applications. The agent deploys modules and monitors their status, while the hub proxies communications with Azure. Every module has a JSON manifest defining its configuration (a module twin,[64] riffing off of the familiar IoT concept of a device twin[65]) for which the agent can retrieve a local copy from the hub when deploying a module. Back-end changes can be made to the twin, and they will be updated in the Edge hub the next time it connects to Azure. From the standpoint of hub clients, they are always and only connected to Azure and unaware they are communicating with a proxy.

---

[63] https://learn.microsoft.com/en-us/azure/iot-edge/iot-edge-runtime?view=iotedge-1.4

[64] https://learn.microsoft.com/en-us/azure/iot-edge/iot-edge-modules?view=iotedge-1.4#module-twins

[65] https://learn.microsoft.com/en-us/azure/iot-hub/iot-hub-devguide-device-twins?view=iotedge-1.4

Azure IoT Edge Runtime

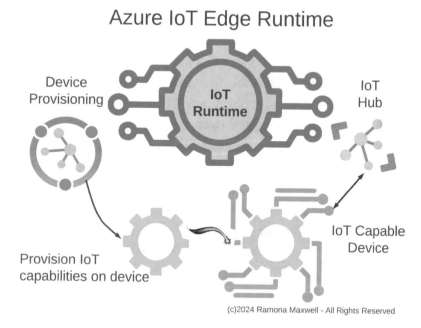

Figure 8-5. *Azure IoT Edge runtime, @2023 Ramona Maxwell*

In December of 2022, Gartner released their Magic scoreboard for industrial IoT and named Microsoft a leader,[66] and it's apparent from their product development approach that they intend to retain that recognition. In November of 2023, Microsoft released in preview Azure IoT Operations.[67] As previously discussed, IoT devices are often purchased and installed at colossal scale, and the IoT Operations suite is intended to make connecting and managing massive IoT fleets manageable. Similar to the newly overhauled Azure Stack HCI, the capabilities of IoT Operations are underpinned by Azure Arc. This proffers the same benefits to IoT assets

---

[66] www.gartner.com/doc/reprints?id=1-2BQFX3BJ&ct=221116&st=sb

[67] https://techcommunity.microsoft.com/t5/internet-of-things-blog/
accelerating-industrial-transformation-with-azure-iot-operations/
ba-p/3976702

that any other Arc-enabled resource has – they become native to Azure and as Azure resources can belong to an RG, have tags, and be managed via the Azure API or via the Azure IoT Operations Experience. Most importantly, these IoT assets are now defensible using Azure Monitor, Defender, and Policy. Core services such as Arc-enabled data services and machine learning enable preprocessing and storage of data at the edge, while cloud connectors make post-processing available with Microsoft analytic and event processing tools such as Event Hubs, Fabric, Power BI, and more.[68] Two appealing features are a device registry at the edge and an automated device discovery and registration tool, Azure Akri,[69] born of the CNCF Akri project[70] which can scan your network for devices and expose them in your Kubernetes cluster. The very definition of a leader is to provide the most secure and straightforward route to a goal, and overcoming the hurdles of creating a well-integrated IoT solution at scale with IoT Operations puts Microsoft on a path to retain its leadership title when that product becomes generally available [GA].

Creating a Policy Feedback Loop

The importance of policy as a tool for systems management cannot be overstated, and when you extend the reach of the Azure Policy engine via Arc, you are able to manage multi-cloud systems seamlessly. When you first install the Connected Machine agent on VMs outside of Azure, the application of policies mandating installation of AMA and DCR can also be automated, and this approach can accelerate both GitOps and SecOps.

---

[68] https://learn.microsoft.com/en-us/azure/iot-operations/manage-devices-assets/overview-manage-assets

[69] https://learn.microsoft.com/en-us/azure/iot-operations/manage-devices-assets/overview-akri

[70] www.cncf.io/projects/akri/

When you consider the complexities of maintaining large multi-cloud Kubernetes installations and the additional configuration of service mesh, networking and more Kubernetes maritime analogies are especially apt. An ineffective or incomplete policy implementation is akin to an adrift vessel at risk of capsizing or being DITW when pirates attack. By contrast, policy will provide systematic injection of quality from the GitOps processes used to build your fleet to the security and supply chain protections needed to keep it afloat.

To continually nourish and protect your systems, it's vital to hydrate your feedback loop through logging and other types of monitoring that have been mentioned in this chapter. The aggregated data continually informs policy, including both what is a base policy implementation and the design of customized overlays specific to the business model. Policy is then applied, and the failure or success of the controls it imposes plus any remediation triggered by policy emanate back into the monitoring stream so that it is continually tuned and regenerated. The tools within Azure's ecosystem are purpose-built to this end, with the management and automation disciplines core to the CAF for hybrid and multi-cloud.[71] Core recommendations include careful design of LA workspaces and efficiency around installation of monitoring agents, achieving consistency and enforcing governance via automation wherever possible (and it is the author's recommendation that if you find a gap, you fill it with a scripted solution, using hand-built automation as necessary until it is closed) across all of your infrastructure and the workloads it carries. In terms of automation architecture, CAF notes there are at least six different ways to onboard servers to ARC from the PowerShell, CLI, and REST API options that should satisfy those of your admins whose hands never leave the keyboard to Azure Portal, Windows Admin Center, and Azure Automanage

---

[71] https://learn.microsoft.com/en-us/azure/cloud-adoption-framework/scenarios/hybrid/

for their GUI colleagues. VMware VMs can still be onboarded individually but now in preview is the option to Arc-enable an entire VMware vSphere,[72] thus operationalizing enterprise scale Arc adoption for VMware shops. This highlights the importance of design in accordance with the skills possessed by your IT staff, the current complexion of your systems, and your overall governance strategy. The stability of your systems requires a uniform approach, precisely what Arc enables, and also lets you choose which method you can apply with regularity.

For instance, enabling the Azure Policy extension[73] places large portions of your validated Kubernetes infrastructure[74] into the policy feedback loop without further initiative on your part as long as your clusters are registered with Microsoft Defender for Cloud; however, a resource that existed prior to your installing the extension wouldn't have policies applied until it was rescheduled on to a new pod. The feedback from the policy implementation is then exposed in policy and gatekeeper logs so that the policy lifecycle can provide immediate protection via built-in policies and begin to inform the areas in which you will further customize and tune both policy and remediation based on the feedback received.

Microsoft Purview is a monitoring product that grew out of Microsoft Compliance Manager, rolling in new data discovery and monitoring capabilities.[75] It is well suited to monitoring SaaS data and can assess its lineage as well as track its movement. In the subsequent chapter, we

---

[72] https://learn.microsoft.com/en-us/azure/azure-arc/vmware-vsphere/overview

[73] https://learn.microsoft.com/en-us/azure/governance/policy/concepts/policy-for-kubernetes?toc=/azure/azure-arc/kubernetes/toc.json&bc=/azure/azure-arc/kubernetes/breadcrumb/toc.json#install-azure-policy-extension-for-azure-arc-enabled-kubernetes

[74] https://learn.microsoft.com/en-us/azure/azure-arc/kubernetes/validation-program#validated-distributions

[75] https://learn.microsoft.com/en-us/purview/concept-insights

will examine the change in approach toward data movement as opposed to managing and aggregating data stores in place to mitigate or even eliminate common challenges of large data corpuses such as migration risks, uneven implementation of RBAC controls, and obstacles to data discovery. Purview starts down the rainbow road that leads to the new Microsoft Fabric pot of gold by letting you apply data ownership policies from a very high-level view of your data assets held in Arc-enabled SQL Servers,[76] rather than down in the weeds of each database.

Purview collects the metadata that swirls around data providing context that can be reaped by developers and analysts targeting an API but is also readily accessible to business users via its own portal. It makes use of labels to classify sensitive information to meet both compliance and data loss prevention [DLP] objectives and can discover unlabeled sensitive data using sophisticated content analysis. Purview integrates smoothly with many other Azure features such as eDiscovery and can be a data source for Defender and Sentinel. If you turn on the policy enforcement option when registering a data source with Purview, it then integrates with the policy engine in order to achieve these goals, making purview a solid partner to Defender in providing automated governance through policy feedback loops across all facets of your organization's information technology assets.

Cost Monitoring

As Microsoft continues to build out Monitor, they're also establishing a pricing model for its usage,[77] and as of midyear 2023, most activities on the platform are billable. While in line with industry norms, and in part

---

[76] https://learn.microsoft.com/en-us/purview/how-to-policies-data-owner-resource-group

[77] https://azure.microsoft.com/en-us/pricing/details/monitor/

negotiable under enterprise service agreements, the cost of running a comprehensive monitoring operation must itself be monitored. Habits of ignoring masses of low-level alerts that might have been tolerable in wholly owned infrastructure certainly won't be acceptable if there is a monetary ding for every batch of a thousand. A comprehensive monitoring strategy is nevertheless one of the best ways to achieve cost control across your organization. It's important to look at Arc from both the aspects of the observability it enables and enhances relating to cost savings across Azure and the cost of observing Arc itself.

A few features of Arc such as RBAC, querying the Resource Graph, and some templates and automation are currently free to use, but the features you will want after you make the effort to configure Arc-enabled servers, data platforms, and Kubernetes clusters are not.[78] For instance, the free version of Defender does not extend to resources on other clouds – the raison d'être you would use Arc. You are not the only one trying to curb costs as Google, Meta, Microsoft, IBM, AWS, and more have all made announcements about extending the depreciable lifespan of their servers by one or two years.[79] That doesn't mean they aren't spending money on the cool toys (such as Nvidia GPUs for AI[80]), but excepting some nice advances in storage technologies, most of the hardware from four or five years ago still admirably meets today's compute requirements. There is a saying among enterprise architecture professionals that we shouldn't "gold plate" the solutions by recommending an entire suite of top-tier offerings

---

[78] https://learn.microsoft.com/en-us/azure/cloud-adoption-framework/scenarios/hybrid/arc-enabled-servers/eslz-cost-governance#how-much-does-azure-arc-enabled-servers-cost

[79] www.datacenterdynamics.com/en/news/google-increases-server-life-to-six-years-will-save-billions-of-dollars/ and www.wsj.com/articles/big-tech-expects-some-assets-to-last-longer-but-the-boost-to-profit-is-temporary-66ce9f98

[80] https://techcrunch.com/2023/08/24/nvidia-earnings-flying-high/

but instead search for the minimum viable product [MVP] that gives a working solution while minimizing the expenditure to achieve it. What is important for both massive cloud providers and your enterprise is to determine the apex of profitability from your cloud spend.

Most of the product offerings mentioned in this chapter have multiple ways in which you could be charged for their usage. Monitor, for example,[81] charges for things like log ingress and retention, and states queries are free unless you happen to query logs that have been archived. Whether the pricing structure is a "gotcha" or not depends on how you perceive it, but it is a fact that using all available platform tools to regulate spend is advisable, and it's also true that platform experts in your organization who understand the nuance of cost control will be essential in determining cost-effective placement of resources, advantageous pricing eligibility such as volume requirements for commitment tier purchasing, and deep familiarity with usage patterns to support the negotiation of enterprise agreements.

Entire companies devote themselves to cost control efforts on cloud platforms, and their remuneration is usually a percentage of what they save the client on services, a blatant example of how much money is hanging in the margins of a typical cloud budget waiting to be gleaned. According to a Q3 2022 Forrester Cloud Cost Management and Optimization report,[82] cloud vendors themselves are starting to provide cost optimization features in the face of customer's "intense desire for tooling that can help optimize spend and rein in unnecessary costs." Forrester also recommends that such products integrate well with your existing monitoring and ITSM solutions and, very much in harmony with the practices outlined herein, states they should also "Enable intelligent usage policy creation and enforcement."

---

[81] https://learn.microsoft.com/en-us/azure/azure-monitor/usage-estimated-costs?view=azureml-api-2

[82] www.forrester.com/report/the-forrester-wave-tm-cloud-cost-management-and-optimization-q3-2022/RES176395

Microsoft considers the Cost Management discipline[83] one of the five key pillars of the CAF governance model, and policy is one of just three primary tools to achieve it. Another is Cost Management and Billing[84] which can provide guided assistance and alerts as well as a calculator and budgets. Microsoft is expanding caps on some alerts such as those to rein in the cost of maintaining an LA workspace[85] by including Defender for Cloud data types. Inverse to the desire to limit costs, there may be situations in which you wish to escalate and expand your use of Azure resources in order to fulfill a consumption commitment made as part of an enterprise agreement [EA] in exchange for steep discounts. While EA discounts can be a bit of a gamble if the business climate in your industry regresses, they are extremely advantageous under growth conditions, and thus many customers find them irresistible. Even if you are not party to a large agreement, you may purchase a certain commitment tier (formerly referred to as a capacity reservation) and want to fully utilize your purchase. Azure Savings Plans[86] are another option that offers a steep discount on typical Pay-As-You-Go rates over a disparate range of services based on your purchase of one- or three-year blocks of a certain amount of consumption per hour.

Lighthouse has been mentioned previously as a tool for oversight of large enterprise or Managed Service Provider [MSP] client operations, but it is also a powerful emissary in your mission to regulate spending across multiple Azure tenants since you have access to query the Graph API in their behalf and discover things like forgotten POCs and improperly

---

[83] https://learn.microsoft.com/en-us/azure/cloud-adoption-framework/govern/cost-management/

[84] https://learn.microsoft.com/en-us/azure/cost-management-billing/cost-management-billing-overview

[85] https://learn.microsoft.com/en-us/azure/defender-for-cloud/upcoming-changes#change-to-the-log-analytics-daily-cap

[86] https://learn.microsoft.com/en-us/azure/cost-management-billing/savings-plan/savings-plan-compute-overview

scaled workloads that are draining cash every moment they run. Shadow copies of departmental resources in an old subscription, applications that never gained velocity within an organization, duplication of storage, failed deployments that left artifacts behind – perhaps all sprawled across multiple clouds and DCs – plus many more albatross that you needn't pay to feed can be found and eliminated.

Since speed is essential in responding to an emergency, automation is a nonnegotiable requirement for security responses. The benefits of automation though are core to business velocity overall, and in the next chapter, we will look at how the maturation of machine learning and artificial intelligence can maximize the value extracted from technology.

CHAPTER 9

Automation in the Era of ML and AI

Automation in the Era of AI

No discussion of process automation can overlook the explosion of artificial intelligence [AI] into the public consciousness, now that what just a few years ago might have been referred to as machine learning [ML] input put to intelligent use for Robotic Process Automation [RPA] has come to be thought of as AI. To apply the term "artificial" to what is being produced is only truthful in the sense that the calculations and deductive reasoning are not being performed by a biological intelligence. The output itself is not artificial in the sense of being fake, any more than a calculator producing an answer to an equation would make the answer invalid. We are in the industrial age for brain laborers, and the opportunities that presents are exciting in terms of velocity for business growth and solutions for previously unresolved technical roadblocks for the same.

The growth we are experiencing now has been anticipated since the 1950s at least and hoped for long before that. A Brazilian consultancy specializing in AI[1] opines that it dates back to discoveries like Aristotle's

---

[1] https://industriall.ai/blog/history-of-artificial-intelligence

© Ramona Maxwell 2024
R. Maxwell, *Azure Arc Systems Management*,
https://doi.org/10.1007/978-1-4842-9480-2_9

Posterior Analytics[2] in which two known factors create a supposition of an unknown fact or the calculator designed by Leonardo Da Vinci, while Wikipedia has an exhaustive two-millennia list of projects[3] that at least demonstrate humanity's deep interest in empowering itself via automation.

For the fun of it, I started looking back at my own materials on the process. In 2009, I wrote an article titled "Predictive Analytics and Your Bottom Line"[4] that discussed the challenges of building a useful analytic model (still applicable) and lamented compute power limitations blocking the full utilization of what was technically feasible. It's that second limitation that's fallen away, and in fact the compute power available utilizing one or more clouds is limited only by the amount you're willing to spend on those resources. A 2011 article discussed Microsoft's FAST Server for SharePoint,[5] the technology for which had been scooped up for $1B+ in 2008.[6] The FAST engine performed analytics on the underlying data corpus being searched so that when a query was executed, the results would be relevant based on the context of the user – again a straight line could be drawn to model training methodologies for AI.

In 2020, in a presentation on RPA at my then employer's annual Tech Summit in Minneapolis, I noted "Robotic Process Automation introduced bots and *AI routines* able to respond intelligently to events in a way that was previously impossible without human intervention." Really, the eager anticipation around the possibilities of full-on AI in the technology community was such that when ChatGPT and its cohorts hit the scene, the reaction in some quarters was finally! Now yesterday's RPA buzzword

---

[2] https://study.com/learn/lesson/posterior-analytics-aristotle.html

[3] https://en.wikipedia.org/wiki/Timeline_of_artificial_intelligence

[4] https://ramonamaxwell.com/assets/09-12-28%20Predictive%20Analysis%20and%20Your%20Bottom%20Line%20-%20Ramona%20Maxwell.pdf

[5] https://ramonamaxwell.com/assets/FAST%20Search%20for%20the%20Enterprise%20-%20Ramona%20Maxwell%202011.pdf

[6] https://en.wikipedia.org/wiki/Microsoft_Development_Center_Norway

has become passe in favor of AI-infused process automation, and many companies have updated their product descriptions in order to hitch a ride on the bandwagon of enthusiasm around AI. When examining products for your use case, it's worth noting whether the marketing hype represents actual updates to functionality or is just a relabeling of automation features already present in the application. Google succinctly defines AI[7] as "enabling a machine or system to sense, reason, act, or adapt like a human" and also describes it as an umbrella technology with many subfields under discussion here such as ML and deep learning.

At the Databricks 2023 Data and AI Summit,[8] Marc Andreessen (famous for being the coinventor of the first graphical web browser as well as for influencing the development of many well-known companies as a venture capitalist) described AI as an 80-year journey running alongside development of supporting technology that is "just now starting to work."[9] Commenting on the large amounts of data is required to make AI work; he stated, "we're there now" and encouraged the audience to look at his recent treatise on the future of AI that he boldly titled "Why AI Will Save the World."[10] Whether or not that utopian view is a stretch, one appreciable point made in his article is that AI is machinery and data manipulated by humans is "not going to come alive any more than your toaster will." As we discuss expanding our reach over enterprise systems using Azure Arc for the purposes of machine learning and automation, the AI that we are referring to is the ingestion of voluminous data and the execution of processes based upon it that are designed, controlled, and understood by humans.

---

[7] https://cloud.google.com/learn/artificial-intelligence-vs-machine-learning

[8] www.databricks.com/dataaisummit/

[9] www.databricks.com/dataaisummit/session/data-ai-summit-keynote-thursday/

[10] https://a16z.com/2023/06/06/ai-will-save-the-world/

Per Microsoft's Vasu Jakkal who is a corporate VP of Security, 2023 was slated to become the "inflection point" year where the union of AI, hyperscale data, and threat intelligence formed "Security-Specific AI" tools powerful enough to overcome currently insoluble onslaughts of computer crime that organizations worldwide are facing.[11] Like Andreessen, she expresses the positive, life-changing potential of using this particular technology revolution to create a more equitable social landscape and particularly to empower "defenders" of the data she describes as "the new gold" against cybercrime. To achieve the sort of transformation these two visionary leaders are so passionately describing, companies cannot hesitate in terms of understanding how to utilize AI to their advantage.

Extending Jakkal's apt analogy of data as gold reminds us that fabulous riches aren't easily extracted and that failure is often incidental to their pursuit. This is particularly true for ML and AI initiatives, and we will see how Arc in particular increases the odds of success.

Acquiring, Maintaining, and Modeling Your Actionable Data

Much of what was discussed in the last chapter revolved around data emanating from systems and workloads that could be captured with monitoring. In many cases, the feedback loop of monitoring combined with policy design and application will be sufficient for operational and security control automation, and specific Azure policies should be implemented as you design your AI/ML workspaces.[12] However, it will be vital to discover areas where incomplete or misinterpreted information could be creating an oblique view of just how effective the current

---

[11] www.youtube.com/watch?v=ek4sjb3iLKI

[12] https://github.com/MicrosoftDocs/azure-docs/blob/main/articles/ machine-learning/how-to-integrate-azure-policy.md

feedback loop is in order to determine whether policy alone is enough or if the identified concerns are worth the significant investment of ML/AI. For large organizations, AI-driven security tools are likely obligatory, simply due to the fact that the onslaught of attacks is greater than the capabilities of security teams to review, and the analytics performed on anomalies to determine whether they represent actual risk greatly reduces the problem of alert exhaustion. Policy is a static tool akin to a door lock, while AI/ML is dynamically searching for threats and actively addressing them, so use policy to create a vault around confidential assets and then AI/ML as an army of warriors to keep marauders far away from the guarded assets. Among SIEM providers, a recent Forrester report[13] ranked Microsoft Sentinel third behind Splunk and Elastic in terms of strategy while noting in the case of both the Sentinel and Splunk products that their effective use will entail hefty budget allocations and capable security teams.

There are abundant use cases in which targeting monitoring data with ML/AI tools will be propitious, but it is also likely that a primary use will be to extract profitable insight and actions from a company's LOB data. This is where Arc becomes particularly advantageous as this data may have geographic or other restrictions that make assembling a credible ML pipeline and assuring it remains fresh each daunting endeavors. Aside from these construction and maintenance hurdles there is the ever so politely named impolite problem of "model collapse"[14] which occurs when various types of models trained on prior models continually degrade as to their usefulness and accuracy with each training cycle.

As machine learning requires massive amounts of data ingestion, where this information is stored will be a key part of how your ML solution is architected. For instance, a pharma company developing a new medication based on a clinical trial containing the personal health

---

[13] https://reprints2.forrester.com/#/assets/2/682/RES176427/report
[14] www.techtarget.com/whatis/feature/
Model-collapse-explained-How-synthetic-training-data-breaks-AI

data of the individuals participating in the trial may be required to keep patient data and intellectual property off the public cloud and perhaps also guarantee full network isolation. The approach that Azure Arc takes is to process ML data in an Arc-enabled Kubernetes cluster; therefore, edge and disconnected scenarios are fully supported. The Azure Machine Learning extension must be deployed to the cluster(s) which can then be enabled for model training, model deployment, or both of those purposes. As with any Arc-enabled Kubernetes deployment, it should be made secure and repeatable by the use of GitOps and governed by policy.

Another issue relating to voluminous datasets is the capacity limitations of your DC or conversely the great expense of taking advantage of what is virtually unlimited capacity in the cloud (excepting occasional constraints imposed by cloud providers when they themselves occasionally reach a capacity limit). Capacity though is not the only fulcrum on which your decision to store models in the cloud or in an on-premise data center will turn. The nature and purpose of your model also impact your choice of storage in that if you have a dependent workload that requires high performance from your model, the latency of cloud storage may not be acceptable.[15] This again is a use case for Arc since it is agnostic as to where you choose to store model data and by extending processing capabilities for ML to on-premise or competitor clouds gives you the ability to colocate model processing with data for efficiency and cost savings. If on the other hand your model is not impatient, perhaps consuming volumes of research data that are to a model that is not expected to be updated instantaneously, then low-cost cloud storage might be optimal. Again, the ability to operate anywhere and yet use the tools that are available in Azure is the advantage that Arc provides.

---

[15] www.techtarget.com/searchstorage/news/366537138/Storages-role-in-generative-AI

While the models themselves will be much smaller than the dataset on which they are trained, they along with other ML/AI artifacts require a storage and versioning strategy which is typically accomplished by a model registry.[16] While you could get by with Azure ML Git integration,[17] which allows you to use any flavor of Git repository for model development that you can authenticate to, a model registry captures key metadata for a model version such as the dataset it's based on and the features it was trained with. A private registry provides proper access control as well as an audit trail and additionally will be accessible through an API for integration into your ML pipeline. There are a number of open source model registries, the best known of which is perhaps the MLflow Model Registry[18] which can be set up as a private registry[19] when configured with a dedicated server and is also compatible with an Azure ML workspace.[20] Azure offers a model registry with the assumption that you'll be using Azure cloud storage, and the same is true of Google's Vertex AI Model Registry which is free to use excepting that you'll be purchasing storage for your models from Google. When you access certain models within the Azure ecosystem, such as those pertaining to Responsible AI governance, you are pulling from Azure's own instance of its model registry. Craig Wiley, a founding contributor for both AWS SageMaker and Google Vertex, now Sr. Director of Product, AI/ML, at Databricks, lamented the fact that when he asks "Where is your model registry?", the frequent reply is Excel, stating "That can't be the answer in 2023!" and further explaining

---

[16] https://towardsdatascience.com/ml-model-registry-the-interface-that-binds-model-experiments-and-model-deployment-f6df00f0b695

[17] https://learn.microsoft.com/en-us/azure/machine-learning/concept-train-model-git-integration?view=azureml-api-2&tabs=python

[18] https://mlflow.org/docs/latest/model-registry.html

[19] https://techcommunity.microsoft.com/t5/ai-machine-learning-blog/announcing-registries-in-azure-machine-learning-to/ba-p/3649242

[20] https://learn.microsoft.com/en-us/azure/machine-learning/how-to-manage-models-mlflow?view=azureml-api-2

Databricks' approach that the models and their management should be integrated with the data layer itself, one advantage of which is models inheriting the governance of the data they are based on vs. having to set up additional RBAC controls for a registry. While you are not locked into using Azure's ML registry by the fact of running AI/ML workloads on Arc-enabled clusters, to do so is advantageous since it keeps management of the AI/ML assets within Azure, a key rationale for using Arc to begin with.

Azure AI/ML consists of a plethora of offerings including everything from speech and image recognition to prebuilt offerings that can be integrated into an application without custom model development. In most instances, organizations will prefer purpose-built models, and Azure has a large and well-organized AI/ML ecosystem. As shown in Figure 9-1, an ML workspace in Azure connects to a data store using stored credentials from Key Vault. No data is migrated or duplicated; the data store simply contains references to the data you perform filtering queries upon in order to create the dataset on which you wish to train your model. Models are stored and versioned in a repository just as any other development artifact until you are ready to deploy them.

Contributing to the rapid growth of AI/ML are the languages of data science that have created a common foundation on which to build AI/ML models. Among the dominant languages in the space are Python and R for model development, but C languages also play a major role even when they are not the tool in the hands of the developer as their superior speed and computational accuracy underpin the ability to process large volumes of data through complex computational filters. R has typically been used by statisticians and data scientists and so has a specialized and devoted audience, while Python has long been valued for not just AI/ML but is also commonly used to develop large commercial websites, with some sources claiming it's used in approximately 14% of sites live on the Internet in 2023. It is popular not only because its declarative programming style is refreshingly easy to work with, it is also platform independent, and, perhaps most importantly, it greatly speeds the inner loop of application development because it does not have to be compiled. An ML developer can literally see the impact of code changes in near real time as they type. Python is one of the languages used in creating Jupyter and other proprietary notebooks that take a unified natural language approach to development and consolidate assets directly into the development flow. Things that usually aren't exposed short of reading logs or running tests are quickly discernable, for instance, you can look at how each variable affected the result of a code run. If you are developing large models, you'll want programmers from multiple disciplines, as knowledge of lower-level languages which perform the heavy computational lifting will aid in troubleshooting anomalies that aren't apparent until code reaches the outer deployment loop.

Azure AI/ML Overview

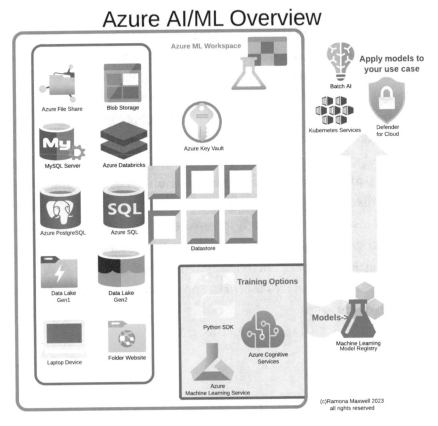

Figure 9-1. *An introductory view of the Azure ML/AI ecosystem*

Another benefit intrinsic to using Arc as the control plane for ML infrastructure is the separation of the responsibilities of data scientists from those of the operations team. The operations team can continue to use their fully developed GitOps routines to deploy the clusters that you dedicate to machine learning with simple tunings in the pipeline in order to make them suitable for this purpose, the security team can apply all of the proper network segregation and private endpoint requirements that your governance plan requires, and your data science team can be merrily focused on models and their application rather than drowning in a sea of deployment troubleshooting.

The balancing act when ingesting extraordinarily large volumes of data for purposes of model training is well portrayed in a brief article released by the Meta engineering team[21] describing how it became necessary to rewrite storage algorithms in order to gather training data without unnecessary and expensive iteration over irrelevant data. Hard limits on not only hardware capacity but also caps on power consumption have forced these innovations forward in an admirable way, but the fact that Meta encounters them again illustrates the value and cost optimization potential of flexible options for storage and processing infrastructure.

While Meta took the path of customizing storage and retrieval solutions with their exabyte-scale storage system,[22] they are not the only ones taking a hard look at what it takes to deal with colossal amounts of data. The days where migration was an assumed approach toward data warehousing may be fading into the rearview. At Databricks 2023 Data and AI conference, JP Morgan Chase Head of Global Tech Strategy Larry Feinsmith, who described JPMC's technology culture as "data driven" throughout his 15-year tenure with the bank, commended Databricks on their platform which fit with his proffered strategy to "efficiently move the data once and then manage the environment." As a rationale, he explained that "...once you start moving data around it's a nightmare to manage, it's highly inefficient, you break data lineage...,"[23] succinct arguments for leaving data in place and aggregating at the control plane level.

Concerns around breaking data lineage are an important consideration for enterprises of any type. Two major lawsuits and counting have been filed against AI frontrunner ChatGPT by authors and

---

[21] https://engineering.fb.com/2022/09/19/ml-applications/data-ingestion-machine-learning-training-meta/

[22] https://scontent-sea1-1.xx.fbcdn.net/v/t39.8562-6/24710006 9_301176064865170_8801733765234032327_n.pdf?_nc_cat=105&ccb=1-7&_nc_sid=ad8a9d&_nc_ohc=fr2Bad-efiIAX8WK_sQ&_nc_ht=scontent-sea1-1.xx&oh=00_AfDOjtnYUdOibPJSHnqGyXo1OsAIg2RLWUP_GLYweMtSHA&oe=6510AD7F

[23] www.youtube.com/watch?v=DoAomvtE_AM

publishers who claim their copyrighted works were vacuumed up by its Large Language Model [LLM].[24] If your enterprise has access to proprietary information via subscriptions and you consume this into your model, it might be considered similarly to analytics companies that have long run on their data feeds. But if your own clients have access to the model, will this usage still be in compliance with your subscription agreement? While those are questions that business negotiators and their legal departments are competent to resolve, answering the question of where data originated is likely to fall directly on the IT side of the house. Preserving identifying metadata of data flowing through systems is an important aspect of risk management that is made easier when management of data stores is done from a central control plane.

Databricks calls its data aggregation strategy the Lakehouse[25] and claims it will relegate classic data warehouse architecture to the history books as organizations become aware of the advantages of being able to query and manage data no matter where it lives, a premise very similar to that of Arc. There is genius in the simplicity of the approach taken to achieve this in that a versatile and cost-effective file format, Parquet,[26] provides the interface enabling diverse types of storage to be queryable as a single entity. The second of Databricks' one-two knockout punches is that security is addressed via their Unity Catalog – one set of authorizations to data resources no matter where in your hybrid and multi-cloud ecosystem they live. Microsoft and Databricks have partnered

---

[24] https://variety.com/2023/digital/news/openai-chatgpt-lawsuit-george-rr-martin-john-grisham-1235730939/ *and* www.cnbc.com/2023/12/27/new-york-times-sues-microsoft-chatgpt-maker-openai-over-copyright-infringement.html

[25] https://docs.databricks.com/en/lakehouse/index.html

[26] www.databricks.com/glossary/what-is-parquet

throughout the growth of Databricks' data platform, and it has resulted in an interesting synergy between Microsoft's own Intelligent Data Platform built on Databricks Lakehouse technologies[27] and an Azure Native offering of Databricks.[28]

Indeed, there are many commonalities between Microsoft's Databricks offering and its newest SaaS data and analytics platform, Microsoft Fabric.[29] Fabric rolls many of Microsoft's well-developed analytics solutions such as Power BI, Synapse, and Data Factory into a consolidated solution that abstracts away the complexities of setting up these products separately and makes them all available to data stored in what Microsoft also refers to as its Lakehouse, with an official title of OneLake. As a SaaS product, there are some feature differences between Fabric and Microsoft's stand-alone data and analytics tools,[30] but the overall multi-tool approach will empower many midsize organizations that lack large data science teams to tackle big data problems and unify their approach to analytics.

Model Feeding and Care

Per Matei Zaharia, Apache Spark inventor and CTO at Databricks, "naively adding an LLM assistant doesn't work"[31] for the reason that the context of the business domain may be missing from the model, giving it limited usefulness in solving the real business problems encountered by the

---

[27] www.linkedin.com/pulse/powering-future-analytics-microsoft-databricks-pablo-junco-boquer/

[28] https://techcommunity.microsoft.com/t5/azure-data-blog/microsoft-and-databricks-deepen-partnership-for-modern-cloud/ba-p/3640280

[29] https://learn.microsoft.com/en-us/fabric/get-started/microsoft-fabric-overview

[30] https://learn.microsoft.com/en-us/fabric/data-engineering/comparison-between-fabric-and-azure-synapse-spark

[31] www.youtube.com/watch?v=h4z4vBoxQ6s at 45:07 forward

organization. He cited the same problem addressed many years ago by the creators of FAST, that identical terms vary in meaning according to their domain context, and then described Databricks Lakehouse IQ tool for examining data sources from aspects such as query frequency, associations, and more to develop the accurate context needed to prepare data prior to creation of a useful model. Similarly, Google recently added AutoML[32] to its Vertex AI product, allowing visibility into the data shaping a model from its lineage to its impact on the model being designed. IBM promotes Watson Studio[33] as a tool to "Operationalize enterprise AI across clouds" and claims it will "Increase model accuracy by 15% to 30%." AWS meanwhile touts its 20-year history as an AI/ML fueled company[34] and offers sophisticated model prep tools such as SageMaker Data Wrangler[35] to assess data quality issues prior to model training. The tools mentioned earlier are only a sampling of what is available from each large vendor, as all have tried to balance a fully automated approach that can be brittle and inflexible with the opposite of a fully composable model development process that tends to push enterprises toward large teams of data scientists and ML ops engineers. Both Databricks and AWS, perhaps others also, opine that the democratization of machine learning technologies through simplification will make their use accessible to a broader swath of people across the business landscape. The efforts toward making AI/ML accessible from different vantage points and skill levels are also running apace with AI/ML capabilities being offered in Power BI,[36] Python

---

[32] https://cloud.google.com/automl

[33] www.ibm.com/products/watson-studio

[34] https://aws.amazon.com/blogs/machine-learning/announcing-new-tools-for-building-with-generative-ai-on-aws/

[35] https://aws.amazon.com/sagemaker/data-wrangler/

[36] https://learn.microsoft.com/en-us/power-bi/connect-data/service-tutorial-build-machine-learning-model

worming its way into Excel,[37] and even Databricks' Wiley calling models "fancy functions" and noting that with Unity Catalog in the mix models can be run as user-defined functions by SQL analysts.

Critical to the growth of AI's commonality, usability, trustworthiness, and overall maturity as a mainstream technology is a platform that enables an organization to deemphasize where data is hosted in a way that is not limited to ML technologies, but also attempts to offer the macrocosm of purposes for which a technology stack exists. Microsoft's bet is not based on owning every piece of infrastructure to which you deploy but rather that by facilitating the right environment to foster business growth and reliable, secure operations through a comprehensive suite of native and integrated tools, Azure will become the preferred vantage point from which you construct and govern your IT agglomeration.

Another advantage in terms of multi-cloud MLOps is the ability to distribute ML workloads in a cost-efficient manner. For instance, you might want to take advantage of Parameter-Efficient Fine-Tuning of large-scale LLMs[38] on cheaper hardware vs. the risk and expense of retraining an entire model. Deploying Azure's machine learning extension[39] on Arc-enabled Kubernetes clusters will allow you to run either training jobs or inference workloads in your multi-cloud infrastructure. Additionally, Azure ML supports any Git-compatible repository for Machine Learning Operations [MLOps].

---

[37] https://techcommunity.microsoft.com/t5/microsoft-365-blog/introducing-python-in-excel-the-best-of-both-worlds-for-data/ba-p/3905482

[38] https://huggingface.co/blog/peft

[39] https://learn.microsoft.com/en-us/azure/machine-learning/how-to-deploy-kubernetes-extension?view=azureml-api-2&tabs=deploy-extension-with-cli

Adjacent tasks such as monitoring and governance are part of a comprehensive MLOps implementation and you must implement tagging for cost control to be effective.[40] You can deploy your model to an Azure hosted machine learning endpoint or to provision an endpoint on your Kubernetes cluster of choice.[41] Your deployed model can answer either real-time or batch queries as to the result of running the model on the data you provide. For instance, a mortgage loan processor might want to compare the data of a single borrower against the model in real time when deciding whether to approve a mortgage application for a customer visiting their branch or in a different scenario send an entire batch of data to process if considering buying a block of loans. Real-time inferencing is specifically for scenarios where immediate feedback to a query is desired.

Deploying to an endpoint (or endpoints for A/B testing) is an important part of the ML pipeline so that you can test the inferencing provided by your model. Azure Monitor can offer a very thorough picture of events emitted by your ML endpoints[42] from the success or failure of deployments to audit information and performance metrics. The reverse approach of running machine learning tasks in the Log Analytics workspace of Azure Monitor[43] might be one of the primary use cases for ML in your organization and one that starts to open up endless possibilities for extracting value from the AI/ML toolset given the breadth

---

[40] https://learn.microsoft.com/en-us/azure/machine-learning/how-to-view-online-endpoints-costs?view=azureml-api-2

[41] https://learn.microsoft.com/en-us/azure/machine-learning/concept-endpoints-online?view=azureml-api-2#managed-online-endpoints-vs-kubernetes-online-endpoints

[42] https://learn.microsoft.com/en-us/azure/machine-learning/how-to-monitor-online-endpoints?view=azureml-api-2

[43] https://learn.microsoft.com/en-us/azure/azure-monitor/logs/notebooks-azure-monitor-logs

of information collectible with Monitor. Event Grid hooks to actions based on the ML event stream are also in preview,[44] opening up the wide world of things like Logic Apps, webhooks, Azure functions, and more.

The partnership between Microsoft and mega-startup Databricks is interesting in that as of this writing Microsoft is the only one of the three major cloud providers on which Databricks is a "first-party service, sold and supported directly by Microsoft"[45] rather than a third-party integration. Not only that, Microsoft has based its own OneLake[46] on a lakehouse paradigm of a single data lake per tenant organization with discrete governance applied and is recently rumored to be working on an AI service together with Databricks[47] that is more customizable than the one provided from their partnership with OpenAI. Being able to have a full implementation of Databricks within the Azure ecosystem is really a best-of-both-worlds scenario for enterprise-scale ML/AI, and the two companies have a great deal of synergy in terms of their approach to security and integration of ML/AI into an overall business strategy.

Databricks has another claim to fame besides the way they've built their Lakehouse and that's Unity Catalog. What Unity Catalog [UC] achieves is a centralized permissions store and query path. Much like Meta's massive file store, the UC achieves its coverage of mass and disparate data stores through a metadata layer living atop the actual data that functions like a compact directory for a huge metropolis. This meta layer provides a record of underlying data stores and their relationships

---

[44] https://learn.microsoft.com/en-us/azure/machine-learning/how-to-use-event-grid?view=azureml-api-2

[45] https://azure.microsoft.com/en-us/products/databricks *and* https://learn.microsoft.com/en-us/azure/databricks/machine-learning/

[46] https://learn.microsoft.com/en-us/fabric/onelake/onelake-overview

[47] https://aibusiness.com/companies/microsoft-courts-openai-rival-databricks-to-power-azure-ai-tech

and facilitates securing individual assets at a granular level. It eliminates a singular problem of model skew with AI/ML models which occurs when a model trained on data available in a development environment may produce different results when run against production data. The intent is to have your models become native to your data, a harmonious part of your data corpus that remains faithful to the original source of truth that defines the model. When running on any of the three major cloud providers, the metadata layer of UC runs at the level of the region, while individual UC instances run in the account (AWS), subscription (Azure), or project (GCP). UC uses a managed identity to access the actual data, so users are *not* provisioned directly on the underlying stores. One impact of this architecture is that cross-region metastore queries can result in egress charges.

Models cannot remain static if they are to be effective. I recently encountered an example of this when I used Bing's AI search while upgrading my personal website from an early version of Angular to version 16 and asked for a sample of router modifications using stand-alone components. The answer as of early 2023 was that only samples of Angular 13 were available because the model had a cutoff date from 2021. By September 2023, OpenAI responded to this limitation with the announcement that "ChatGPT can now browse the internet to provide you with current and authoritative information, complete with direct links to sources. It is no longer limited to data before September 2021."[48]

My case was inconsequential, but for a large enterprise relying on models that shape sales data or hunt for security anomalies, keeping the model fresh is essential. To do that, your model development efforts will need a pipeline as indicated by the terms Microsoft prefers, "AIOps" and "MLOps." New information flowing into your model must be validated as meeting the standards of content and accuracy for your model by thorough testing. Keeping adequate flow of healthy input to your model will provide

---

[48] https://twitter.com/OpenAI/status/1707077710047216095?s=20

currency and will drive toward the goal of closing the delta between what the model predicts will happen and the actual outcomes which determine whether the expense and effort of maintaining a model has sufficient ROI.

Bias and the Greater Impact of Model Corruption

Data professionals and application developers have long referred to having a "single source of truth" to assure the integrity of data so that critical facts affecting the business can be relied upon. The issue with model training though is that truth is entirely subjective. It's not so much a garbage in, garbage out issue, although that is also applicable, as the fact that models synthesize data using mathematical comparisons[49] such as frequency of terms and their proximity to one another. Validation can be accomplished with comparisons of a data point with an authoritative source, but if your model is trained only on the data itself, then if it is skewed your model will be also. Unfortunately, some types of information that may be valuable in terms of predictive analytics are not necessarily binary or easy to validate. Vanessa Otero, founder of news curation provider Ad Fontes Media, eloquently explains why this issue exists in an article[50] that is a bellwether for some of the intrinsic problems that must be addressed for the models relied upon for AI to be viewed as trustworthy. Issues such as hallucinations,[51] where the output of a generative AI model is seemingly unrelated to its foundational data and training, have caused immediate alarm around casual adoption of AI in areas that could have direct impact such as healthcare recommendations, approving or denying financial

---

[49] www.datacamp.com/blog/machine-learning-models-explained

[50] www.linkedin.com/pulse/ai-struggles-detect-false-information-because-finding-vanessa-otero/

[51] https://direct.mit.edu/tacl/article/doi/10.1162/tacl_a_00563/116414/Understanding-and-Detecting-Hallucinations-in

transactions, and evaluating applications to educational institutions or jobs. GeeksForGeeks[52] published a charming summary of the problem, citing an image processing AI struggling to distinguish between chihuahuas and blueberry muffins with the concluding comment, "there is an immediate need to develop algorithms or methods to detect and remove Hallucination from AI models or at least decrease its impact."

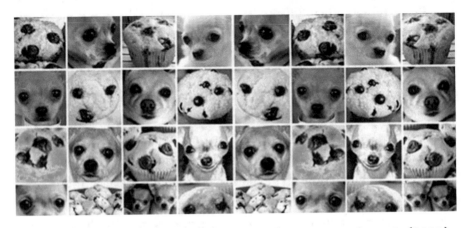

Figure 9-2. *Wetnose or juicy blueberry? (Source: Niederer, S. (2018). Networked Images: Visual methodologies for the digital age)*

Because of this potential for model corruption – whether deliberate or incidental – proponents of AI bear great responsibility for its ethical usage and insertion into the daily services on which people depend. The business risks posed by a bad model are already surfacing with lawsuits such as those by Joseph Saveri Law Firm[53] on behalf of several best-selling authors citing theft of intellectual property by LLM creator

---

[52] www.geeksforgeeks.org/hallucination/

[53] https://llmlitigation.com/

ChatGPT. The provocatively titled JD Supra Racist Robots 2.0: AI Liability for Discrimination[54] highlighted a recent lawsuit by the United States Equal Employment Opportunity Commission [EEOC][55] which penalized an employer whose AI had screened out older employment candidates with the reminder that liability for automated discrimination could be extensive. These accounts illustrate that poorly trained models can quickly consume the profit that was originally hoped for down a drain of legal fees or regulatory penalties. Meanwhile on the Digital Asset Management side of the house, VentureBeat points out that companies like Adobe[56] and Shutterstock are offering indemnity with their AI-created images to their risk-averse corporate buyers, and OpenAI recently followed suit[57] in an effort to reassure corporate customers using its model that they will not be exposed to legal risk.

You might assume a bad model could simply be shut down and given a fresh start, but the extremely high cost of creating large models makes this approach unpalatable. AI models are described as having an "unlearning" problem in that they don't easily filter and discard information. Even if you remove problematic information from your training data and attempt to refresh your model, it does not eliminate all of the summary calculations made with the original training.[58] This is why nonpublic models built from proprietary data are destined to become a standard for the enterprise and will likely be the only way to assure an AI investment is suitable for certain

---

[54] www.jdsupra.com/legalnews/racist-robots-2-0-ai-liability-for-2042826/

[55] www.msba.org/ai-first-eeoc-settles-first-ever-ai-discrimination-lawsuit/

[56] https://venturebeat.com/ai/adobe-brings-firefly-commercially-safe-image-generating-ai-to-the-enterprise/

[57] www.theguardian.com/technology/2023/nov/06/openai-chatgpt-customers-copyright-lawsuits

[58] https://fortune.com/2023/08/30/researchers-impossible-remove-private-user-data-delete-trained-ai-models/

critical or confidential business processes. A product like Arc makes it possible to secure your data estate, and that will be foundational in assuring lineage for models that reflect and support corporate standards in a manner that protects your company from unnecessary litigation.

Stereotypes live in models because they live in our culture and inside us as humans. Is a male engineer more likely to be an insider threat? Or is this assumption skewed because there is not yet a large enough sampling of the behavior of engineers who are women or nonbinary? If you track gender for HR purposes, then how will you guide the ways it is associated with other data such as salary, absenteeism, promotions, or healthcare? Do you evaluate a person's cost to your health and welfare plans based on the number and type of dependents they have and then feed that back into your compensation algorithm? Whether it's wise or possible to engineer social justice is still under discussion, but what is immediately pertinent is whether you will discover your model's weaknesses before an opportunistic lawsuit does. Governing your data so that it is protected against intrusion, pollution, duplication, and neglect is the job of consolidated systems management and policy and can be facilitated in very large organizations with Arc because it can manage the large number of operational tasks required to accomplish these multiple complex objectives across large multi-cloud and hybrid IT estates.

If you have protected the data, then you have provided a clean source on which to build your data and analytics and can proceed with additional tools to accomplish the task of ML itself in a way that is reproducible and allows you to validate both the inputs and outputs of the models you create. This sounds reasonable and easy until you consider that complex models with one or many neural processing layers begin to escape the reach of governance simply because we do not yet have the tools to unravel where a logic failure in a complex model occurred.

Azure's ML toolset tackles the foregoing challenges in model development through their Responsible AI framework.[59] Based on overarching principles of transparency and accountability into four key pillars of Fairness, Reliability and Safety, Privacy and Security, and Inclusiveness, it comes with its own standards document[60] that is basically an implementation guide stating how Microsoft thinks those core principles can be applied for an organization aiming toward AI/ML governance maturity. Microsoft's Responsible AI Dashboard allows you to implement and monitor the outcomes of initiatives based on the governance framework. It contains tools you can run against your models for things like *Interpretability*, for example, can you explain why your model gave the result it did? You can explore the shape of the underlying data model in terms of raw statistics, and if there are errors, perform an analysis to learn where those are concentrated. There is an open source tool called Fairlearn[61] included in the dashboard that can help you assess how your model is performing in terms of fairness, but the documentation makes clear that you will have to customize it to match desired goals – it cannot automatically discern or dictate what those should be.

The what goes in the model is followed by the how to get it there, with Microsoft's set of tooling to make implementation possible from the aforementioned data management frameworks to specific feature and inference training and test tools. One of the challenges of model development is very similar to that faced by first-generation mobile device developers who attempted to release usable apps on multiple versions of mobile OS, including not only Apple and Android but also Blackberry and Windows Phone, all running on assorted hardware that varied in both

---

[59] https://learn.microsoft.com/en-us/azure/machine-learning/concept-responsible-ai?view=azureml-api-2

[60] https://blogs.microsoft.com/wp-content/uploads/prod/sites/5/2022/06/Microsoft-Responsible-AI-Standard-v2-General-Requirements-3.pdf

[61] https://fairlearn.org/

capabilities and methods of interfacing with the device. Model training is a little like that as a model may need to be deployed to vastly different hardware and integrated with a plethora of language frameworks in order to serve its intended purpose. Much like Parquet paved the way for data sharing protocols, a consortium of AI Partners including Microsoft have worked on a common file format and operators for ML known as the Open Neural Network Exchange[62] [ONNX]. ONNX Operators[63] refer to the mathematical operators used in model training. Microsoft has been involved in ONNX since its inception at Meta, and the two companies were initial proponents of establishing its open standard. Hardware vendors and others caught on and began to design to the standard.

Microsoft has since deepened its investment by developing the ONNX Runtime[64] which bridges both the programming and device issues. This means that when developers incorporate the ONNX Runtime as part of the ML pipeline, using their choice of C, C#, C++, Java, or Python, ONNX will automatically optimize the model to run on target hardware, taking into account whether the deployment is trying to run on a CPU in a dev box or a fully equipped GPU-based production setup. And if that is not just enough ML geek euphoria, summer 2023 brought the release of ONNX script[65] which normalizes ONNX development by wrapping it in familiar Python conventions. To ML developers, this could be what TypeScript was to JavaScript, a huge step toward standardization and productivity.

---

[62] https://onnx.ai/

[63] https://onnx.ai/onnx/operators/

[64] https://onnxruntime.ai/about.html

[65] https://cloudblogs.microsoft.com/opensource/2023/08/01/introducing-onnx-script-authoring-onnx-with-the-ease-of-python/

Another Azure tool intended to provide velocity to larger organizations that may have multiple teams working on a number of AI/ML projects is the Azure ML managed feature store,[66] which allows you to publish a feature set to a catalog. This could be a great governance tool, for example, if you are a fintech and want all your teams to use identical calculations for certain types of analysis. The feature store serves the features directly so that you can entirely bypass development and accelerate the pace of model training significantly.

All of us have had a part in training LLMs; Google, for example, acknowledges that the CAPTCHA "prove you are human test" in common use across the Web trains ML, explaining, "Every time our CAPTCHAs are solved, that human effort helps digitize text, annotate images, and build machine learning datasets."[67] When Microsoft first introduced the ability to run Azure's OpenAI service on a customer's own data,[68] rumors were started that Microsoft was inviting their customers to contribute their private corporate data to OpenAI, leading Microsoft to publish a clarification[69] explaining that the data collected is not fed back to a stateless Microsoft copy of OpenAI's model, but rather simply allows customers to see how that model adjusts when inputting actual business data – which remains securely within the customer's tenancy. The fine-tuned superset of the model resulting from this customization can then be used for applications relevant to specific LOB applications.

---

[66] https://learn.microsoft.com/en-us/azure/machine-learning/concept-what-is-managed-feature-store?view=azureml-api-2

[67] www.google.com/recaptcha/intro/?zbcode=inc5000

[68] https://techcommunity.microsoft.com/t5/azure-ai-services-blog/introducing-azure-openai-service-on-your-data-in-public-preview/ba-p/3847000

[69] https://learn.microsoft.com/en-us/legal/cognitive-services/openai/data-privacy

The security issues surrounding massive, open LLMs are gargantuan. A fall 2023 Forbes article[70] highlights the access of criminal organizations to these models is the same as anyone else and that is quickly being used for purposes like emulating biometric IDs to gain access to financial accounts, creating voiceprints for telephone fraud schemes and deepfake video productions to entice people with fake endorsements. While AI can also be put to use on the security side to fight fire with fire, one vendor lamented to the author that if security models aren't continually updated, protection from their use is significantly weakened. Further, the human firewall is still a weak link. A VentureBeat security article[71] describes a social engineering attack that was successful just because the thieves took the time to study the LinkedIn profiles of the people they impersonated and commented, "Shutting these attempts down requires a balance between the contextual intelligence humans provide and AI-based data analysis and risk prediction." Per a Gartner predictive assessment of the upcoming security landscape,[72] "contextual human intelligence" is expected to remain in short supply as security professionals are as rare as nurses and equally missed when their services are required. Their remediation suggestions revolve around the idea that security must be a top-line revenue expense, and its implementation should permeate the culture. One analyst contributing a section on zero trust architecture to the report commented, "Ensure that zero trust is not seen as a technology or even technology-first effort, but is a shift in mindset and security approach." This is particularly true in the context of Arc and the impressive range of security enhancements it facilitates through identity management, authorization,

---

[70] www.forbes.com/sites/jeffkauflin/2023/09/18/how-ai-is-supercharging-financial-fraudand-making-it-harder-to-spot/
[71] https://venturebeat.com/security/ai-needs-human-insight-to-reach-its-full-potential-against-cyberattacks/
[72] www.gartner.com/doc/reprints?id=1-2D7XIUC3&ct=230413&st=sb

private networking, threat detection, and automated remediation – however, all of these require dedicated effort to correctly and consistently implement.

Significant security concerns don't mean that large public models like OpenAI's ChatGPT or Meta's Llama 2 will not be adopted by businesses. They are far too useful in terms of their massive aggregation of data and the way they lower the barrier to AI/ML entry vs. the expenditure and technical capabilities required to develop a model from scratch. Amazon has a new service named Bedrock specifically to make what the industry terms Foundation Models available on its platform, and its release announcement[73] makes it clear they're aware of the inherent risks, but also the business value as noted earlier. They manage these risks by storing the model you will access securely on their platform and also making sure that the read relationship is one-way. You can incorporate the model into your work, but the model can't train on yours.

Both Amazon and Microsoft[74] are using a Red Team approach to proactively guard Foundation Models offered through their platforms, and Microsoft has teamed with MITRE and additional stakeholders to develop the Adversarial Machine Learning Threat Matrix.[75] Google in turn has committed $20M to its AI Futures project[76] to support ethical AI research being done by academic and private institutions. Each of the big three cloud vendors are individually and jointly deeply involved in AI stewardship. Whether you look at big cloud companies being at the helm of AI's future in our world as the foxes guarding the henhouse or not, they

---

[73] www.amazon.science/news-and-features/amazon-bedrock-offers-access-to-multiple-generative-ai-models

[74] www.microsoft.com/en-us/security/blog/2023/08/07/microsoft-ai-red-team-building-future-of-safer-ai/

[75] www.mitre.org/news-insights/impact-story/mitre-microsoft-and-11-other-organizations-take-machine-learning-threats

[76] https://blog.google/outreach-initiatives/google-org/launching-the-digital-futures-project-to-support-responsible-ai/

are certainly vested in its path to usability and adoption as ultimately its success or failure is largely their own. While the ML/AI community as a whole can and does contribute to the trajectory of its success, doing what's required to set AI on the right path and keep it there through upcoming industry and societal challenges requires industrial muscle in terms of talent and funds that only these leading companies have.

Mitigating Environmental Impacts of AI

Another cost to consider is the impact of model development on the planet. A recent article by Bernard Marr in Forbes[77] highlights ESG concerns around AI models, specifically the environmental impact of maintaining the large datasets required for an effective model, and suggests that a model's environmental impact be listed alongside its claims of efficacy and other metrics. Not only in terms of model development but across entire IT estates, it is becoming critical for organizations to consciously manage their carbon footprint to comply with regulatory imperatives such as the European Union's Corporate Sustainability Reporting Directive [CSRD][78] that extends accountability for product impact substantially. Microsoft is enabling its customers to meet the emerging regulatory challenges in a way that demonstrates an interesting convergence of AI technology governance challenges being met with an AI-based solution.

How will Microsoft promote sustainability when their profitability is based upon your consumption of their compute and storage resources? By productizing the complex process of achieving measurable results

---

[77] www.forbes.com/sites/bernardmarr/2023/03/22/green-intelligence-why-data-and-ai-must-become-more-sustainable/?sh=3d8461067658

[78] https://corpgov.law.harvard.edu/2022/11/23/eus-new-esg-reporting-rules-will-apply-to-many-us-issuers/ and https://corpgov.law.harvard.edu/2023/02/18/esg-eu-regulatory-change-and-its-implications/

toward customer's sustainability objectives, whether those are voluntary or mandated by regulatory bodies and Microsoft Cloud for Sustainability[79] is their consolidated offering for this purpose. Microsoft Sustainability Manager can be purchased as part of an enterprise agreement or through a Cloud Solution Provider and offers visibility into consumption per billing account. In preview as of this writing are an entire set of APIs[80] to monitor your consumption of cloud resources that go beyond the typical financial views and look at how efficiently your compute strategy reduces your water consumption and waste emissions. Microsoft estimates that the efforts they've made to engineer their DCs to reduce negative environmental impact mean that running on their cloud will be better in terms of achieving a carbon neutral stance than running in your own DC (in fact, claiming, "Transitioning workloads to Microsoft Azure can produce up to 98 percent more carbon efficiency and up to 93 percent more energy efficiency than on-premises options"[81]). They've released a Power BI ESG dashboard[82] for Azure (there is also one for M365) to aid monitoring, including statistics from your own DC – but those rely on your estimation. There is significant business benefit to this tracking, particularly in claiming carbon credits[83] which may be required contractually, by statute, or even be resaleable for those uses, and the Sustainability Manager API includes credit tracking capabilities.

---

[79] https://learn.microsoft.com/en-us/industry/sustainability/

[80] https://learn.microsoft.com/en-us/industry/sustainability/api-overview?source=recommendations

[81] https://learn.microsoft.com/en-us/industry/sustainability/build-it-infrastructure?source=recommendations#workload-migration-to-the-cloud

[82] https://learn.microsoft.com/en-us/industry/sustainability/sustainability-manager-import-data-emissions-impact-dashboard-connector

[83] https://interwork.org/wp-content/uploads/2021/05/Voluntary_Ecological_Markets_Overview_Revised.pdf

For Azure Arc however, the main play Microsoft seems to make making in terms of sustainability is to promote the use of Azure Stack HCI.[84] This makes sense since Microsoft cannot control how infrastructure is managed on competitor clouds or in your DC, and further, self-contained computing solutions consume less resources than those distributed across a public cloud. Their assertion[85] is that the best paths forward in reducing carbon footprint are either to host your workloads on their infrastructure, which is continually optimized to meet sustainability objectives, or to reduce your footprint by adopting an Arc-enabled edge solution such as those from Dell[86] that incorporate sustainability principles and promise to deliver more compute power using fewer physical resources. Dell itself has made a hard commitment to sustainability in the near term,[87] promising that by 2030 100% of its packaging and 50% of the electronics it produces will be recycled as part of its stewardship of a circular economy for manufacturers through the Circular Electronics Partnership.[88]

Capturing the Money in Your Models

An internally developed AI model is a valuable intellectual property and can distinguish your business either in terms of the capabilities it enables relative to your marketplace or as a premium asset to be sold. Much like businesses in the early days of the Internet that failed to secure their own

---

[84] www.youtube.com/watch?v=y8MpXuMfwh4

[85] https://msazurepartners.blob.core.windows.net/media/1%20 New%20Resources%20Page/Hybrid%2BMulticloud/Azure%20hybrid%20 SustainabilityWP.pdf

[86] www.delltechnologies.com/asset/en-us/products/converged-infrastructure/technical-support/azure-stack-hci-techbook.pdf

[87] www.dell.com/en-us/dt/corporate/social-impact/reporting/goals.htm

[88] www.wbcsd.org/Programs/Circular-Economy/News/Circular-Electronics-Partnership-CEP-The-first-private-sector-alliance-for-circular-electronics

domain names often paid a hefty fee to recover them, companies that do not retain sovereignty over their proprietary models will likely regret that oversight. Beyond the concerns around ownership for business profitability, sovereignty issues are also being closely examined as the European Union as one example expresses deep concern over whether dominance in the field of AI will also impact the political standing of countries that fall behind in owning and managing their own models.[89]

In either case, and others such as proprietary business information, it would be difficult to govern and control both your model data and the intellectual property of the models derived from it without a comprehensive solution that addresses visibility and protection of the entire IT estate as a solution like Arc provides. Azure has long provided API security and accessibility through API gateway, and that is now possible to enable on Arc-enabled Kubernetes clusters.[90]

An article in *New York* magazine in collaboration with *The Verge*[91] offers a fairly horrifying outtake on the use of human annotators to build LLMs. Its discussion of the cavalier way in which annotators have been engaged to work on some of the largest models we depend on could do serious damage to their reputation as an authoritative resource – a problem it describes the industry as responding to by starting to build standards around annotation to assure that contributors have knowledge of the topics they annotate. This underscores the business value of models that are traceable and the opportunity to produce the same on a governed platform that allows documentation of data sources, and because permissions to training roles can be governed by RBAC, annotations can

---

[89] https://futurium.ec.europa.eu/en/european-ai-alliance/blog/towards-sovereignty-ai-7-tier-strategy-europes-technological-independence-generative-artificial

[90] https://learn.microsoft.com/en-us/azure/api-management/how-to-deploy-self-hosted-gateway-azure-arc

[91] https://nymag.com/intelligencer/article/ai-artificial-intelligence-humans-technology-business-factory.html

also be audited. The value of verifiable models will continue to increase in market value as the drawbacks of cheaper off-the-shelf models become more apparent.

Figure 9-3. *There is sometimes a human behind the AI curtain*

Assuming the burden of model training allows you to maintain privacy guardrails around its underlying data and also to control costs by determining the most effective training approach. However, the greatest gain might be in the use of an API to extract full value of the model. When looking at the ways an API can extract revenue from a model, it's helpful to flip the equation to look first at the APIs a company already owns and how AI/ML could increase the effectiveness of established lines of business. An API provides the interface over which your applications can communicate with your models, and if you compare the heavy lifting an application might have to do in order to extract the data it needs and the time constraints around the execution of those requests, it becomes clear that being able to instead utilize preprocessed data in an ML model is an accelerator. Here again, the fusion of existing DevOps pipelines for application development with MLOps on an integrated platform accelerates the ability to drive product into production.

In looking at how AI/ML practice impacts a business, an effective use of the technology can flip a negative outcome. Recently, the federal government began to regulate the use of algorithms used to manage patient care under Medicare Advantage[92] due to occurrences of blatantly short-sighted application of coverage restrictions made by automated systems that in many cases overruled the discretion of the attending physician in determining what care a patient needed. In truth, it isn't the use of algorithms that has caused these difficulties; rather, it is the use of *improperly trained* algorithms that failed to integrate contextual data about the patient and their entire constellation of health conditions, living situation, medical history, and other factors that if properly applied could lead to better outcomes. Simple factors such as whether a patient could walk or feed and medicate themselves seem to have been overlooked with heavy consequences in a personal sense to those who were improperly denied coverage, but also costly in terms of providing care if incorrect decisions led to secondary injury and more treatment than would have been necessary with a correct initial decision. This lack of product maturity is not new and has been faced for many years by industries relying on Custom Off The Shelf [COTS] software that gathers up its customer base when it is in the whizbang new and great stage, but doesn't stay ahead of security or other core development tasks once its product is embedded in a customer's business and the python style hug of vendor lock-in takes hold. In the rush to develop new AI solutions, methodical development practice that takes advantage of every tool that will contribute to its efficacy throughout the entire product lifecycle is essential not only to

---

[92] www.news-medical.net/news/20231005/Feds-rein-in-use-of-predictive-software-that-limits-care-for-Medicare-Advantage-patients.aspx

the profitability of a particular offering but to prevent damage to the computing industry that occurs when regulations have to be imposed that constrain its growth. Much like retail shrinkage raises prices for everyone, immature software products that have been rushed to market in a quest for profit are bad for the technology industry.

In attempting to make best use of the remarkable and constantly transfigured tools for automation, a foundational approach that is always underpinned by core business objectives, is as simple as possible given the requirements generated by those objectives, and is consolidated into a uniform approach that is not subject to one-off vagaries when an obstacle is encountered will offer the best outcomes over time. As with API development, finding areas where it is advantageous to deploy ML should start with processes that are already vital to the business. Azure Monitor is an excellent tool to begin mining for tasks that could be automated and to discover processes that are inefficient, circular, or just unnecessary so that you can distinguish what is low-hanging fruit and what is an exercise in overengineering.

A serious pain point in previous attempts at automation has been the tendency to step out of an automation loop exhibiting a problem and manually resolve it, recreating dependence on an individual being present to run very slowly what should have executed as part of the automation. With the additional burden of scrutinizing tremendous volumes of data and processing resulting actions accordingly, such manual interventions pose more risk to timely execution and accuracy than ever before no matter how skilled the data wrangler. Wherever possible, use policies to prevent circumvention of automation.

The final chapter of this book will look at the incredible body of work that led to a product like Arc being possible and explore where the fulcrum lies that might pivot an organization toward or away from Arc.

CHAPTER 10

Azure Arc – History and Horizons

The Metamorphose of Enterprise Computing Platforms

From bi-quinary wooden abacus[1] to the vacuum tube electronics of the Colossus code-breaking machine used in WWII.[2] From mainframe to personal computers to the advent of quantum computing. From programming that had to account for and reuse infinitesimally small pieces of the memory register to RAM that can carry massive loads of computational data. From IBM's 20-foot-long 236GB mass storage system[3] half a century ago to the prospect of storing a quarter-million terabytes in one gram of DNA.[4] Changes in the capabilities and scale of the technologies invented within the last century have exceeded the ability of their creators to fully manage them well before AI was factored in, and that divergence is part of what makes AI/ML fully necessary. When the

---

[1] https://en.wikipedia.org/wiki/Bi-quinary_coded_decimal
[2] https://en.wikipedia.org/wiki/Colossus_computer
[3] www.computerhistory.org/timeline/1974/
[4] www.labiotech.eu/startup-scout/biomemory-dna-hard-drive/

© Ramona Maxwell 2024
R. Maxwell, *Azure Arc Systems Management*,
https://doi.org/10.1007/978-1-4842-9480-2_10

breathtaking reality of the reorganization by technological advancement of not only human lives but our very environment sets in, then tools like Arc[5] begin to seem not utilitarian but heroic as we use them to meet the challenges we have laid out for ourselves.

To this point, we have discussed multiple spaces where an effective enterprise control plane bridles and directs the incredible power we have at hand such as

- Software supply chain security and consistency

- DevOps pipelines that are governed, streamlined, and well equipped to manage the application lifecycle without sinking into a morass of legacy code and loose secrets

- GitOps to provide uniform and secure deployments at speed and scale

- Governance through a combination of policy guardrails, discovery, and monitoring feedback loops

- End-to-end security using RBAC and principles of least privilege along with aggressive defense mechanisms applied at edge and every gate leading inward to core data and operations

- Visibility and access to data no matter where it is stored

---

[5] This book's subject, but also referencing control planes that are the passionate endeavor of organizations such as Google, AWS, VMware, RedHat, CNCF, and others

- Analytics, ML, and AI that turn raw data into outputs directly traceable to human achievement, health, and monetary gain

- Automation and observability into all of the above which can enable not only business objectives but implementation of ESG and other initiatives protective of the environment and people technology is able to serve

The creative pressures that led to products with outsize obligations and impact like container hosting, data encryption, and control planes that attempt to manage the entire stack of technology interaction have also been detailed. Those pressures continue apace with cyber risk specialists IT Governance[6] reporting, "114 publicly disclosed security incidents" (organizations that are private and not subject to regulatory disclosure may not publicize an attack) and "867,072,315 records known to be breached" *in October of 2023 alone.* The Microsoft Customer story of Centro Hospitalar in Portugal[7] flipped those statistics while managing a huge inventory of IoT devices and improving access to healthcare services with new APIs, while Arc played a central role in their ability to manage both devices and facilities. Multinational energy provider Tecnicas Reunidas[8] needed a way to manage regulatory compliance obligations that varied by the country in which operations were being conducted, to reinvent themselves as a data-driven company, and despite their focus on ESG-related businesses such as carbon capture and zero waste, to defend themselves from threat actors well known to target utilities.

---

[6] www.itgovernance.co.uk/blog/data-breaches-and-cyber-attacks-in-october-2023-867072315-records-breached

[7] https://customers.microsoft.com/en-us/story/1650842079078735000-chtmad-health-provider-azure-en-portugal

[8] https://customers.microsoft.com/en-us/story/1662899805786944041-tecnicas-reunidas-energy-azure-arc

Arc was instrumental in each of those goals being accomplished, and their Customer story featured comments about how Arc facilitated a uniform approach to operations, provided effective security with Sentinel, and met their data-centric business objective with Arc-enabled SQL Server.

What Is the Fulcrum for Arc?

A recent TechTarget article highlighted how recessionary pressure may drive businesses back to the data center,[9] citing a company who'd done just that to reduce costs along with another whose cloud-agnostic approach to compute purchases keeps them well positioned to negotiate with vendors. However, for prodigious companies, the impact of streamlined operations, monitoring, enhanced security, and governance can have a near instantaneous benefit both in terms of ongoing costs and also in enhanced market opportunities due to the company's ability to pivot quickly into new ventures without undue concern about whether they will be able to enable additional workloads. Conversely, massive enterprises often struggle with uneven outcomes where some IT teams "run like a top" (and without falling over), while others circumvent policy and take dangerous or costly shortcuts. The justification for lapses in governance is sometimes expressed as a concern that standards and agility are not compatible – in fact, proper guardrails could be compared to a freeway to allow your agile teams to drive much faster toward business objectives, with lowered risk factors and repeatable processes contributing to velocity. In those situations, the power of Arc lies in the ability to standardize approaches to common tasks and to assure that policy has the reach it needs to be effective. With Lighthouse in the mix providing panoramic clarity and the power of AI/ML to aggregate what is observed, tools like Arc provide never before realized capability to achieve governance and security objectives.

---

[9] www.techtarget.com/searchitoperations/news/366537339/Cloud-repatriation-vs-multi-cloud-IT-seeks-cost-relief

The Global Finance news site has an interesting live chart ranking the ten largest companies in the world by market capitalization over 2022,[10] and during that span, the top four companies were often the big three cloud providers along with Apple. Apple has its own success story based on top-tier consumer products and its lock on hardware for digital design companies, but the other three have risen to their respective pinnacles by providing the business platforms along with specialized software and search algorithms that power the rest of the world's business. There is some natural interdependence amid their intense competition, such as AWS rumored $1B purchase of Microsoft 365 seats,[11] which if proved true subsequent to this writing would be a nod to the extreme investment Microsoft has made in securing its cloud – since a prior objection of AWS to onboarding business operations to the Microsoft cloud was the protected storage of internal documents. Sometimes, these companies compete within their cloistered circle, as demonstrated by Google having to provide a legal defense for its purchase of default search engine status on Apple devices,[12] something Microsoft also admitted they would have been willing to pay for given Apple's consumer reach.

Somewhere below those lofty standard bearers of the corporate behemoth live the 80% of companies that run our world from automobile manufacturers to highway and bridge builders, from manufacturing of the universe of household goods and the homes that store them to the consumables the people inhabiting them need. These companies are likely to face relentless competition in their vertical amid a constantly changing business landscape while often being accountable to a board and investors with limited sympathy for failures that affect profitability.

---

[10] https://gfmag.com/data/biggest-company-in-the-world/

[11] www.windowscentral.com/software-apps/amazon-and-microsoft-to-sign-dollar1-billion-megadeal-for-cloud-productivity-says-internal-document

[12] www.nytimes.com/2023/10/26/technology/google-apple-search-spotlight.html?partner=slack&smid=sl-share

It is those companies that stand to gain the most from adopting Arc, and the further across the IT estate they expand its control plane, the better their ROI will be.

Microsoft's bet is on your ability to distinguish advanced platform capabilities such as those provided by Arc from competing with other cloud providers on commodity IaaS or PaaS offerings. Even if Microsoft preferred that all of your needs for compute and storage were met on their platform, that isn't always realistic. They recognize that customers are cost-conscious and that commodity margins are thin, akin to trying to make a profit in the grocery industry. Additionally, Microsoft and their compatriots also face capacity constraints in the race to meet consumer demand. In a July 2023 earnings call, CFO Amy Hood noted that DC capacity additions are aimed at both overall commercial cloud demand and building out capacity for AI.[13]

Can small and medium businesses benefit from Arc adoption? Many organizations will find Azure Management Groups to be sufficient to manage even a few large subscriptions, particularly if they are not attempting a multi-cloud setup; however, businesses in every stage of growth can benefit from Arc features to some degree, even those at the beginning of a journey toward cloud computing. It's established that a move off of cloud computing platforms and back to the DC is expensive and difficult. If your rationale to move included the costs of upgrading and expanding infrastructure, negating the not insignificant investment of moving toward the cloud to begin with along with the capital investments necessary to assure your current DCs will be able to run whichever workloads you previously migrated is not likely to be advantageous compared to other approaches to cost control, and DC repatriation is generally precipitated by very specific governance or operational concerns beyond those of cost. If a business is at a point of pivotal growth which

---

[13] www.microsoft.com/en-us/investor/events/fy-2023/earnings-fy-2023-q4.aspx

their own DC cannot accommodate, onboarding to Arc is a fantastic premigration move since the visibility into resources it provides will create transparency around which assets are the best targets for initial migrations to cloud hosting in terms of both management and ROI. When migration decisions are made with all of the dark corners of existing architecture lit up, the outcome is much more likely to meet the business goals of the project and its desired ROI.

Cost is a realistic pivot in the decision process as you define a technology road map. Microsoft's general advice around this is to never cut corners on security, and, instead, if you can't afford to secure the innovative solution you're imagining, you should scale back to something simpler that utilizes built-in roles and guardrails rather than operating in a vulnerable state. When it comes to trade-offs between cost and operational excellence, the suggestion offered is to utilize PaaS services for pricing that spreads the cost of the underlying infrastructure across many Azure customers rather than bearing the heftier expense of building your own. Businesses are often advised to prepare carefully to negotiate their cloud spend so as to not only take advantage of available discounts based on expected usage but also product trials, support needs, training, and other benefits to which they may be entitled. Another objective is to assure that costs remain stable and aligned to business growth. Changing market conditions can and do affect the ROI of cloud spend; just imagine your LOB was residential mortgage lending once interest rates began to rise or ERP for commercial real estate when everyone left the office. Accurately estimating the capacity you need to buy is key not only to receiving discounts, but properly using the ones you've been granted. Yes, you can turn off a server that is not in use, but if you've purchased a block of capacity that doesn't return the funds you've agreed to spend, you only gain if you find a productive way to repurpose it. The view of your workloads and their supporting infrastructure through the lens of Arc's control plane has passed Hubble in clarity and James Webb in scope so that you have Euclid's wide view[14] of the galaxies making up your IT universe. With this comprehensive overview, it becomes much easier to assess the value of particular workloads, manage them with efficiency, look for opportunities to streamline and optimize, and in preparation for purchase negotiations be able to accurately assess what you should buy and at what cost.

Microsoft Global Black Belt Alexander Ortha helps Microsoft's EMEA customers as a Senior Specialist for Hybrid Solutions. He describes the client base in Europe as being judicious about the technology they implement and apt to require validation of the security and efficacy of solutions they adopt – particularly when these are running in the cloud rather than in a customer-owned DC. Often, a key enticement for these customers to explore the overall capabilities of Arc is the ability to automatically update Arc-enabled servers. The opportunity exists to combine this benefit with the newly available Extended Security Updates[15] for Windows and SQL Servers that have reached the end of product support. The generous three-year term of the extension allows new customers to gain immediate benefit from an initial investment in Arc and to become familiar with the advantages of single control plane management.

The next step according to Ortha is often an investment in security that is facilitated by wrapping the Azure ecosystem with its advanced monitoring including XDR and SIEM tools around vulnerable workloads and infrastructure. In discussing the shift in thinking necessary for even an experienced on-prem systems administrator to become cloud savvy, Ortha noted he encourages that at minimum they study for and take the AZ-900 certification exam,[16] stating that "without this understanding this

---

[14] www.esa.int/Science_Exploration/Space_Science/Euclid/Euclid_s_first_images_the_dazzling_edge_of_darkness

[15] As discussed in Chapter 8 and its footnote #37

[16] https://learn.microsoft.com/en-us/credentials/certifications/resources/study-guides/az-900

information it's almost impossible to have a successful cloud project." This particular certification, which focuses on three core areas (cloud concepts, Azure architecture and services, and Azure management and governance), is also heavily encouraged at many Microsoft-centric consulting firms for the same reasons. He also highlighted the need for a new operations management approach, taking into account that the intent behind Arc is to streamline and simplify processes. If the proper training is provided, then the risk of having disparate and siloed management teams, one for cloud and one for on-premise, can be avoided. This approach opens up the horizons of what is possible in Azure as he notes that when someone comes from a perspective of writing a script for individual tasks and then "you project servers into the cloud and as soon as you do this you open the Azure framework... you realize what you can do now and that is incredible..." in terms of what the Azure ecosystem offers.

At times, the vision for a product might be labeled "Star Trek syndrome" in that what it is imagined to be exceeds its actual capabilities, and at its inception this could have been said of Arc. However, Ortha noted the goal of a "unified operations model" is now achievable with Arc whether workloads are running on Azure Stack HCI, VMware vSphere, or somewhere else. A prior disparity in the ability to manage VMs with Arc as compared to Arc-enabled servers is dissipating as the underlying object model is standardized. As Ortha also commented when discussing these technologies, Azure is "the North star" for which these integrations aim so that all workloads benefit from uniform application of policy, RBAC and Azure monitoring and security tools. He commented that in the past when customers requested the ability to run Azure in their own DC, he would say, "yes – of course you can!" but a decade ago that meant they had to buy a shipping container stocked with private cloud hardware or more recently just a rack or two progressing down to a "couple of servers." But now, *you don't need to buy anything!*" and can Arc-enable on-prem workloads independent of where they are (AWS, Alibaba "wherever") or which hypervisor they run under.

Another key customer advantage Ortha cited is the ability to meet strict compliance requirements imposed by the European Union's General Data Protection Regulation[17] [GDPR] which describes itself as "the toughest privacy and security law in the world." Per Akamai,[18] the EU has granted its citizens a right to privacy for almost three quarters of a century since the 1950 European Convention on Human Rights. Companies all over the world are impacted as GDPR governs how they will do business with EU citizens, and Ortha states that compliance with GDPR is a first priority for Microsoft providers in the EU. To effectively meet this challenge, Ortha states that Microsoft offers transparency into the data that Arc and every associated service can collect. There also has to be a process of education around the levers that control data flow and how to assure they are set correctly so that no disallowed data or metrics are collected incidentally. These very practices are also a constant source of friction in the United States, where Google recently agreed to a nearly $400M settlement for tracking locations in behalf of advertisers after users had revoked tracking permission,[19] and there is another suit pending regarding a claimed misuse of website analytics.[20] In that regard, GDPR regulations have provided a training ground for the industry in how to protect personal characteristics and activities of the users of software. Ortha further explains that Microsoft provides "precise documentation" of the networking flow (unidirectional), firewall rules (all ports closed by default), and encryption standards and takes very seriously the obligation to provide a platform on which customers are not exposed to the risk of violating GDPR regulations.

---

[17] https://gdpr.eu/tag/gdpr/

[18] www.akamai.com/glossary/what-is-gdpr

[19] https://time.com/6233752/google-location-tracking-settlement-privacy/

[20] https://caselaw.findlaw.com/court/us-dis-crt-n-d-cal/114823778.html

As a priority for EU enterprises, Ortha points out that conversations around how data will be managed often occur well before customers may learn about powerful tools such as the policy engine that can actually make a public cloud far safer than a DC that is built by hand.

Ortha also noted distinct differences between Azure Arc and Azure Stack HCI which are sometimes confused as being equivalent products. While Azure Stack HCI has a dependency on Arc to function, Arc has no such dependency on HCI and as a control plane sits above and enables HCI's virtualized workloads. HCI stands for hyper-converged computing infrastructure, and the idea is that rather than having to manage separate portions of infrastructure, its compute, storage, and networking are compressed into a single layer. While greatly streamlining the process of spinning up, for example, a complete operation at an edge location, it also takes away some choices such as how you might customize storage IOPS[21] for a specific workload by swapping portions of the hardware. Primary vendors like Dell attempt to sidestep that limitation by offering at least a few choices[22] so that you can tilt toward the model that best suits your workloads. HCI takes the art of virtualization to its logical limit by not stopping at the VM and virtualizing storage and networking as well, and Azure Stack HCI adds the special sauce of integrating your edge installation into Azure from its inception with Arc. An HCI installation consumes only a small footprint (between 1 and 16 physical servers hosting a proportionately larger number of virtual instances in each Stack) but still offers a full array of Azure services including Azure Virtual Desktops for workers at remote locations. They are also a cost-effective approach for keeping subsets of data on-premise when business or regulatory

---

[21] https://www.techtarget.com/searchstorage/definition/
IOPS-input-output-operations-per-second
[22] www.delltechnologies.com/asset/en-us/solutions/infrastructure-
solutions/technical-support/dell-integrated-system-for-microsoft-
azure-stack-hci-spec-sheet.pdf

requirements make this necessary. Managing Azure Stack HCI resources via the Arc control plane is an area of rapid growth, and there have been some bumps in the road for those participating in the preview at the time of this writing. A new version that improves the CLI and supports static IP addresses is a breaking change that requires reinstallation.[23] Nonetheless, avoiding duplication of administration duties by centralizing management of Azure Stack HCI VMs from the Azure portal should contribute to cost control efforts and also allow for consistent application of governance and security across an organization that includes remote locations.[24]

Azure Arc Landing Zones

The "In the beginning" moment of creation for an IT estate hosted on Azure starts with a landing zone [LZ], and in the case of organically grown installations that start to go awry, exporting an environment to look for ways to realign with the templated approach Microsoft provides in landing is often a recommended course of action. A template in this instance doesn't imply a cardboard cutout or universal sizing. Microsoft recognizes that analysis of complex business scenarios may need to take place in preparation for LZ architecture and provides tools to help. In the case of Arc, that help comes in the form of customized templates. LZs for hybrid and multi-cloud computing have special considerations around secure networking, perhaps Kubernetes installations and their GitOps deployment pipelines, whether you will run Arc-enabled data services, and much more. As emphasized in previous chapters, this is the juncture where the architecture counts and the investments made in design will

---

[23] https://learn.microsoft.com/en-us/azure-stack/hci/manage/azure-arc-vms-faq#what-does-this-breaking-change-on-azure-stack-hci--version-22h2-mean-for-me-and-my-workloads--

[24] https://learn.microsoft.com/en-us/azure-stack/hci/whats-new?tabs=2402releases

return scalable, performant, and secure systems that are able to support the profit-making ventures of your business. Failure to adhere to proper design principles in response to project deadlines or budget pressures can have disastrous consequences to both your business and your bottom line, and it is because of those ever-present tensioners that the use of specialized LZ templates that can be used in a modular fashion to build out fairly large and complex installations is recommended.

For smaller organizations that are willing to manage their infrastructure a click at a time through the Azure Portal, there is a list of LZ accelerators that will allow you to deploy entire portals very rapidly using common defaults.[25] A larger or more operationally mature organization is likely to pursue the IaC[26] approach to both the initial LZs created and expansion into further customized LZs, which not only reflect the purpose of the LZ but also further enable specific features needed by your organization. There are LZ templates for High Performance Computing [HPC], SAP, Spring apps, and many more, and of course some are unique to Arc such as those for an Azure Arc-enabled SQL Managed Instance landing zone accelerator[27] and one for Azure Arc-enabled Kubernetes.[28] While you can mix approaches by firing the build-it button on an accelerator and then later exporting the ARM template to your IaC repository, taking adequate time to plan (and at the very least to fully understand what each template under consideration deploys) is the best approach. The fact that an entire LZ architecture can deploy to Azure so rapidly offers amazing velocity to your business, but it's good to paint the deploy button red to remind yourself that the bill starts the moment you push it.

---

[25] https://learn.microsoft.com/en-us/azure/architecture/landing-zones/landing-zone-deploy#application

[26] https://aws.amazon.com/what-is/iac/

[27] https://techcommunity.microsoft.com/t5/azure-arc-blog/announcing-landing-zone-accelerator-for-azure-arc-enabled-sql/ba-p/3647623

[28] https://techcommunity.microsoft.com/t5/azure-arc-blog/announcing-landing-zone-accelerator-for-azure-arc-enabled/ba-p/3380797

Azure Lighthouse[29]

Customers with established tenants or those newly onboarding to Azure services may choose the Managed Service Provider [MSP] approach if there are insufficient resources or time to independently approach the adoption of desirable cloud services. What Lighthouse enables is the management of your subscription from within the provider's tenant. They may provide a specific service such as security enablement or cost control auditing for your business and many others directly from their own Azure tenant. As a customer of an MSP, you set the scope of access that will be needed in order for them to perform the requested service and can also audit each action taken by the MSP as well as remove access if that becomes necessary. The process of authorizing this access to your tenant is called delegation as you are delegating management of your resource(s) to the MSP, and you can delegate your entire subscription or a single resource group where the MSP's product is utilized. Given that you are opening the doors of your subscription to a third party, not only is the security protocol through which they gain entry important, you should also assure that the MSP itself has implemented best-in-class security controls. An attack on an MSP is often seeking the higher value target of access to their customers.[30] Although Lighthouse is designed to restrict MSPs from accessing their customer's data by utilizing strict predefined RBAC that cannot be modified with custom roles, the restrictions may not be absolute. This risk has been acknowledged by Microsoft[31] and

---

[29] https://azure.microsoft.com/en-us/products/azure-lighthouse/

[30] https://techcommunity.microsoft.com/t5/microsoft-defender-for-cloud/announcing-microsoft-defender-for-cloud-capabilities-to-counter/ba-p/3876012

[31] https://learn.microsoft.com/en-us/azure/lighthouse/concepts/tenants-users-roles#role-support-for-azure-lighthouse

was highlighted in a blog by data security provider Symmetry Systems[32] explaining why they began using an Application Security Principal in the customer's tenant instead of Lighthouse to ensure they did not have incidental access into the very data they were commissioned to protect. In the classic conundrum of whether you can trust the partner you need to grow your business, Symmetry's customers were fortunate to find one whose ethics led them to protect their customer from "emergent behavior[33] with serious implications for data security."

For MSPs, Lighthouse is a powerful tool to centralize operations performed in behalf of customers since service offerings can be managed from a single control plane, and solution provisioning in subscriptions where authority has been delegated is automated using ARM templates, just as it would be within a subscription owned by the tenant. It is a collaboration offering that is unique to the Microsoft ecosystem and in conjunction with Arc can enable a service provider to manage very large IT estates for their customers. For business organizations that don't want to assume the burden of running an IT organization to manage part or all of their infrastructure, the ability to farm this out to one or more MSPs may be appealing, especially for companies that have no standing IT operations and are looking for an entry point or those whose current operational needs have significant gaps that cannot be quickly filled internally. Further, MSP offerings aren't limited to operations but can include custom applications that are hosted in the MSP tenant.[34]

---

[32] www.symmetry-systems.com/blog/unintended-third-party-access-to-data-through-supported-azure-built-in-roles/

[33] https://en.wikipedia.org/wiki/Emergence

[34] https://learn.microsoft.com/en-us/azure/lighthouse/concepts/isv-scenarios#saas-based-multi-tenant-offerings

Arc Horizons
VMware Shops Get the Love They Deserve

As the omnipresent basic tool for server virtualization for more than 30 years, VMware is present in many, if not most, large enterprises. It consists of the vSphere virtualization platform or virtual DC, one or more vCenter servers which are centralized configuration management consoles for virtual hosts, and thirdly ESXi is the hypervisor which is installed on those bare-metal hosts for virtual machines. The durable value of VMware's virtualization offering is evident in the recent purchase offer of an estimated 61B by silicon giant Broadcom.[35] In November of 2023, Microsoft announced that Arc-enabled management of the workloads running on VMware is now GA.[36] This does not liberate you from the vSphere in terms of administering your VMware operations as a whole, nor does it offer any GitOps goodness in terms of a deployment pipeline, but it does enable full lifecycle management of the workloads themselves so that you can "create, resize, delete, and power cycle operations such as start/stop/restart on VMware VMs consistently with Azure."[37] Once Arc enabled, the VMs, networks, and storage are all visible to you in Azure and can benefit as any other onboarded server from the management and security tools available in Azure.

For Arc-enabled VMware vSphere, as well as Arc-enabled System Center Virtual Machine Manager [SCVMM] and Azure Stack HCI, simply installing an agent is not sufficient. Projecting these workloads into Azure

---

[35] www.crn.com.au/news/broadcom-misses-vmware-deal-closing-date-601856
[36] https://techcommunity.microsoft.com/t5/azure-arc-blog/bring-azure-to-your-vmware-environment-announcing-ga-of-vmware/ba-p/3974305
[37] https://learn.microsoft.com/en-us/azure/azure-arc/vmware-vsphere/overview

requires the installation of the Azure Resource Bridge,[38] a virtual appliance which hosts a Kubernetes cluster that runs alongside vSphere in your own DC. The Resource Bridge device communicates through the vCenter server for all operations on workloads under that vCenter's purview, and the Bridge has a large capacity, so one Bridge can Arc-enable multiple vCenter servers if the total of VMs they are running is less than 10,000 VMs. The Bridge requires an outbound connection to Azure, and as Private Link was not yet available for this at the time of writing, you must ensure traffic is encrypted. While you will immediately have the fabulous freebie of a complete inventory of the vCenter's resources, including VMs, storage pools, and so on, you must select which ones you will manage in Azure. This gives you discrete control over how you apply the Arc control plane to your workloads while still assuring they appear in the inventory which is continuously synchronized with Azure via the Bridge.

SCVMM, for those not familiar, is Microsoft's vSphere equivalent that allows management of Hyper-V hosts of virtual machines and indeed can also manage VMware ESXi hosts. However, with Arc enablement now available for both, the logical choice is to manage the workloads for both from Azure. Like its VMware peer, SCVMM continues to manage the hosts, but their workloads can be managed directly in Azure via Arc.

Resources for Arc Adoption

Play is a sneaky education tool, helping people learn to do things that equip them to meet real-life challenges. The Arc Jumpstart team built the playground quite some time ago, and but now they've outdone themselves with Jumpstart Agora[39] which intends to provide working scenarios for

---

[38] https://learn.microsoft.com/en-us/azure/azure-arc/resource-bridge/overview

[39] https://techcommunity.microsoft.com/t5/azure-arc-blog/announcing-jumpstart-agora/ba-p/3887199

real-world industries and enterprise-scale use cases such as IoT and data services. If your organization is in the beginning stages of Arc deployment, offering experienced engineers the chance to experiment with Jumpstart and see ready-to-go complex deployments in action will likely provide much quicker upskilling than hours spent poring over the docs.

At Microsoft's 2023 Ignite conference, Lior Kamrat (who at the time of his presentation was a Principal Product Manager for Edge and Platform leading development of Arc Jumpstart at Microsoft and is now a Principal Product Manager Lead) announced that Jumpstart is now officially considered a product rather than a project in development by Microsoft.[40] In a subsequent one-on-one interview, Kamrat explained that over four years ago he was thrilled to see the first ten or so customers who were able to benefit from Jumpstart, but that now he sees Microsoft Partners build out a five-day engagement for their client and regularly include Jumpstart as part of that sales effort.

The early Jumpstarts served primarily as a technology map, but grew into full environments with the introduction of several iterations of ArcBox beginning in May of 2021[41] that offered a full sandbox environment with the only prerequisite being an Azure subscription. Kamrat notes that the release of Agora is a significant milestone in that it begins left with an industry scenario and builds on real-world use cases to create the correct architectural context for its deployment model from that industry's domain story and language. This is a tremendous expansion from the initial Jumpstarts that simply demonstrated the implementation of Arc. The transformation toward a scenario-based approach was largely driven by observations that customers were interested in building POCs most closely

---

[40] https://ignite.microsoft.com/en-US/sessions/b50aad74-4289-4c1f-807c-772a9895816b?source=sessions

[41] https://techcommunity.microsoft.com/t5/azure-arc-blog/announcing-jumpstart-arcbox-a-complete-azure-arc-sandbox/ba-p/2376039

aligned with their objectives, for example, building an Arc-enabled data platform is not necessarily an indicator that the customer has the same level of interest in Arc-enabled Kubernetes. The list of Agora Jumpstarts as of this writing aligns very well to the topics covered in previous chapters:

- Arc-enabled servers

- Arc-enabled SQL Server

- Arc-enabled VMware vSphere

- Arc-enabled Kubernetes

- Arc-enabled data services

- Arc-enabled app services

- Arc-enabled machine learning

- Arc, Edge, and IoT Operations

- Arc and Azure Lighthouse

and an Agora Jumpstart for manufacturing is expected to be available in 2024. Because of an approach Kamrat describes variously as "Lego coding" or "continuous code synergy," improvements to the underlying libraries benefit every Jumpstart that might utilize a particular service area of Azure since they all derive from the same codebase, and this cycle of continuous improvement also means the Jumpstarts stay closely aligned with the latest updates to the Azure platform.

The effectiveness of the Jumpstart approach has led Microsoft to expand their use, with the Jumpstart team announcing they had created HCIBox[42] for Azure Stack HCI to provide the same onboarding experience for edge

---

[42] https://techcommunity.microsoft.com/t5/azure-arc-blog/announcing-jumpstart-hcibox/ba-p/3647646

compute customers that those adopting Arc enjoy. Although the Azure Stack HCI Evaluation Guide[43] had been created along with deployment scripts,[44] customers were running into roadblocks attempting to build out the sample on their own without a running POC to reference, a problem neatly solved by a Jumpstart.

Perhaps a tribute to the success of Arc Jumpstart is Google's new and interestingly named Jump Start collection of solution guides[45] for the GCP platform. At the present time, the offerings range from a three-tier web application deployment to examples demonstrating how to set up a data warehouse, analytics, and ML. Each sample helpfully incorporates a detailed cost calculator so that those new to GCP can see the costs of running the solution in the long term. Microsoft is likely to see more imitation as flattery from competing cloud platforms wishing to increase consumption as customers become aware of the significant benefits to seeding their projects this way. Kamrat estimates that POC creation time is cut by 30–60% among his customers through the use of Jumpstart, and a Jumpstart is always contained within a single RG so that it can be instantly knocked down to sidestep the expense of running it longer than is needed to examine suitability, thereby encouraging sampling of various Jumpstart scenarios. Kamrat sees customers, a large segment of which hail from the IT industry, taking advantage of the ephemeral nature of a Jumpstart environment to conduct training or present a POC and then delete it immediately.

Kamrat notes that the Jumpstart project started as a way to "mitigate a pretty fundamental gap in context of Azure Arc and our documentation" for multi-cloud customers wishing to home on Azure since Microsoft Docs aren't designed to provide instruction as to how you run workloads on

---

[43] https://learn.microsoft.com/en-us/azure-stack/hci/guided-quick-deploy-eval?tabs=global-admin
[44] https://github.com/Azure/AzureStackHCI-EvalGuide
[45] https://cloud.google.com/architecture/all-jss-guides

GCP or AWS – and yet that is exactly what Arc is designed to do. Kamrat notes that Jumpstart has been open source "since day one" and that his philosophy is to encourage adoption through enablement, not by holding information hostage. He calls Jumpstart "a way for us to not be in the room as Microsoft" and believes "the docs should speak for themselves" and even noting that "if we have to be in the room then we've done a bad job" of enabling the customer because "if you have questions that I could have answered in the doc or ... architecture diagram or ... improving an automation that means that I dropped the ball, not you as a consumer." There are experiential customer stories backing up that approach such as when a client is introduced to Arc through a Jumpstart and comes back "a month later with the things they created" as well as hard data when a customer utilizes Jumpstart and there is a spike in the number of Arc-enabled resources in production at that organization a short time later. Per Kamrat, this was the experience of a large bank that deployed the SQL flavor of ArcBox for IT Pros[46] (a version of ArcBox that included monitoring, security, and supported ARM templates written in Bicep or Terraform), and after a couple weeks of receiving assistance from Arc specialists at Microsoft, they then performed "internal bashing" on their POC before they "started scaling up" independently without any further help from Microsoft.

Jumpstart grew from an experiment in customer enablement to a product team relied upon as the "source of truth" within Microsoft for Arc enablement largely through the devotion of the people building it.[47] When I asked Kamrat who on the Arc Jumpstart team had made particularly significant contributions, he refused to highlight individuals. This "all for one, and one for all"[48] zeal for the success of the Jumpstart project likely contributes much to its growth leading to its recent productization

---

[46] https://azurearcjumpstart.com/azure_jumpstart_arcbox/ITPro
[47] https://github.com/microsoft/azure_arc/graphs/contributors
[48] https://en.wikipedia.org/wiki/Unus_pro_omnibus,_omnes_pro_uno

by Microsoft. The stamp of legitimacy added by Microsoft officially designating Jumpstart as a member of their product suite[49] is a significant milestone for the Arc Jumpstart team, but not its destination, and the use cases for this sort of working model documentation are abundant. Kamrat would like to use Agora to showcase scenario innovations by Microsoft partners who specialize in Arc deployments, although since Microsoft itself doesn't charge for Jumpstart, the reward for this appears to be largely reputational. The opportunity to contribute is not limited to partners and follows conventions typical for open source software.[50]

As noted in prior chapters, Microsoft's Cloud Adoption Framework [CAF] is where to start for new Azure deployments, and in a former role as lead for Arc's worldwide field engineering team, Kamrat developed a hybrid accelerator for hybrid and multi-cloud LZ deployments.[51] The special challenge in accomplishing this lay in the fact that CAF wasn't initially designed with the objective of deploying resources outside of Azure. This accelerator marked the first time the CAF was applied anywhere external to Azure, and the degree of integration the new LZ template provided for those newly onboarding to Microsoft's cloud platform as a control plane for large IT estates was the "silver bullet" needed for Arc to be seamless with the Azure platform as a way to keep customers on the *All Azure – All the Time* channel.

If you are a visual person with an appetite for a 95-slide PowerPoint, it's worth diving into the Microsoft Cybersecurity Reference Architectures [MCRA][52] that are part of the Microsoft Security Adoption Framework.[53]

---

[49] https://azurearcjumpstart.com/

[50] https://arcjumpstart.com/contribution_guidelines

[51] https://learn.microsoft.com/en-us/azure/cloud-adoption-framework/scenarios/hybrid/enterprise-scale-landing-zone

[52] https://learn.microsoft.com/en-us/security/cybersecurity-reference-architecture/mcra

[53] https://learn.microsoft.com/en-us/security/ciso-workshop/adoption

Everything discussed in this book hinges on security for its ultimate success, and the MCRA lays it out in a way that, like the CAF, will strengthen your chances of making your first implementation also a correct one. Slide 49 addressing "cross-cloud and cross-platform" concludes, "***Key Takeaway*** – Microsoft builds security for the 'hybrid of everything' enterprise you have, not just 'security for Microsoft'." When I administered SharePoint farms years ago, I used a 36" plotter to print Microsoft's "Where's Waldo" style posters explaining the complexities of SQL Server Reporting Services and the mechanics of their integration into SharePoint's business intelligence features and hung them around my desk. The slides in this deck pack in an impossible level of detail and are also frame-worthy. One of its authors, 23-year Microsoft veteran security architect Mark Simos, also keeps a running list of updates to this document and relevant parts of CAF.[54]

In addition to Jumpstart, traditional training opportunities for Arc may come through Microsoft partners whom you have hired or directly from your Microsoft Technical Account Manager. Funds can be extended to build a POC for workloads or to fund training opportunities relevant to the specific purchase you are considering.

Arc Adoption

In Microsoft's FY24 First Quarter Earnings call,[55] Satya Nadella states Microsoft has 21,000 Arc customers worldwide, almost one and a half times the number a year prior. During another earnings call six months earlier,[56] large companies like Ikea and Rabobank were highlighted as

---

[54] www.linkedin.com/pulse/marks-list-mark-simos/

[55] www.microsoft.com/en-us/investor/events/fy-2024/earnings-fy-2024-q1.aspx

[56] www.microsoft.com/en-us/Investor/events/FY-2023/earnings-fy-2023-q3.aspx

Arc consumers. What this indicates to those considering Arc now is that Microsoft is supporting a large enough customer base on the product that new customers are unlikely to experience the pain of early adopters for typical uses of Arc.

McKinsey's relatively new Magic Quadrant for Distributed Hybrid Architecture[57] puts Microsoft at the very top of the heap, and the criteria on which their selection is based is meaningful with one of the two "must-have capabilities" being a "vendor-developed infrastructure resource management control plane" – practically a subtitle to describe Azure Arc. You can march down McKinsey's list of standard-to-optional features, and Microsoft's offerings headed by Arc tick virtually every box. I believe credit for this goes to Microsoft's diligence in recent years to play well in the yard, meeting and contributing to the highest industry standards for everything from security to ESG concerns and their willingness to partner with both established and open source collaborators when this is the best path to providing both services and tools to manage them.

Summary

An interesting McKinsey article[58] on the topic of building digital ecosystems highlights the juxtaposition between expanding technical capabilities and aligning this with the business value they will actually provide. Is there actual ROI and who does it benefit, your company or its customers? Is the return measurable and the benefit significant enough to draw notice? Will it enhance your company's ability to scale in its marketplace or branch into adjacent business opportunities? Does it create favorable circumstances to grow in partnership with another company whose offerings are complementary? Microsoft's strategy for Azure itself is

---

[57] www.gartner.com/doc/reprints?id=1-2FG8TML3&ct=231030&st=sb

[58] www.mckinsey.com/capabilities/mckinsey-digital/our-insights/ecosystem-2-point-0-climbing-to-the-next-level#/

a remarkable example of this; when there is not something comparable to another company's offering already built by Microsoft, it partners with the company or project that does have a viable offering so that products like Istio, Databricks, and NetApp are readily available to Azure customers.

A primary factor in the failure of organizations to secure their IT estate is the meteoric expansion rate of technological development. The business landscape itself is fluid, and continually reengineering both fronts can lead to unnecessary fragility. Companies should run the absolutely leanest but also most muscular stack possible that will accomplish their business objective using the highest quality product available to them. Cost savings should be achieved by avoiding sprawl and buying what can be well managed. For that management effort to be successful, it's essential to have a correct toolset, and if you are running a large hybrid enterprise, the path Arc opens to Microsoft tools on every cloud is the best available in today's market.

If you think about the strategy Microsoft has taken with Arc by facilitating the use of other clouds as if they are native to its platform, it was both anticipatory and bold. With the cloud itself becoming a commodity item, they were willing to look beyond profits from consumption of compute, storage, and services to open up their platform to competitors' offerings. The true differentiator in terms of intellectual property are the innovations across Microsoft's product line that let customers move fast *without* breaking things whether their LOB is running an oil rig in the Arctic sea or selling flowers in Seattle. This "it's all just Azure" approach simplifies training for an organization's technologists, and working on with a unified set of tools accelerates the path toward full automation. My prediction for Arc in the long term is that it will become intrinsic to how Azure works rather than productized separately and that while moving to Azure might include some migration of assets, it will primarily mean that Azure is home base for all of a company's IT operations.

Thank you for reading, and I hope the points discussed are helpful both in terms of evaluating control plane offerings and also in promoting the interests of security and innovation in the technology community. I am grateful for the opportunity to write this book and owe many thanks for the support I received in doing so, especially to

- Apress editors and assistants including Ryan Byrnes for his encouragement as the project drew to close as well as his assistant Gryffin Winkler, and formerly at Apress as a Senior Editor, Joan Murray, who guided the structure of the project with readers first in mind

- Mike DeLuca, who was invaluable as a technical editor who *knows* the Azure platform from the standpoint of someone who has been part of its development from the early days of offloading basic compute from the DC to the superabundance of its offerings today

- Former employers such as Magenic and Avanade who treated their customer's interests as superior to their bottom line and promoted technical expertise at a level exceeding industry norms

- Contributors from Microsoft cited in the book whose dedication to developing Arc and its integrations with the Azure platform produced compelling solutions worth writing about

- My husband who helped me host years of user group meetups and continues to be cheerful about big collections of PC parts taking the place of food on our kitchen table, climbing on the roof to adjust the Starlink, assembling 3D printers, putting up with racket from the loudest Cherry MX keyboard I can find while always kindly encouraging me to follow my interests

- The love and support of my wonderful family with
  whom, along with the fun we have together, reciprocal
  encouragement is the norm, and some of the snippets I
  got while writing were "have a goal," "it's worthwhile, I
  think you should stick with it" (in response to my
  indulging in a bit of whining minus the cheese), "Is the
  book done yet?", "Good job Mom!", and "I'm so happy
  for you !! Really the smartest person I know ♥♥♥♥♥"
  (from my dear Mya-Louise who is super young and
  hasn't met very many people yet)

Index

© Ramona Maxwell 2024
R. Maxwell, *Azure Arc Systems Management*,
https://doi.org/10.1007/978-1-4842-9480-2

Printed in the United States
by Baker & Taylor Publisher Services